CROSSBLOODS

Intro - contemp examples
of North Am. Indians
being savaged in prin-
people type - doing
damage - don't get the
culture.
murderer - cultural
schizophrenia - 34. -

---

interesting - using contemp
theory to argue for
Native Am lits - postmodernism,
language, etc.

also by Gerald Vizenor

GERALD VIZENOR

CROSSBLOODS

BONE COURTS, BINGO, AND OTHER REPORTS

University of Minnesota Press

Minneapolis

Published by the University of Minnesota Press
2037 University Avenue Southeast, Minneapolis, MN 55414.
Printed in the United States of America.

Library of Congress Cataloging-in-Publication Data

Vizenor, Gerald Robert, 1934–
    Crossbloods : bone courts, bingo, and other reports / Gerald
Vizenor.
        p.   cm.
    ISBN 0–8166–1853–4. — ISBN 0–8166–1854–2 (pbk.)
    1. Ojibwa Indians—Politics and government.   2. Ojibwa Indians—
Economic conditions.   3. Ojibwa Indians—Social conditions.
I. Title.
E99.C6V58   1990
973'.04973—dc20   90–32973
                                                                        CIP

CONTENTS

CONTENTS

✛ Introduction

> *The main interest in life and work is to become*
> *someone else that you were not in the beginning. If*
> *you knew when you began a book what you would*
> *say at the end, do you think that you would have*
> *the courage to write it? What is true for writing*
> *and for a love relationship is true also for life. The*
> *game is worthwhile insofar as we don't know what*
> *will be the end.*
>
> MICHEL FOUCAULT
> *Technologies of the Self*

The new woodland tribes bear their agonistic totems from
that wild premier union with the fur trade and written languages, and earlier, a brush with lethal pathogens; that
first touch, the deceptions of missionaries, the phraseolo-
gies of treaties, and the levies of a dominant consumer culture induced postmodern emblems.

The agonistic survivors are crossbloods; their stories and
totems are indwelt, a new survivance that enlivens an interior landscape. Crossbloods hear the bears that roam in
trickster stories, and the cranes that trim the seasons close
to the ear. Crossbloods are a postmodern tribal bloodline,
an encounter with racialism, colonial duplicities, sentimental monogenism, and generic cultures. The encounters are

comic and communal, rather than tragic and sacrificial; comedies and trickster signatures are liberations; tragedies are simulations, an invented cultural isolation. Crossbloods are communal, and their stories are splendid considerations of survivance.

The reports and essays in this collection were first published in newspapers, magazines, and journals. The earliest reports arise from my experience as an advocate in tribal communities, urban and reservation, and as an editorial writer for the *Minneapolis Tribune;* later, from my encounters as director of Indian Studies at Bemidji State University, and as a professor at the University of Minnesota and the University of California at Berkeley.

More than a century ago my crossblood relatives published the first newspaper on the White Earth Reservation; my reports in this collection and my remembrance of that time are a continuation of an agonistic tradition of crossblood journalism.

The first issue of *The Progress,* edited by Theodore Hudon Beaulieu and published on March 25, 1886, was critical of land allotment legislation and the Bureau of Indian Affairs. Federal agents confiscated the newspaper and ordered that the crossblood editor and publisher be removed from the reservation. Several months later, following a trial in federal district court, the second issue of the newspaper was published.

The United States Indian Agent at White Earth saw the newspaper as a threat to his fascist control of activities on the reservation. He wrote to the publisher that the newspaper was circulated "without first obtaining authority or license so to do from the honorable Secretary of the Interior, honorable Commissioner of Indian Affairs, or myself as United States Indian Agent."

The editor wrote, "We began setting the type for the first number of *The Progress* and were almost ready to go to press, when our sanctum was invaded by T. J. Sheehan, the United States Indian Agent, accompanied by a posse of the Indian police. The composing stick was removed from our hands, our property seized, and ourselves forbidden to proceed with the publication of the journal. . . . We did not believe that any earthly power had the right to interfere with us as members of the Chippewa tribe, and at the White Earth Reservation, while peacefully pursuing the occupation we had chosen."

At the turn of the last century metropolitan newspapers advanced the racist notions of savagism and civilization at the same time that the editor of *The Progress* opposed the Dawes Severalty Act, or General Allotment Act, the federal legislation that allotted communal tribal land to individuals and opened the White Earth Reservation, and other tribal communities, to timber companies. The editor wrote, "We shall aim to advocate constantly and without reserve, what in our view, and in the view of the leading minds upon this reservation, is the best for the interests of its residents."

The *Minneapolis Journal*, on the other hand, reported on July 16, 1906, that "with the minds of the White Earth Indians muddled by liquor, and their eyes dazzled by money, of which they know little . . . the White Earth Indian Reservation will soon be a thing of the past." The Dawes Severalty Act, not beverage alcohol, was the problem; in any case, the reservation is not a "thing of the past." Such racialism has turned to liberal fascism in the present; however, in recent newspaper and television stories, the romantic simulations of tribal people have been overturned by more critical attention to economic development and the politics of reservation governments.

Some of my reports center on paraeconomic survivance in the past two decades, from tribal entrepreneurs, and reservation services, to the political management of tribal enterprises; for instance, the rise of bingo games as a new cash crop. High-stakes bingo operations on reservations, and tribal rights to hunt and fish within the boundaries of original treaties, have been reported in newspapers and magazines more than other issues in the past few years.

Bingo casinos have blazoned reservation communities in more than a dozen states for the past decade; the high-stakes game has tested tribal sovereignties, state jurisdictions, and traditional tribal worldviews; the returns, incredible cash crops, have changed the way some people think about Native American Indians.

The five letters of bingo have been teased in church basements for several decades, the new monotheism, and even children learn to play the game in public schools; however, tribal bingo is a high-stakes game that takes millions of dollars from compulsive gamblers, and the cash debases some tribal communities.

The Lucky Knight casino, for example, was burned in August 1989 by tribal members who opposed gambling at the St. Regis Mohawk Reservation on the Canadian border in northern New York. Victory Adams, the owner of the casino, said the mob tried to burn other casinos on the reservation. The Associated Press reported that the "Mohawks contend they are not bound by state or federal gambling laws since they consider their reservation a sovereign nation."

Jake Swamp, a member of the traditional council, told the *New York Times* that the Mohawk Great Law of Peace "says you always must look seven generations into the future. . . . That's the only way we've been able to survive this far. But we're having a really hard time keeping our traditions intact." Casino gambling has divided the reservation between those who favor economic development, and those who fear the corruption of tribal cultures.

President Reagan signed legislation in October 1988 that established a commission to regulate gambling on reservations or federal trust land. The National Indian Gaming Commission monitors bingo and other games of chance in tribal casinos. Roger Jourdain, the trenchant chairman of the Red Lake tribal council in Minnesota, opposed the new legislation. "We are not going to stand by and let the federal government assume unauthorized and unconstitutional jurisdiction over our reservation," Jourdain told the *Minneapolis Star and Tribune.* "Tribes have the inherent right to govern themselves in all local matters, including the very important area of gambling."

The Fond du Lac Reservation, on the other hand, has turned the smoke and mirrors of state dominions, treaties, and tribal sovereignties, into a festive gaming casino in downtown Duluth, Minnesota. The Fond du Luth Gaming Casino is a preposterous postmodern reservation; the fabrication of this gaming reservation insinuates the signature of a tribal trickster.

The tribal council at the Fond du Lac Reservation, and the mayor of the city of Duluth, proposed a venture casino as a source of revenue for economic development. The enticements were not racial, colonial, cultural, or savagism over civilization in a theater of inversions. Bingo was not a mismeasure of worldviews, or economic trust; wild cash was the lure, and two governments dared to propose the creation of a brand new reservation, a place to gamble downtown on trust land. This reservation was based on bad habits, even postmodern casino vengeance, an unusual measure of tribal paraeconomic survivance. "Gambling Abuse and Addiction Treatment" is a new subject heading in the local telephone directory, and there is a new listing for professional services located a few blocks from the casino.

The Sears building was purchased and converted to a casino that seats more than twelve hundred gamblers downtown under thousands of beveled mirrors. The new commission regulations limit the games to pull tabs, video poker and fruit machines, keno, lotto variations, and other games based on bingo, such as bingolette and bingo jack.

Telly Savalas, the television actor, and other entertainers, were hired to celebrate the opening of the three million dollar urban reservation casino in September 1986. The Fond du Luth Gaming Commission reported that "never before in history had off-reservation land been taken into trust as Indian land for the purpose of gaming."

William Houle, the elected chairman of the tribal council at the Fond du Lac Reservation, pointed out that the creation of the casino had the support of state and federal politicians, James Watt, then secretary of the Department of the Interior, and the Bureau of Indian Affairs. "I don't believe there will ever be a project as unique as this one. You're never going to be able to find a relationship between a tribe and a city to rival the one we have here," said Houle. "Gaming has always been part of our culture, and now it is an integral part of our economy as well."

Indeed, but bingo as the new cash crop is based on losers, compulsive behavior, and most of the downtown gamblers are white; bingo and pull tabs are not moccasin games, and bingo is far from a traditional tribal giveaway to counter materialism. Moreover, the fabricated reservation could break the tribal bank. The tribal council borrowed more than three million dollars to renovate the building, and the city issued bonds to build a parking ramp next to the casino. The *Minneapolis Star and Tribune* reported that the tribal council, or band, stands to lose their investment if the "venture flops. In that case, the city could gain control of the building for its own use and take possession of the band's assets." In the first year of operation the casino had fallen short of expected revenues and was behind in loan payments.

Norman Crooks, former chairman of the Shakopee Mdewakanton Sioux Reservation in Prior Lake, near Minneapolis, established the Little 6 Bingo Palace in 1982, the first high-stakes bingo operation on tribal land in the state and one of the first in the nation. In the first few years the reservation was transformed by new community investments and payments to individuals. Eighteen years later each tribal member might have been paid a total of more than a hundred thousand dollars. The worldviews of tribal children must be altered by so much cash from games; unemployment and poverty turned to wealth and leisure in a decade.

Little 6 Bingo Palace appears on a huge outdoor sign at the entrance to a suburban shopping center; bus loads of white people arrive each night from various parts of the city to play bingo and other games on the reservation. Sweet Shawnee, one of the new video fruit machines, stands in the wide, air conditioned and carpeted trailer, waiting to be played. The simulated tribal woman pictured on the machine is dressed in a bikini and mounted bareback on a pinto; she wears a feathered headdress. Several other tribal casinos have the same machine. Such racial and cultural detractions might have been challenged in a white-owned establishment, but certain issues seem to lose their importance when the games turn a higher profit on reservations.

The American Indian Movement held the most headlines on tribal issues in the late sixties and seventies, a romantic inversion of racialism, and praise for generic cultures. These urban radicals were tribal simulations with dubious constituencies, and their stoical poses, tragic and lonesome, were closer to photographic and video images familiar to a consumer culture; these ersatz warriors were much closer to the invented tragedies of a vanishing race than were the crossbloods who endured the real politics and weather on reservations. My editorial series in the *Minneapolis Tribune* was the only critical report on the racial duplicities of the leaders of the American Indian Movement.

Donald Barnett, mayor of Rapid City, South Dakota, responded with concern to the radical leaders, but then he read their criminal records and changed his mind. "Are these men serious civil rights workers or are they a bunch of bandits?" the mayor asked in an interview. "People working for civil rights do not carry guns. I have seen the records on these men, and you can't sit and negotiate with a man who has a gun." A few days later the American Indian Movement occupied Wounded Knee, South Dakota.

United Press International reported on March 1, 1973, that "members of the American Indian Movement held ten people hostage . . . at this Pine Ridge Reservation town where more than 200 Indians were massacred by Cavalry troops in 1890." There were never hostages, and leaders of the American Indian Movement were never charged with kidnaping or any other crime associated with the taking of hostages. I was close to the village that day, but the reporter for United Press International never moved from his motel room. He ordered a single-engine plane to circle Wounded Knee and filed his simulated romantic story with an aerial photograph of the church, militants, and raised weapons.

The American Indian Movement is more simulation than dread in the eighties, and the crossblood leaders are as close to retirement as those who financed their movement and adventures. The church and state contribute to other causes now, and the media cover bingo, education, reburial, the legal interpretations of treaties, and other tribal issues, with more enthusiasm than the peevish revisions of urban revolutionaries.

Russell Means, however, reappeared in a recent national report on corruption and fraud in tribal programs. "Within the past two years, I have personally attempted to assist seven Indian reservations . . . with economic development," Means told an investigative committee of the Senate Select Committee on Indian Affairs. "I know that the tribal governments do not want economic development unless graft is a major ingredient." Means was hyperbolic, as usual, and did not name the seven reservations.

Dennis Banks, the venerable leader of the American Indian Movement, has returned to the business world and corporate investments in tribal communities. Twenty years ago, before his transformation as a political activist, he wore a necktie and was a recruiter for Honeywell. Banks

Dennis Banks at Augsburg College, 1989

was a fugitive in California for nine years; he returned to serve a three-year prison sentence in South Dakota. He moved to the Pine Ridge Reservation.

The *St. Paul Pioneer Press Dispatch* reported on January 4, 1987, that Banks borrowed money from the tribal council on Pine Ridge to establish his company, Loneman Industries. "Banks spends many of his days working the phone in his cluttered office, an abandoned portable classroom. . . . He's got meetings scheduled with IBM and an appointment with Nissan executives in Japan."

"I should have been a capitalist years ago," he told James McGregor, a reporter for the *St. Paul Pioneer Press Dispatch*. Banks said, "I just click with ideas. There's an excitement to it. I like that excitement." In the past, he needed more stimulation than the mere click of economic ideas; once he posed as a traditional woodland warrior and, with hundreds of other urban militants, armed with new weapons, threatened to attack white fishermen on the opening day of the season and clouded a court decision in favor of the Leech Lake Reservation.

Federal Judge Edward Devitt ruled in January 1972 that the Leech Lake Reservation of the Minnesota Chippewa Tribe had the right to hunt, fish, and gather wild rice on the reservation without restriction from the state of Minnesota. The governor, elected tribal officials, and the state legislature reached an agreement that has become a model of good sense, a wise measure of treaties, and the best management of natural resources. Leech Lake tribal members relinquished the right to commercial fishing, and the agreement established a special state licensing system; the proceeds from license fees, in the millions, have been turned over to the tribal government.

The American Indian Movement, and Vernon Bellecourt in particular, has opposed most agreements with state and federal governments and cash settlements for land and resources; some tribal radicals, supported by romantic liberals and anarchists, would oppose any government and hold to an absolute return of tribal land.

Bellecourt told a congressional committee that he was a "member of the White Earth Anishinaabe nation and the Anishinaabe Akeeng, which means 'the people's land.' We are a coalition of allottees and heirs to the White Earth Anishinaabe nation organized to stop the further taking of our treaty-guaranteed lands and to recover what has been illegally taken from us." White Earth is a reservation, not a separatist nation, and most tribal people are proud to defend constitutional democracies. Once more, tribal radicals have dubious tribal constituencies.

Darrell Wadena supported the White Earth Land Settlement Act in 1986, which would reimburse tribal members

whose allotments were lost to state tax forfeitures and illegal land transactions at the turn of the century. More than
ten million dollars was awarded to the heirs who lost tribal
land in various swindles; moreover, the settlement would
provide six million dollars in economic assistance to the
reservation, and ten thousand acres of land would be returned to White Earth.

Bellecourt is a leader of Anishinaabe Akeeng. He was
once an elected member of the tribal government, but lost
the election for tribal chairman to Darrell Wadena. Bellecourt told the *Minneapolis Star and Tribune* that the settlement was "the most terrible injustice." Wadena indicated
that Anishinaabe Akeeng was urban, not reservation,
born; he pointed out that Bellecourt has traveled to Nicaragua and Libya, and "people don't believe that his association with Gadhafi has any real importance here."

Panama has been added to the nations that Vernon
Bellecourt has visited, according to a newspaper published
at the Minneapolis American Indian Center. *The Circle* reported in September 1989 that Bellecourt sued the Federal
Bureau of Investigation for "illegally obtaining copies of
pictures he took" at a Congress of Indians Conference in
Panama City. "The day after Bellecourt returned to the
Twin Cities he took two rolls of film that he shot while in
Panama to the F-Stop One Hour Photo Store . . . in Minneapolis on March 22, 1989. When Bellecourt returned for
his photos, the store manager informed him" an agent had
demanded that an employee "give him copies of Bellecourt's pictures." A federal judge ruled in favor of the government; his decision was based, in part, on the type of
machine that allows the public to view the process of printing the photographs. Bellecourt said, "If we allow the
judge's order to stand, it'll be a threat to the basic, fundamental constitutional rights of all Americans."

Bellecourt has accused tribal leaders of "selling treaty
rights." Three reservations, Bois Forte, Fond du Lac, and
Grand Portage, agreed to an annual cash settlement of five

million dollars to limit hunting and fishing rights on original treaty land in the Arrowhead region of Minnesota. The reservations agreed to restrict commercial fishing and to abstain from spear fishing. The agreement between the three reservations and the Minnesota Department of Natural Resources was approved by a federal judge in June 1988. The agreement was negotiated, not forced; reservations were permitted to withdraw with proper notice to exercise rights to hunt and fish in the original treaty area outside the reservations. One year later, in June 1989, Fond du Lac voted to withdraw from the agreement with the state and the other two reservations.

Robert Peacock, tribal leader at Fond du Lac, told the *Minneapolis Star and Tribune*, "If one has agreed not to do something, in essence you've put a price on doing it. Once you've put a price on it, it implies it's for sale." He said land was a "gift from the creator. . . . You can't measure love in dollars. You can't measure religion in dollars." The Fond du Lac Reservation would have been paid almost two million dollars annually to abstain from commercial fishing and not to spear fish, which has caused so much racial rancor on lakes in northern Wisconsin.

"The Dairy State has turned sour about fishing," wrote Ron Schara in the *Minneapolis Star and Tribune*. "Specifically, spear fishing in the name of Chippewa treaty rights. . . . Retaining treaty rights that destroy sport fishing and threaten a tourism economy is a hollow victory for Indian leaders. And they ought to know that."

Schara is a popular sports columnist, but his condescension and racialism is misdirected and malicious, a reversion to earlier colonial reports on tribal cultures. Schara has the right to publish racial notions, the tribe has a right circumscribed in treaties; he reports the rancor, the tribe exercises an aboriginal right.

"The story of Native American claims to aboriginal land within what is now the United States is not a story of broken treaties, amended statutes, or breach of the sacred

duty of guardianship. Rather, it is the story of the un-
bridled, unabashed, and undisguised power of the con-
queror over the conquered," Michael Kaplan wrote in *Irredeemable America*.

The Chippewa in Wisconsin spear muskies and walleye
pike when the ice breaks on the northern lakes in the
spring. The tribe has done this for centuries. The rights to
hunt and fish are natural tribal practices, neither conferred
nor alienated, in the tribal sense, by state or political dominions; however, the tribal rights to hunt and fish and
gather wild rice have been contained by treaties with the
government of the United States. In recent court decisions
these tribal rights have been sustained.

The problems over land use started with conquest, political abuses, and racism, not with the aboriginal rights of
tribal cultures; the dominant poses are economic, a mani-
fest protectionism, macho tourism, and the patriarchal
possession of natural resources. The tribal practices are
natural rights that arise from aboriginal worldviews; the
domination and possession of the earth is a Western custom that is not the same as the natural tribal right to use
the land.

"Aboriginal title is a political issue, for the most part, not
a legal one," wrote Michael Kaplan. "The United States
government continued to extend sovereignty over tribal
lands but sustained Indian rights to use and occupancy.
Such use and occupancy has normally been based on exclusive possession antecedent to conquest or negotiated
acquisition of title, as by treaty, and it is not a property
right protected under the Fifth Amendment."

National sovereignties begin with tribal cultures; the
modern sense of tribal sovereignties has been determined
by treaties, state and federal statutes, court decisions, and
other implications, such as land use agreements. Charles
Wilkinson points out in *American Indians, Time, and the Law*,
that the existence of a tribe is maintained independent of
"any federal action." Tribalism is aboriginal, not a federal

source, "but it has become entwined with the federal government. . . . Congress established a comprehensive matrix of laws regulating Indian affairs and effectively limiting the scope of tribal sovereignty. . . . The power exists to enact everything from the debilitating allotment and termination programs to the beneficent child welfare and tax status laws that offer so much promise to Indian people."

The Chippewa are a tribal culture, and their aboriginal rights to hunt and fish on original treaty land in northern Wisconsin were settled in the United States Court of Appeals in 1983. The court recognized the rights mentioned in several treaties more than a century ago when vast territories were ceded to the government and reservations were established. Chippewa rights to hunt, fish, and gather wild rice on lakes, rivers, and lands in the ceded territories of the treaties were restored by the court. Nancy Lurie in the epilogue to *Irredeemable America* points out that at the time of the treaties the tribe "had long engaged in commercial fishing as well as hunting for the fur trade, so commercial activities were covered as a customary right in the treaties. The decision evoked bitter denunciations from white sportsmen's groups supported by generally anti-Indian whites claiming the Indians would wantonly wipe out all the fish and game."

Treaties determined the relations between the tribes and the federal government for several generations. Then, in 1871, Congress declared that the previous treaties would be honored, but in the future the tribes would form agreements with the federal government; legislation, not treaties, would arise from proposals and agreements to manage reservations and the tribes. The cessation of treaties was the end of tribal independence and the sense of national sovereignty. The General Allotment Act of 1887, for instance, provided individual land allotments; the tribes lost a hundred million acres of communal land on reservations. Moreover, Public Law 280 extended state, civil, and criminal jurisdiction on reservations.

The University of Minnesota sponsored the first conference on Indian Tribes and Treaties in 1955. Public officials, anthropologists, lawyers, and tribal respresentatives from various reservations attended the conference. John Killen, then a member of the Minnesota Law Review, reviewed several treaties and the legal issues that arose with state jurisdiction on tribal land.

Joe Vizenor, who was then an elected representative of the Minnesota Chippewa Tribe, argued that when Public Law 280 was presented to the tribe, "we went on record approving it with the provisions whereby we reserved our rights to fish, hunt, trap, and rice on our reservations. That was written in that law, and it seems to me that should clarify it." Vizenor continued, "Well, we have game wardens up there who are pinching Indians right and left for setting nets. We went to our Indian Office and we contacted the United States Attorney and we haven't a decision yet. We should like to know where we're standing, as quick as we can find out." The tribal right to hunt, fish, and gather wild rice was decided in federal court a generation later; the state did not have jurisdiction to enforce state game and fish laws on treaty land.

"To prove a point," Schara wrote in the *Minneapolis Star and Tribune*, "Wisconsin tribal leaders are giving their people old traditions instead of future hope. This isn't 1854. The way of their forefathers was not headlamps and electric trolling motors. . . . Or to put it another way: Does anybody really believe that what the American Indian people need today is all the fish they can spear?" Schara proved a racist point, but he should have asked about the ways of his own forefathers.

Dean Crist is president of Stop Treaty Abuse and the inventor of Treaty Beer, the "true brew of the working man." His partisan beer, and the organization, represent the formal opposition to tribal rights on treaty land. Stop Treaty Abuse, a non sequitur, and other protest associations seem to assume that federal courts created tribal rights to torment white people who fish and hunt for wild game. Rather, federal courts based their decisions on the treaties, an interpretation of aboriginal rights and territorial enclosures that had been abused by state governments for more than a century. Tribal rights were restored, not created, by recent court decisions. Some protesters argue that treaties should be rescinded; in that case, the ceded territories would be restored to the tribes, and white settlers could become criminal trespassers.

"Our argument is not with the Chippewa Indians," Larry Grescher told Kurt Chandler of the *Minneapolis Star and Tribune*. Grescher was executive director of Protect American Rights and Resources; his dubious disclaimer would not ease the racial duplicities of his organization. "We recognize that the Chippewa Indians are doing only what the law allows them to do. We are attempting to put pressure on federal legislators to take a look at . . . rescinding treaties."

An "Annual Indian Shoot" was announced by an anonymous organization in Wisconsin. The circular described a point system for scoring the shoot: plain Indian, five points; Indian with walleye, ten points; Indian with boat newer than yours, twenty points; Indian using pitchfork, thirty points; Indian tribal lawyer, one hundred points. The white circular mentioned "taking scalps," and the prizes included "six packs of Treaty Beer."

In April 1989, at demonstrations on northern lakes in the state, there were signs that read, "Save a walleye, spear an Indian." Pat Doyle reported for the *Minneapolis Star and Tribune* that a "parade of motorboats" followed a tribal man in a rowboat at midnight on Balsam Lake, Wisconsin. Kenny Pardun was in the rowboat; he held a light in one hand and a spear in the other. Someone shouted from a motorboat, "Did you get that light from your ancestors?"

Doyle reported that at Big Butternut Lake there were police in riot helmets to hold back a crowd of about a hundred white protesters, and to protect the rights of tribal people at the boat landing. The crowd shouted at the tribal people in their boats. "Gotta quit handing out those welfare checks so they can't buy a boat," someone shouted. "If we nailed their mailbox shut they'd starve to death." Then a man shouted, "Why don't we go back to our heritage and hunt you guys down?"

Ronald Reagan said, "Maybe we made a mistake in trying to maintain Indian cultures. Maybe we should not have humored them in wanting to stay in that kind of primitive lifestyle." The former president is no trickster, compassionate or otherwise; maybe we should have humored him when he pronounced his unintended ironies. His sense of tribal cultures seems to be based on simulations from western movies. The means to "maintain Indian cultures" were never mistakes; indeed, the bias is in the absence of humor and historical consideration. His voice could be a simulation, the riot and seethe of imperialism in politics and movie scenes. Reagan seemed to be in the movies when he visited Moscow in May 1988, and when he responded to questions about Native American Indians.

The use of the word "Indian" is postmodern, a navigational conception, a colonial invention, a simulation in sound and transcription. Tribal cultures became nominal, diversities were twisted to the core, and oral stories were set in written languages, the translations of discoveries.

Christopher Columbus reasoned that he had reached India, a generous mismeasure, but there were no Indians in India. The origin of the name, according to the *Dictionary of Indian English*, is *sindhu*, river or sea, from Sanskrit. The "name exchanged the initial sibilant for an aspirate" and became Hindu in Persian, a native of India.

Native American Indians are burdened with colonial pantribal names, and with imposed surnames translated from personal tribal nicknames by missionaries and federal agents. More than a hundred million people, and hundreds of distinct tribal cultures, were simulated as Indians; an invented pantribal name, one sound, bears treaties, statutes, and seasons, but no tribal culture, language, religion, or landscape.

The last national census enumerated close to one and a half million tribal people in the United States. The Cherokee are the most populous, followed by the people named the Navajo, Sioux, and Chippewa, the four largest tribes in the country. Some of the least populous tribes are located in New England; however, low populations are not proper measures of tribal interests. The Passamaquoddy and the Penobscot, for example, were awarded more than eighty million dollars in a recent land claims settlement in Maine.

Native American Indians are ever in the news because tribal cultures continue to be dubious measures of civilization and mismeasures of race; tribal shades, names, and poses are collectibles in liberal stories, and the simulated tribes are praised on certain national and religious holidays. Thanksgiving Day, for instance, imposes an aboriginal retinue and celebrants from the wilderness; however, tribal cultures are not honored on Columbus Day.

"From where the sun now stands, I will fight no more forever," is attributed to Chief Joseph of the people named the Nez Perce. From that memorable "surrender speech" to the taxicab driver who "cleaned" a statue of Chief Seattle, the indigenous cultures of this hemisphere have become tribal camp, postmodern translations and simulations. The stories that follow have been selected from recent publications of books, newspapers, and magazines.

"I realize that there was one area I'd never really exploited: my lifelong obsession with American Indians," wrote Oleg Cassini, the costume designer, in *In My Own Fashion: An Autobiography*. "A good many of my American Indian dresses required intricate beading of a sort that was not available in Italy. . . . I'd been told Hong Kong was the place to find such material."

Cassini tried to appease his obsession in an agreement with Peter MacDonald, then the chairman of the Navajo Tribal Council. The couturier announced at the National

Press Club that he would build, as a joint venture with the tribal government, a "world-class luxury resort" on the reservation. The architecture and furnishings of the tourist resort would "have their base in authentic Navajo designs." MacDonald said the resort would "reflect the unique culture and tradition of our people." Moreover, the tribal leader announced: "We are creating a Navajo Board of Standards for all new tourist facilities on the reservation to assure that the Navajo name means quality."

Visitors to the Grand Canyon complain that the view is ruined by air pollution. What some visitors thought might have been smoke from forest fires turned out to be industrial smog, reported *Time* magazine. The National Park Service studied weather patterns, the haze, and determined that the source was the Navajo Generating Station located on the Navajo Reservation near Page, Arizona. "The plant, burning 24,000 tons of coal daily and releasing an estimated 12 to 13 tons of sulfur dioxide from its smokestacks every hour, was found responsible." The plant, one of the largest coal fired generators in the nation, supplies power to Arizona, Nevada, and California. Los Angeles, in a sense, is air conditioned by coal generated power from the Navajo Nation. The *New York Times* reported that the Environmental Protection Agency found "substantial evidence" that the power station was "a major contributor" to air pollution at the Grand Canyon.

The *Seattle Post-Intelligencer* reported that "Cabbie's scrubbing rubs Chief Seattle wrong way." A taxicab driver tried to clean the natural patina from the bronze sculpture of the famous tribal orator; he used an acid that damaged the statue. "I tried to do something good and it turned out bad," said the cab driver. "The Indians in the area need to know that the white man cares." Chief Seattle told Isaac Stevens, the governor of Washington Territory, that "when the last red man shall have perished, and the memory of my tribe shall have become a myth among the white men, these shores will swarm with the invisible dead of my tribe. . . . The white man will never be alone."

The *Los Angeles Times* reported in September 1989 that leaders of the Mormon Church "excommunicated the only American Indian ever appointed to the church hierarchy." George Lee, one of more than forty thousand Navajo Mormons, was the first high official "to be erased from membership rolls" in forty-six years. Lee is reported to be the son of a "medicine man." He was excommunicated for "apostasy and other conduct unbecoming a member of the church." Indians are mentioned in the Book of Mormon.

The *Independent*, a newspaper published in Gallup, New Mexico, reported on July 6, 1989, that Russell Means had been arrested by "Navajo police officers . . . as he attempted to make a citizen's arrest of the Bureau of Indian Affairs area director" James Stevens at the tribal government center in Window Rock. Means was held overnight in the Crownpoint "jail on assault and battery charges." He accused the area director of "interfering in Navajo political matters."

The *Navajo Times* reported that "Means had held a press conference the week before in which he said he would place Stevens under citizen's arrest. . . . Means got him in a headlock." Stevens is a San Carlos Apache; Means is Dakota and is married to a Navajo.

The *Albuquerque Journal* indicated that the area director had agreed to meet with the "Pro-Dineh Voters group, a Navajo organization, seeking reinstatement of Chairman Peter MacDonald." The Navajo Supreme Court had affirmed the suspension of MacDonald by the tribal council, following allegations that he "took kickbacks from reservation contractors and personally profited from the tribe's purchase of the Big Boquillas Ranch." Stevens recognized the appointment of an interim tribal chairman. Means opposed that decision and attempted a citizen's arrest.

MacDonald was "stripped of power by his own tribal council" and faces "bribery and corruption charges,"

Sandy Tolan reported in the *New York Times Magazine* on November 26, 1989. "When MacDonald refused to leave office, he precipitated a five-month crisis in the Navajo government, culminating in a violent confrontation." MacDonald said, "All they want to do is silence people like me who speak out against those who are trying to erode tribal sovereignty."

The Select Committee on Indian Affairs reported that MacDonald "is one example of a tribal chief executive who placed personal enrichment above public service. For years, MacDonald received bogus 'consulting fees,' 'loans' and 'gifts'—and even persuaded the tribe to purchase desert land worth less than $26 million for more than $33 million so that, through a shell company, he could enjoy a secret share of the $7 million markup."

MacDonald was born on a sheep drive near Teec Nos Pos, Arizona. He enlisted in the Marines and became a Navajo Code Talker; later, he graduated from college as an electrical engineer. He returned to the reservation and has been elected to four terms as chairman. Now, he is "likened to a corrupt dictator by many of his own people." Some of his critics contend that he has strayed from the tribal way. "If you cease to live the way of the Navajos, you're going to become less human," Daniel Peaches told Sandy Tolan. "You will have less moral strength."

The *Minnesota Daily* reported in August 1989 that Jim Weaver, an elder member of the Minnesota Chippewa Tribe, would fast until the federal government investigated the White Earth Reservation. Weaver was critical of Darrell Wadena, the elected tribal chairman. "If someone has to die to get this man out," said the elder, "that's what is going to happen." Weaver was serious; he tended his fire. "It's a sacred fire. I keep it going until I either kick the bucket or end the fast." He ended the fast. Wadena told a reporter, "If the news media would just go away and leave it alone, those guys would go home and start eating."

White Earth Reservation politics are postmodern, and the poses are ever terminal.

The *Los Angeles Times* reported in September 1989 that the wild rice harvest was ruined in Minnesota. Overnight the tribal cash crop "fell victim to scientific tinkering, big-time agribusiness, Indian complacency and a wave of greed and hype stretching from the farms in the North Woods to the fertile rice paddies of the Sacramento Valley."

Mahnomin, or wild rice, is not a proper rice, but a coarse, indigenous, annual aquatic grass. The wild is nominal, but the wild harvest is protected by state statutes in Minnesota; however, the rice that is a grass has become a postmodern cash crop on idle, not wild, land in California.

Statutes in Minnesota specify that wild rice harvested on public land be done from canoes with push poles and flails to gather the rice. The regulations are based on the traditional harvest practices of woodland tribes. Mahnomin grows best in shallow lakes and rivers; mechanical harvests are forbidden on public waters. The high price of natural wild rice, between five and ten dollars a pound retail, attracted investors. Minnesota legislators responded to the potential capital investments and supported research to develop a commercial grain that would survive mechanical harvesting on private land.

The specialty market for wild rice has provided a source of income on some reservations. Ikwe Marketing, for instance, a group of tribal women on the White Earth Reservation, listed wild rice, native recipes, and handcrafted birchbark baskets in a recent issue of an alternative holiday gift catalog.

The demand for institutional and industrial wild rice has stimulated the commercial development of the market; for example, broken rice was separated and milled for use in pancake flour. Tribal governments invested in commercial paddies, but the most profitable paddies were subsidized by federal agricultural policies. California proved to be a better location to cash in on commercial wild rice than Minnesota.

"Established white rice growers jumped on the bandwagon," reported the *Los Angeles Times.* "To trim a surplus of white rice, many California growers were getting federal set-aside payments to hold some of their land out of production. But idled land still had to be planted with some sort of grass to prevent erosion. And, because wild rice technically was a grass, it started turning up in more and more idled fields. The growers sold the wild rice and kept the government set-aside money to boot."

Syndicated columnist Jack Anderson, in a report about Jamake Highwater, stated that "one of the country's most celebrated Indians has fabricated much of the background that made him famous." Highwater, the author of several books about tribal cultures, wrote in *This Song Remembers,* a collection of portraits published in 1980, that he speaks eleven languages and "entered the university at thirteen."

Anderson revealed that Highwater admitted that he "lied about many details of his life. Asked why someone of such genuine and extraordinary talent felt he had to concoct a spurious background, Highwater said he felt that doors would not have opened for him if he had relied on his talent alone." He claimed advanced degrees from the University of California at Berkeley, and the University of Chicago. "In fact, he admitted he never got any such degrees."

Highwater may have opened doors with his spurious identities, but he stole public attention, and his bent for recognition may have closed doors for honest tribal people who have the moral courage to raise doubts about their own identities. "I am cautious about my success, and about my visibility," he wrote in *This Song Remembers.* "As a tribal person, I've had the rewarding experience of having Native Americans from all tribal backgrounds say, 'What you're doing is good.' " He said he was born in the "early forties" and "raised in northern Montana and southern Alberta, Canada. I'm not enrolled in the Blackfeet tribe, but I spent my first thirteen years among the Blackfeet and Cree people."

Anderson pointed out that Highwater has listed his birthplace as Los Angeles, Canada, South Dakota, Montana, and Normandy, France. "Vine Deloria Jr. and Hank Adams say flatly that Highwater is not an Indian."

In *Shadow Show: An Autobiographical Insinuation*, published in 1986, two years after the column by Jack Anderson, Highwater wrote, "The greatest mystery of my life is my own identity. . . . To escape things that are painful we must reinvent ourselves. Either we reinvent ourselves or we choose not to be anyone at all. We must not feel guilty if we are among those who have managed to survive." He seems to name his identities in others, a culture consumer; his new stories are autoinsinuations, a literature that abandons his dubious connections to tribal cultures.

Highwater wrote in *Shadow Show*, "I begin to think that our borrowed lives are necessities in a world filled with hostility and pain, a confusing world largely devoid of credible social truths."

Ishi, the last of his tribe, has become the romantic postmodern measure of survivance because he died in a museum at the University of California. His choices were passed over to settlement and civilization; he consented, but he might never have chosen to live and die in a museum.

The Yahi tribal survivor was a popular aboriginal artifact, a voice from the Stone Age. He was a romantic figure in tribal simulations, and was studied with unnatural respect by anthropologists and linguists; however, we must never revise his manners and loneliness as the behavior of a happy slave to science. His tribal identities, and the landscapes he imagined, were translated and transvalued in postmodern education and politics; he lived with one name and an uncommon sinecure, a tenured tribal consultant to enlightened methodologists.

Alfred Kroeber was in New York when Ishi died; he wrote to the curator of the museum, "If there is any talk about the interests of science, say for me that science can go to hell." The distinguished anthropologist anticipated by more than two generations the scientific debate over the reburial of tribal remains.

Ishi was cremated and his remains were placed in a "small black Pueblo jar," the curator wrote. "The funeral was private and no flowers were brought." The inscription reads: *Ishi, the last Yana Indian, 1916.*

Ishi did not choose to live in a museum, but at least his remains were protected by a friend; his bones were not stored in a museum as were the bones of several hundred thousand other tribal people. Some scientists oppose the reburial of tribal remains; others avoid the moral discourse on natural rights and the proposal to establish bone courts to hear and resolve disputes over research interests and reburial.

Douglas Schwartz, president of the School of American Research in Santa Fe, New Mexico, and his associate Jonathan Haas, for instance, have protected their research on tribal remains and their possession of ceremonial artifacts; their research motivation and interests in human remains would be recorded in a bone court.

The distinctions between archaeologists and physical anthropologists are lost in the discourse on reburial. "We archaeologists are bearing the heat for physical anthropologists," Larry Zimmerman told a reporter for the *Chronicle of Higher Education* in September 1989. "We're out there on the front lines at the digs, and they're in the lab not talking to Indians." Zimmerman is a professor at the University of South Dakota. Frank Norick, an anthropologist at the Lowie Museum of Anthropology, University of California, Berkeley, has "gone on record in opposition to such efforts as that of Stanford University to return remains to local tribes."

Thomas White Hawk murdered a jeweler in Vermillion,

Thomas White Hawk leaving a court hearing, 1968

South Dakota. The nineteen-year-old tribal orphan and college student shot the man in his bedroom, beat him on the head in the kitchen, gathered his blood in a bowl, and then raped his wife several times. The crime was heinous, a vicious and horrific scene in an otherwise pleasant university town on the prairie; the handsome murderer was hiding as a child might do in the closet when the police arrived at the house. White Hawk confessed to the crimes and was sentenced to death in the electric chair.

Joseph Satten in South Dakota, 1968

I read about the crime and the sentence in the *Minneapolis Tribune*. I was in South Dakota a few days later to investigate the crime and organized opposition to capital
punishment. I traveled around the state for more than six
months to gather information on White Hawk and his
family. Three thousand copies of my essay on the case,
which is published here, were mailed at no charge to
individuals and institutions around the world. I reviewed
the court hearings and attended the trial of William

Stands, who was with White Hawk at the time of the crime.

Joseph Satten, the psychiatrist from the Menninger Clinic, reported that White Hawk suffered from psychotic episodes and lapsed into "transient" dreams. "His Indian background would tend to make him place a high value on stoicism, emotional impassivity, withdrawal, aloofness, and the denial of dependence on others. In addition, the tendency of some in the dominant culture to devaluate Indians and the Indian culture would tend to accentuate his feelings of loneliness and suspicion." Satten, in the end, supported my narrative description of "cultural schizophrenia."

The governor commuted the death sentence, but the parole board recommended that no further commutations be made in the future. Without the possibility of parole, White Hawk faces a natural death sentence in the state penitentiary. Many people in the state believe that is more than he deserves for his crimes.

I visited White Hawk at the penitentiary in June 1987. I had not seen him for twenty years; he never told me how he felt about my critical essay on the murder, his motivation, and the sentence. He said he would not have changed a word. White Hawk wrote to his lawyer Douglas Hall, "I have done some heavy thinking and I have been unable to come up with any feasible method for altering Gerald Vizenor's journal to suit our purposes now. . . . Vizenor's work was superbly written and the only elements which I believe we could alter at all would be the placement of the transcript quotes he used. Otherwise, I would change nothing."

PART 1
CROSSBLOOD SURVIVANCE

✚ Crossbloods and the Chippewa: Treaties, Bingo, and Tribal Simulations

The transvaluation of roles that turns the despised and oppressed into symbols of salvation and rebirth is nothing new in the history of human culture, but when it occurs, it is an indication of a new cultural direction, perhaps of a deep cultural revolution.

ROBERT BELLAH
The Broken Covenant

Gaming has always been part of our culture, and now it is an integral part of our economy as well.

WILLIAM HOULE
Tribal Chairman
Fond du Lac Reservation

The White Earth Reservation has become a dubious measure of colonial abuse and rapacious federal policies that dominated the land, and dislocated communal cultures; crossblood realities, and bitter revisions of a romantic past, would haunt the most common political decision on that reservation.

The first part of this essay considers the racial encounters with tribal cultures at the turn of the last century and reviews institutional strains from treaties to allotments, and postmodern adventures in high-stakes bingo. The second part is a presentation of tribal religious and educational experiences, from shamans to boarding schools, peyote ceremonies, radical movements, and other essential revisions of untouchable bureaucracies. These overtures to tribal histories, crossblood identities, personal remembrance, and the separations of imperialism, become a political discourse based on the translated responses of those tribal people who testified to the committee that investigated fraudulent land allotments on the White Earth Reservation.

HYPERREALITIES AND RACIAL EXPOSITIONS

Minnesota Governor Alexander Ramsey reported that "education and agricultural efforts can only hope for useful results when Indians are removed in pursuance of treaties . . . . and when manual-labor schools" are established "to educate their rising generation in the arts, conveniences, and habits of civilization." Ramsey expressed the racial preconceptions of his time; the nation, at the turn of the last century, had removed tribal cultures to federal reservations and then condoned imperialism with romantic notions that the tribes would vanish.

The last "savages" were captured in emulsion by celebrated photographers, "specimens" were paraded at international expositions, and tribal cultures were revised in colonial histories and dioramas. At the 1901 Pan-American Exposition in Buffalo, for example, Vice President Theodore Roosevelt visited a Native American Indian concession and named a newborn tribal child Pan-Anna.[1]

W. J. McGee, an anthropologist at the Bureau of American Ethnology, advanced his theories of racial progress at the 1904 Louisiana Purchase Exposition in Saint Louis. His aim, as head of the anthropology department at the fair, was to "present human progress from the dark prime to the highest enlightenment, from savagery to civic organization, from egoism to altruism." McGee, who was identi-

4

fied as the "overlord of the savage world" in a local newspaper, believed in "cephalization" and emphasized "Indian school work, America's best effort to elevate the lower races."[2]

Stephen Jay Gould, in *The Mismeasure of Man*, points out that "racial prejudice may be as old as recorded human history, but its biological justification imposed the additional burden of intrinsic inferiority upon despised groups, and precluded redemption by conversion or assimilation." Christian credence and conversions seldom embraced tribal cultures with pleasure, or a sense of human sameness; the tribes were to be saved from their color and delivered to the thresholds of colonial domination.

OUTSIZED SHOES AT BOARDING SCHOOLS

The time is twelve minutes before twelve at the turn of the last century; the window shades are drawn in a classroom at a reservation boarding school where sixteen students are posed with their heads down for a photograph. The words "crayfish," "crusty fill," "streams," "stones," and "sand" are written on the blackboard; two bird nests and broken branches are mounted near a window. The open door at the right of the photograph reveals a private residence, with a chest of drawers. The classroom is heated with wood and coal.

In the back rows of the classroom eight boys with short hair, dressed in uniforms, dark coats and vests, concentrate on manual skills, perhaps basket weaving. The eight girls in the front rows are sewing; their hair is braided. New readers or textbooks are stacked in two neat rows on the front bench.

The girl in the left front seat is distinguished from the others in the photograph by a laced boot that appears to be *twice the size of a normal foot* for her age; she would not complain. The outsized boot is emblematic of federal domination on reservations—never a proper meet. Lewis Meriam

5

Turn-of-the-century reservation boarding school

reported that the shoes provided to children at federal boarding schools were "bought on the lowest bid" and were of poor quality. "Another serious factor is the fitting of shoes to the individual child. In some instances accurate measurements are not taken."[3] The student in the front row with the outsized boot might have been Mahgeet, Isabelle, Catherine Goodman, or Be Be Shank.

Catherine Goodman testified on Friday, July 28, 1911, before the House of Representatives committee that investigated the White Earth Reservation. She was questioned by James Graham, chairman of the committee, and Marsden Burch, an attorney with the Department of Justice, about the sale of allotments on the reservation; the interpreter was Margaret Warren.[4]

"Catherine Goodman is my English name," she said.

"What is your Indian name?"

6

"Kah deen," she answered.

"How old are you?" asked Burch.

"Seventeen. . . . "

"Do you have an allotment of land?"

"Yes. . . . "

"Whom did you sell it to?"

"Some one at Waubun. . . . "

"Do you remember the color of his hair?"

"His hair was almost white. . . . "

"How much did you get for the land?"

"Two-hundred dollars. . . . "

"Are your father and mother full-blood Indians? . . . "

"My father, I think is a full-blood," said Catherine Goodman through the translator, "and my mother a mixed-blood."

"How much white blood? . . . "

"I do not know."

"Does she show the white blood in her face. . . . ?"

"I do not know," she answered.

"What did you do with the two-hundred dollars that you received that day for your land?" asked a committee member.

"I paid two dollars each trip to Waubun and back for a hired team," answered Catherine Goodman. The committee members were eager to understand who bought the allotment and what became of the money.

"What did you do with the rest of the money?"

"I bought a sewing machine and a bed and some provisions and clothing. . . . " Catherine had learned to sew at school and the sewing machine was a sign of civilization.

"Can you read English?"

"A little," she answered.

"What reader were you in school?"

"In the third reader."

"Can you write your name?"

"I can write my English name."

7

"Why did you not write your name at the time you were at the bank and put your hand to the pen?" asked James Graham, the chairman of the committee. Catherine testified that the bank held some of her money but did not give her a record of the amount on deposit.

"I could not write then. . . . "

"Who asked you to come to Washington?"

"My mother."

"What did she say to you?"

"My mother told me that someone had come for me to come here, and advised me to come to try and get my land back," she answered.

Lewis Meriam reported in 1928 that the "allotment acts opened several ways through which the whites could obtain possession of the Indian lands. The surplus land remaining after allotments had been made was sold and the proceeds paid into the tribal funds. When an allotted Indian was declared competent, he received a fee patent to his land and could thereafter sell it without government supervision. . . . In some instances acts of Congress have resulted in the wholesale exploitation of the Indians, as was the case among . . . the Chippewas of Minnesota."[5]

Be Be Shank was sworn in by the chairman of the committee and she was questioned by Marsden Burch, an attorney with the Justice Department, and other committee members.

"Have you been to school?"

"Yes, sir."

"Where?"

"At White Earth."

"How many years?" asked Burch.

"Probably three years."

"Can you give the Indian name of your father?"

"His name was Kah don shis."

"Can you give the name of your mother?"

"Nah zhe wah quay," she answered.

8

"Can you read or write?"

"No, sir."

"How long were you at school at White Earth?"

"Three years."

"Did you ever see the land you owned?"

"No sir."

"Who told you that you owned land?"

"My mother."

"Did you sell this land?"

"Yes, sir. . . . "

"Whom did you sell it to?"

"To a man at Waubun. . . . "

"Did you make out any paper or sign any paper?"

"I signed one by a thumb print. . . . "

"What part of the year was it?"

"It was in the summer time," answered Be Be Shank.

"Do you know the Fourth of July?"

"Yes, sir."

"Was it before the Fourth of July?"

"It was probably after the Fourth of July."

"Do you know how to count money?"

"No, sir. . . . "

"Was the money paid, then, to anybody by this man?"

"The money was paid to me."

"What did you do with it?" asked the attorney.

"I went to the store."

"Did you spend the money? . . . "

"Yes, sir."

"What did you buy, if you remember?"

"One horse and a colt. . . . "

"What did you do with the horse?"

"He died."

"Did it have a colt?"

"Yes, sir," answered Be Be Shank.

"Did the colt die, too?"

"Yes, sir; it died, too, when it was quite big."[6]

NINE TREATIES WITH THE CHIPPEWA

The Chippewa or Anishinaabe tribe participated in nine treaties and several legal agreements with the United States. These treaties, signed in one generation between 1826 and 1867, are the legal foundation of tribal, federal, and state government relationships; specific articles in these treaties defined boundaries, ceded land, granted minerals, natural resources, and other rights to the tribe and to the federal government. For example, the right to gather wild rice, to hunt and fish in ceded territories, was "guaranteed to Indians." These were aboriginal rights, or natural rights, not privileges conferred by the federal government; these rights would be argued as tribal sovereignties.

In 1837, in consideration of vast land cessions in the Territory of Wisconsin, the federal government agreed to provide the tribe, annually for twenty years, "nine thousand five hundred dollars, to be paid in money; nineteen thousand dollars, to be delivered in goods; three thousand dollars for establishing three blacksmiths shops, supporting the blacksmiths, and furnishing them with iron and steel; one thousand dollars for farmers, and for supplying them and the Indians, with implements of labor, with grain or seed, and whatever else may be necessary to enable them to carry on their agricultural pursuits; two thousand dollars in provisions; five hundred dollars in tobacco."[7]

In 1847 the Pillager Band of Chippewa Indians received annually, for five years, three-point blankets, cloth, kettles, tobacco, five barrels of salt, and other sundries, for land cessions. Moreover, the "parties to this treaty, shall receive as a present two hundred warranted beaver-traps and twenty-five northwest guns."

The 1867 treaty with the Chippewas of the Mississippi created the White Earth Reservation. In consideration of ceded land estimated at two million acres the government agreed to the following: "Five thousand dollars for the

10

erection of school buildings upon the reservation. . . . Four thousand dollars each year for ten years, and as long as the President may deem necessary after the ratification of the treaty, for the support of a school. . . . Ten thousand dollars for the erection of a saw-mill, with grist-mill attached. . . . Five thousand dollars to be expended in assisting in the erection of houses. . . . Five thousand dollars to be expended, with the advice of the chiefs, in the purchase of cattle, horses, and farming utensils, and in making such improvements as are necessary for opening farms. . . . Six thousand dollars each year for ten years, and as long thereafter as the President may deem proper, to be expended in promoting the progress of the people in agriculture. . . . Twelve thousand dollars each year for ten years for the support of a physician, and three hundred each year for ten years for necessary medicines. . . . Ten thousand dollars to pay for provisions, clothing, or such other articles as the President may determine, to be paid to them immediately on their removal to their new reservation."[8]

The schools and houses on the new reservation were meager and bare, according to several investigative reports. Children were in need of clothing and medical care; there were few real improvements in farm operations, as the treaties had promised to provide. Lewis Meriam reported that tribal people did not know the value of the land they were allotted; they did not know how to use their allotments and "the government as a rule did not send to them persons competent to teach them its uses."[9]

Meanwhile, unscrupulous land dealers and bankers bought individual allotments while government agents worried about mixedbloods on the reservation, or those who were "competent" to sell their allotments. The cash from the sale of "surplus" tribal land was deposited in government accounts and used to cover the maintenance of schools on the reservation. In 1911 the tribe had almost four million dollars in the United States Treasury that had "accrued from the sale of land and timber." Some of this money was used for the "support and civilization of the White Earth Indians."[10]

MIXEDBLOODS AND LAND ALLOTMENTS

In 1887, after a decade of public debate, the Dawes Severalty Act, or the General Allotment Act, was passed; the new law divided communal reservation land into allotments, and individual ownership was advanced as an operative measure of civilization. Meanwhile, betterment was no more than a colonial connivance; lumber companies penetrated the reservation with legislation that favored their interests, and, at the same time, released a new wave of racism based on the perverse arithmetics of the mixture of white and tribal blood; the division of "blood quantum" became a racial measure of "civilization."

The tribe had no choice in the land allotment laws on the reservation, and no real choice in the location of allotments; despite the vast land cessions and promises in treaties, tribal money, from the forced sale of "surplus" communal land, paid the cost of education and other services on some reservations. Furthermore, boarding schools are "supported in part by the labor of the students. Those above the fourth grade ordinarily work for half a day and go to school for half a day."[11]

James Graham, chairman of the committee that investigated the White Earth Reservation, reported that tribal "people are the descendants of a race which for centuries had held trade and commerce in contempt. . . . Indeed, the real Indians seem to be without what might be called the business instinct. On the other hand, the white men and the 'near white' Indians are the descendants of a race which for thousands of years has followed trade and commerce" and struggled for "political advantage or supremacy." His racist notion of "political advantage" would include the Clapp amendment, which was approved in 1906; the act allowed mixedbloods to sell with no restrictions

12

their timber and allotments on the White Earth Reservation. This legislation provided that the restrictions on "full bloods . . . shall be removed when the Secretary of the Interior is satisfied that . . . full-blood Indians are competent to handle their own affairs."[12]

Marsden Burch, the attorney who questioned Catherine Goodman and Be Be Shank, told the committee that tribal people formed two lines when they assembled for allotments on the reservation: "When the allotments came to be made, it is a singular circumstance that the most valuable of the pine was allotted to the mixed blood." He pointed out how difficult it was to know "who was an adult of the mixed blood or who was a minor of the mixed blood." Catherine Goodman, a crossblood, testified that she was fifteen years old when she sold her allotment; she had been to school but she was not able to read or write at the time.

E. B. Linnen, an inspector with the Department of the Interior, reported to the committee that no "reliable list of full bloods had been established" on the reservation. When mixedbloods were allowed to sell their allotments "the full bloods sold theirs as well; not only their lands but the pine timber, and a concerted effort seems to have been made by the land buyers to establish every full-blood Indian who had valuable land or timber as an adult mixed blood, which was done by false, fraudulent, or forged affidavits. . . .

"It is safe to say that these Indians, as a whole, did not receive one-tenth of the value of their lands or timber. The land men were aided by numerous educated mixed bloods, who act as interpreters and aid in defrauding these Indians. In scarcely any instance was the Indian paid the amount promised him. In numerous cases they sold their lands when intoxicated, and in many cases the Indian was put under the influence of liquor in order to defraud him out of his land. They were traded old, worthless horses, wagons, buggies, harnesses, and other articles at excessive

13

prices for their lands in lieu of cash. Mortgages were placed on their lands running for periods of ten years and the interest collected in advance from the moneys advanced to them. The persons who secured these mortgages invariably got title to the lands within a short period."[13]

These problems, or imposed structures, were investigated by government committees; general news and editorial articles appeared in local and metropolitan newspapers. *The Progress*, a newspaper edited by two crossbloods on the White Earth Reservation, published controversial editorials and critical comments on government policies. "The novelty of a newspaper published upon this reservation may cause many to be wary in their support, and this from a fear that it may be revolutionary in character," the editor wrote in the first number, March 25, 1886. Later, this headline appeared: "Is it an Indian Bureau? About some of the freaks in the employ of the Indian Service whose actions are a disgrace to the nation and a curse to the cause of justice."[14]

Prior to 1934 and the passage of the Indian Reorganization Act, "two goals had guided federal Indian policy: the acquisition of Indian lands and the cultural transformation of Indians into Euro-Americans—in a word, 'assimilation.' Those goals were enshrined in the Dawes Act, which heralded the age of 'allotment.' Washington broke up much of the tribal land base, withdrawing some property from Indian ownership and distributing other, often marginal, lands to individual tribal members. 'Surplus' lands, more often than not the richest, were then sold off to white settlers."[15]

The *Minneapolis Journal*, more concerned with manners and social behavior than racial violence, reported on July 16, 1906, that "with the minds of the White Earth Indians muddled by liquor, and their eyes dazzled by money, of which they know little, the White Earth mixed-bloods are in a fair way to lose all the Government allotments recently

14

given to them. The land is fast passing into the hands of scheming land-grabbers, and if the present campaign of the sharks is maintained the White Earth Indian Reservation will soon be a thing of the past."

At the turn of the last century tribal newspapers published stories on government intrusions and dubious resolutions to reservation problems; at the same time, metropolitan newspapers supported racialism and notions of savagism and civilization and reported on tribal members as tragic victims. In the past two decades, on the other hand, those romantic testimonials attributed to bourgeois white liberals, a sentimental bereavement over the assumed loss of "traditional" tribal cultures, now seem to echo a new narcissism, a new "liberal fascism," or an ideological variation on a structural theme in public media; the revisions and simulations of the past would serve neocolonialists in the present.

American Indian Movement leader Vernon Bellecourt, for instance, wrote that his "real name, Wabuninini, translates to Dawn, New Day, or Day Break Man. I am a member of the White Earth Anishinaabe nation and of Anishinaabe Akeeng, which means 'the people's land.' We are a coalition of allottees and heirs to the White Earth Anishinaabe nation organized to stop the further taking of our treaty-guaranteed lands and to recover what has been illegally taken from us." His editorial article was adapted from testimony given before congressional committees.[16] Bellecourt was bitter because he had lost a tribal election to Darrell Wadena on the White Earth Reservation.

Louise Erdrich, in a *New York Times* magazine article, pointed out the immediate legal and political disputes over original federal allotments and the current ownership of land on the White Earth Reservation. Erdrich, a novelist, with Michael Dorris, her anthropologist husband, wrote that the "acrimonious conflict over land ownership" involves several tribal factions, "small farmers against bureaucrats, and politicians against their constituencies. No

15

one disputes that decades ago local Indians were unfairly deprived of hundreds of thousands of acres that were guaranteed to them in perpetuity by solemn treaty; yet no one can agree about what should be done to correct that injustice today."[17] Erdrich reviews the most obvious voices of contention, but she neither explains the various allotments in the past century nor elucidates the complications of more than three generations of heirs to disputed reservation land; some allotments were sold by tribal members and are neither solemn nor disputed.

Erdrich concludes that the protagonists in the "dispute see themselves as righteous and heroic, for each is in the position of defending a birthright, a territory paid for by labor and affection and long residence, the immutable inheritance they have hoped to pass on to their children." She construes a romantic resolution, a simulation of the past.

MOCK VICTIMS IN FEDERAL COURT

Nine treaties, and numerous other written agreements with state and federal governments, are material connections to historical identities; however, in the tribal oral tradition these chronicles are dubious interpretations of tribal dreams and experiences. Tribal cultures have been rendered indistinct in the racist binaries of savagism and civilization; various romantics, autistic conservatives, and culture cultists have homogenized tribal philosophies and transvalued tribal visions into counterculture slogans and environmental politics.

Meanwhile, reservations and new tribal governments endure with assured democracies and favorable decisions on treaties in federal courts. The Minnesota Chippewa Tribe, a federation of six reservations in the state, White Earth, Mille Lacs, Leech Lake, Fond du Lac, Nett Lake, and Grand Portage, was established under the Indian Reorganization Act of 1934. Fifty years ago, John Broker became the first president of the federation; since then, the

16

responsibilities of an elected representative on the reservation have multiplied with new programs and legal interpretations, from child care, tribal courts, and water rights, to bingo and new measures of tribal sovereignties.

In January 1972, for example, Federal Judge Edward Devitt ruled that members of the Leech Lake Reservation had the right to hunt, fish, and gather wild rice on reservation treaty land without state restrictions. The state had assumed jurisdiction over the reservation in violation of treaties and tribal sovereignties. In 1972, Leech Lake created an independent conservation department and reached an agreement with the Minnesota Department of Natural Resources that allows "a licensing system permitting the Indian Band to charge an extra fee for non-Indian hunting and fishing within the reservation." Governor Wendell Anderson, who negotiated the agreement with tribal representatives, said that while the "accord applies only to the Leech Lake area, we are hopeful that the pattern established here will be adopted for all open reservations in Minnesota." Tribal leaders, however, are more cautious in negotiations than were their grandparents and distant relatives who signed treaties with the federal government. Tribal trust in the written word has been eroded by misdeeds and bureaucratic malevolence.

The Minnesota Chippewa Tribe opposed the proposal for special state licenses that could be used on six reservations. Tribal leaders argued then that not all reservation governments in the state are interested in opening their lands and resources to public tourism and recreation.[18]

The White Earth Reservation maintains a conservation program under state law but has never reached an agreement with the state to issue special licenses to hunt and fish on the reservation. Other reservations continue to negotiate with the state, and there is at least one new federal lawsuit over tribal rights to hunt and fish on land that was ceded in treaties.

17

Curtis Gagnon, a member of the Grand Portage Reservation, was arrested by a state game warden for hunting moose on treaty land. The hunter and the reservation claim that the state does not have the right to control hunting and fishing in that treaty area. Kent Tupper, the attorney who represented the Leech Lake Reservation in a similar federal lawsuit, said in 1985 that he did not "expect as much community backlash in the Arrowhead region as there was at Leech Lake and White Earth."[19]

In the past century, or three generations, tribal cultures have moved from colonial domination, isolation, and deprivation on reservations, to independent elected governments, assertive remedies in state and federal courts, high-stakes bingo, and educated constituencies; and for the first time in tribal histories there are more tribal people living in urban areas than on reservations, according to the last census.

BINGO SOVEREIGNTIES AND PAVED ROADS

Martha Thomas asked Al White, head of the Prairie Island Sioux tribal council, and then the assistant manager of the new Island Bingo, "Does bingo for profit go against the grain of your heritage?" White, who is a sculptor and graduate of the Institute of American Indian Arts in Santa Fe, responded with allegoric stories:

"Before our students get on the bus to go to school," he said, "they're really open and really boisterous. But when they get in the classroom, the teachers will say, 'That kid's a slow learner. He's not even looking at me when I talk to him. . . . ' Actually, a lot of our children were classed as slow learners. But they were really putting on a face to cope with the classroom."[20]

Island Bingo has earned millions of dollars for this small tribal community near Red Wing, Minnesota; roads have been paved, each child in the community has a trust fund, health and dental care are provided, and members of the

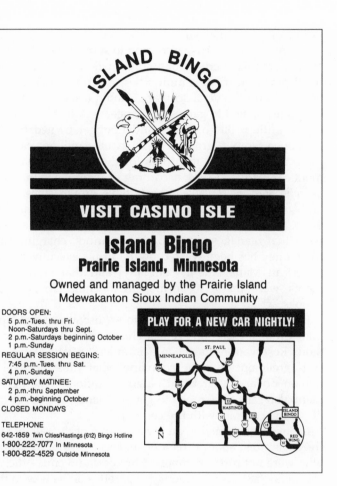

tribal community receive a cash dividend once a month.
Where other economic development ventures have failed,
high-stakes bingo has resolved the unemployment problem in the first few months of operation.

Bingo, however, is a dubious economic resolution on
some reservations; this high-stakes game, unlike simple
fund raisers in church basements, is much less than a tribal

19

vision or a cardinal virtue whispered on the altar. The enormous cash returns, according to some critics, have attracted organized crime. Behind the wild cash and instant fiscal power in tribal communities, a serious concern has been voiced by several scholars: should tests of tribal sovereignties be tied to games of chance?

The Little 6 Bingo Palace and Lounge, owned by the Shakopee Sioux, "grossed about twelve million, earning three million dollars in profits for the tribe and management company" in 1984, according to an article in the *Minneapolis Star and Tribune*. Profits have grown since then, and so have the problems of management. The Shakopee Sioux filed suit in federal court "seeking to oust the company that manages . . . two bingo parlors, charging that the money has been wasted by the firm's executives [Pan American Management Company] and that secret payments were made to former tribal chairman Norman Crooks."[21]

Jim Parsons reported that auditors "discovered that Norman Crooks, the controversial chairman of the Shakopee Sioux Reservation, has been paid at least $104,500 in a secret agreement with the company" that runs the twelve million dollar a year tribal bingo operation. "The agreement also calls for Crooks to get another $91,000 over the life of the contract with the company."[22]

Crooks was named in an investigation of the sale of tax-free cigarettes, about three dollars less a carton, to people who were not tribal members. Minnesota revenue officials seized an "$81,000 shipment of cigarettes on its way to the Shakopee Mdewakanton Sioux community in Prior Lake" in June 1988, according to the *Minneapolis Star and Tribune*, because people other than tribal members purchased the cigarettes in violation of state and federal laws. The state does not have the power to tax tribal members on federal trust land. "We've got Indians with light complexions and red hair," said Crooks, who owned a "smoke shop" for more than a decade in the tribal community. "What are we

20

supposed to do,'' he asked Kevin Diaz, a reporter for the *Minneapolis Star and Tribune,* ''give them cards and put feathers in their heads?''

There are close to a hundred bingo operations located in tribal communities and on reservations in the nation. These games generate an estimated three to four hundred

21

million dollars a year. There are eleven bingo centers on or near reservations in Minnesota. That much money must invite problems of management. The Little 6 Bingo Palace has been involved in a lawsuit over alleged contract violations by an outside management company. The Island Bingo operation has been managed by Red Wing Amusements, a corporation of local investors. During the ten-year contract to manage the operation, according to the tribal attorney, "we select the accountant who has the right to audit anytime, unannounced."[23] Prairie Island and other reservation governments have negotiated more control over the operation of games and cash accounts.

The Prairie Island Mdewakanton Sioux community negotiated an agreement in December 1988 to buy the interests of the company that managed their bingo operation. Part of the buyout payment was a loan provided by the Bureau of Indian Affairs. Federal agencies have been eager to support tribal gaming operations in the wake of federal assistance, program funds, and grants on reservations. The Fond du Luth Gaming Casino, for instance, was created in downtown Duluth; various state and federal agencies participated in the trust land simulated reservation to establish the casino.

Federal courts have ruled in favor of certain tribal rights based on treaties; for instance, state regulations over taxation and overdue tax foreclosures, licenses, hunting and fishing, now bingo and other forms of gambling, have been issues based on the interpretation of treaties and advanced as tests of tribal sovereignties.

The critical question is whether state and local governments have the right to regulate high-stakes bingo on reservations. Several states have argued in favor of some control over bingo, while tribal governments argue against state regulations; their arguments are based on tribal sovereignty. On the one hand, bingo profits have rescued tribal programs and services at a time when federal funds

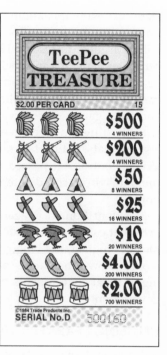

Popular pull tabs at Little 6 Bingo

have been reduced; on the other hand, state governments are concerned that high-stakes reservation bingo is an invitation to organized crime and that the tribes will open casinos, horse racing, and other gambling operations.

"The tribes argue that their land should be seen as entirely separate from state territory," said Karen Funk, an analyst for the National Congress of American Indians, "and that states should have no more authority to regulate gambling on Indian land within the borders of the state than they should on gambling that occurs in adjacent states."[24] Notwithstanding the new wealth on reservations, some leaders are troubled that tribal sovereignties will be argued, tested, and lost on a bingo game. The concern over gambling in tribal communities, however, could be resolved with legislation: some public officials favor the creation of a federal gambling commission to control bingo and other games on reservations. Others, more concerned with the threat of organized crime on reservations, have argued that existing federal laws, such as the Organized Crime Control Act passed in 1970, are enough to protect the public from coordinated criminal activities on reservations.

President Ronald Reagan signed legislation in October 1988 that established a federal commission to regulate and monitor high-stakes bingo on reservations. The legislation would allow other forms of gambling, such as horse racing, if tribal governments negotiate agreements with state governments.

CLIMBING LEARNERS' HILL

Julia Spears moved to White Earth in 1870, two years after the reservation was created, and opened the first school there; forty students attended her first class on the new reservation. The following year the federal government established an industrial boarding school; other buildings were completed, she wrote in a letter, "including the large school-house and boys' building, also industrial hall where the Indian women were taught housework, including cooking, sewing, knitting, carpet-weaving," and other domestic duties in the dominant culture.[25]

Way quah gishig, like many other tribal children, was forced to attend a federal boarding school where he was given the name John Rogers and taught that his traditional tribal language was inferior, his spiritual solace pagan, and his culture irrelevant in the new white world.

24

Rose Belle Beaulieu (left) with friends at Genoa Indian School, Nebraska

Rogers is an unusual person, not because he learned to read and write under colonial duress—thousands of tribal children have survived cultural disunities in federal and mission boarding schools—but because he used his new language to write a sensitive book about his experiences. Rogers was born on the White Earth Reservation at the turn of the last century. He returned from boarding school after six years and learned that his parents had separated; his mother lived alone in a wigwam.

"I was anxious to see my mother and be home again," he wrote in *Red World and White: Memories of a Chippewa Boyhood*. "Mother was seated on the ground working on some fish nets. . . . As she stood up with outstretched arms her eyes sparkled as does the sun on laughing water."

Rogers, despite his adverse experiences in a racist world, wrote with a sense of peace about the changes he observed on the reservation when he returned. He seemed suspicious at times, dubious of the promises made by white people, but his published remembrance is not ideological, bitter, or consumed with hatred; rather, he made use of his time at boarding school and seems to approach the world with a sense of adventure. His brothers and sisters were also forced to attend boarding school.

"She started talking joyously, but we couldn't understand very well what she said," Rogers wrote about his mother, "for we had forgotten much of the Indian language during our six years away from home. . . . During the days that followed we had a happy time getting acquainted after those long years of separation. . . . I was pleased to feel that I would grow into a strong young brave, and so I tried very hard to please her and to learn once more the Chippewa language.

"Mother promised to teach me the ways of the forest, rivers and lakes—how to set rabbit snares and deadfalls, how to trap for wolves and other wild animals that roamed this land. . . . Soon came the time for the leaves to turn

26

brown and yellow and gold. The forest was beautiful and the wind rustled the dry leaves. We just couldn't resist the temptation to gather those beautiful colored leaves and the empty bird nests.

"At school, if we brought in a nest or a pretty leaf, we were given much credit, and we thought we would also please mother by bringing some to her. But she did not like our doing this. She would scold and correct us and tell us we were destroying something—that the nests were the homes of the birds." Rogers moved in nature without philosophical hesitation; his thoughts were gentle, and his metaphors were simple and direct. "I had learned to love the primitive life which had for so many, many generations influenced and shaped the existence of my ancestors. . . . Nothing the white man could teach me would take the place of what I was learning from the forest, the lakes and the river.

"I could read more in the swaying of the trees and the way they spread their branches and leaned to the wind than I could read in any books that they had at school. I could learn more from the smiling, rippling waters and from the moss and flowers than from anything the teachers could tell me about such matters."

Rogers remembered the time he climbed to the top of the tower to oil the gears on the windmill: "As I stood there breathing hard from my climb upwards, I noticed how some trees were taller than others. And then I knew for the first time how the forest and fields and lakes looked to the bird that sailed so freely and happily about. . . . Looking down again on the school grounds, the children appeared like dolls as they walked along the paths or ran about at play.

"As I observed these things, I did not, for a moment, regret my leaving the forest home. . . . Perhaps there were advantages that would make up for what I had left behind!"[26] Indeed, there were some advantages, but the

27

Will Antell, Indian educator, 1970

tribal past seemed hard to hold in common when survival in the white world demanded so much attention.

Will Antell, one generation later, shared similar "advantages" in public schools; he was born in a small shack on the White Earth Reservation. Now, with degrees from several universities and experience as a public school teacher, he has become an important administrator in state education. "When I was young I rejected my Indian ancestry," he said in an interview, "because in the school I attended, which was predominately white, I found out that it wasn't to my advantage to be an Indian. . . .

"In a sense they assimilated me at a cost; I lost something in the heart, and it wasn't until I had a family that I fully realized what had happened. . . . When I was young it was not a good thing to be an Indian; a student would

28

feel much better about being Indian if he could see more Indians around. . . ."[27]

Lewis Meriam, in his 1928 report, argued that tribal families were strained when the government "sacrificed real and vital adult education to the formal education of children in institutions . . . Indians have little to show to repay them for the sorrows of broken homes.

"The loss of children tends still further to disrupt the family through the loosening of marital ties. Normally husband and wife have a strong bond in their common responsibility for children." John Rogers learned that his parents were separated when he returned home. While boarding school was an adventure for some tribal children, it was not the best education. Meriam reported that "the teaching taken as a whole is not up to the standards set by reasonably progressive white communities." He wrote that "several of the industries taught may be called vanishing trades."[28]

John Howard, superintendent of the White Earth Indian Agency, testified in 1911 that the principal of the reservation school earned $720 a year; the assistant matron, a tribal woman, $45 a month; the assistant teacher about $40 a month; and the seamstress, the cook, and the laundress, about $35 a month. Howard reported that the farmer at Pine Point, an "expert farmer" and instructor on the reservation, was paid $1,200 a year; he earned $480 more than the principal.[29]

Maggie Hanks remembered the ride on the old hog cart down the hill from the mission boarding school; as a child she first attended the federal school and when the building burned she moved to the White Earth Catholic school where she made her first communion at the turn of the last century.

Sister Carol Berg interviewed Maggie Hanks on the reservation and writes in her dissertation, "Climbing Learners' Hill: Benedictines at White Earth 1878–1945," that

"[Maggie] also remembers learning to knit and crochet, noting that she and her classmates did well enough to be able to have their work exhibited at fairs."

Alice Clark, who was a student at the mission school, also remembered the hog cart ride down the hill. Seventy years later she could repeat the processional lyrics the students chanted as they moved in columns to and from the school:

We are climbing learners' hill, march along, march along;
we are climbing learners' hill, march along, march along.
We are climbing learners' hill, we're climbing with a will:
we are climbing learners' hill, march along, march along.

Rose Shingobe Barstow, a former language teacher in the Department of American Indian Studies at the University of Minnesota, told Sister Carol Berg that she remembered the boarding school with some sadness but not with bitterness. "Asked to describe what the mission school did for her in the long run, Rose says the school aimed at giving a general education. The sisters taught basic skills. . . . Rose recalls that the curriculum focused on reading, writing, arithmetic, with a heavy concentration also on catechism and bible history. . . . Her amusement still evident, Rose told of a small deception played with the collaboration" of two sisters. "Rose's father regularly sent fifteen dollars a quarter for piano lessons but Rose did not care to take them. She let another girl take the lessons in her place. A skill Rose did care for and excelled at was that of crocheting. For three and a half years she worked at crocheting an altar lace, seventeen feet long, which was later used for the first time at a solemn High Mass. Since she was supposed to 'preserve' her hands, Rose was not allowed to do the usual chores other students did at the time."[30]

Will Antell was one of the first college graduates from a reservation. Thirty years ago there were about fifteen tribal members in Minnesota colleges and universities; the number of students and graduates more than doubled in the next few years. Federal programs encouraged tribal members to attend college; moreover, there was a radical turn in public consciousness about the bitter histories of tribal cultures, and new civil rights legislation.

The University of California at Berkeley, and the University of Minnesota, established the first Native American studies programs about twenty years ago, the first in the nation. In the past two decades thousands of tribal people have earned college degrees, and the number of advanced degrees has increased. Native American Indian studies has survived at Berkeley with an outstanding graduate program in Ethnic Studies, but departments at many other universities have been reorganized or discontinued in the past decade.

Bonnie Wallace, director of the American Indian Student Support Program at Augsburg College in Minneapolis, has one of the best programs in the nation. In the past decade the enrollment in her program has increased from two tribal students to more than forty in attendance; the retention rate, about eighty percent, and the number of graduates has also increased. Thirty-seven tribal students have graduated in the past ten years from Augsburg College. These are real achievements because the number of tribal students entering college has decreased in the same period of time.

Bonnie was born on the Fond du Lac Reservation. She graduated from the University of Minnesota and has dedicated her career to higher education. In 1967 she arrived in Minneapolis, a single parent in need of work; she applied at the American Indian Employment Center. In the interview she told the director of the center that she had no real work experience or qualifications; she had no idea, at that time, what line of work she would pursue. Impressed with her direct and honest manner, the director hired her as an interviewer; she would interview tribal applicants from the reservation and contact employers until she found an in-

31

Bonnie Wallace (left) *and Cindy Peterson, Augsburg College, 1989*

teresting job for herself. Instead, one year later she enrolled in a special program at the University of Minnesota
and earned a degree in social welfare. "We are humble
people, sometimes, but what saves us is our humor," said
Bonnie. "We hit bottom, laugh, and go on. Many people
helped me go on, and I am amazed at how much we have
accomplished in higher education."

FATHER ALOYSIUS AND THE CROSSBLOOD CHOIR

Father Aloysius Hermanutz, one of the first missionaries at White Earth, delivered monotheistic assimilation to the tribal people of the reservation. He was born in Germany and ordained two years before he arrived in the woodland, at age twenty-three, to begin his dedicated conversion of tribal dreams and oral traditions.

Father Aloysius, who had been a priest on the reservation for thirty-three years, testified on February 9, 1912, at the hearing on the "Investigation of the White Earth Reservation." He was questioned by James Graham, chairman of the committee, and later, by Gustav Beaulieu, a crossblood who published the reservation newspaper.

"Are your parishioners mostly of Indian blood? . . . "

"They are mixed blood."

"Have you any white people in your congregation?"

"In my parish at the present time there are six white families who are located somewhere in the mission. . . . "

"What is your income, or do you mind telling?"

"Well," said Father Aloysius, "I don't mind, but I can say my regular income comes from what we call the mixed bloods, they supply me." He testified that there were seven Sisters of Saint Benedict at the mission school and about a hundred students, four were boys. The school maintained a farm, about ninety acres in cultivation, with poultry and livestock.

"Have you a choir connected with your church?"

"Yes."

"All Indian?"

"All my school children. . . . "

"Are they efficient as singers?"

"They are excellent singers."

"They enter into the spirit of it, do they?"

"They have talent, musical talent, especially the mixed bloods," responded the mission priest.

"Lessons on the piano?"

33

"Yes."

"Do they learn quickly?"

"They learn quickly."

"Become capable performers, do they?"

"Yes, sir."

"The full-bloods as well, the full-blood children?"

"Well, they are a little slower on account of the fingering, and so on," he answered, "but the mixed bloods are especially talented in regard to music. They are often passionately fond of music. . . . "

"Do you still speak in Chippewa?"

"I preach every Sunday, Chippewa and English in the parish."

"For those who understand both languages, which one do they prefer that you preach in?" asked the chairman of the committee.

"Well," the priest answered, "the older Indians, of course, and the older mixed bloods, they prefer Chippewa. . . . "

"You think, then, it is a good thing for Indians and whites to come together, that is, mix up and live together?" asked Gustav Beaulieu.

"Yes, sir."

"It is, in fact, the only way to teach the Indians to become civilized and self-sustaining?" asked Beaulieu.

"That is one reason, and the other reason is more or less like it—on account of intermarriages between them, especially the mixed bloods. That would improve that situation."

"There are nearly all mixed bloods upon the White Earth Reservation—largely in the majority?" asked Beaulieu.

"They are in the majority now."[31]

Sister Carol Berg pointed out that tribal languages were not taught in the mission school on the reservation. Several missionaries, however, learned a few words and phrases, enough to communicate their compassion over rites of passage with the school children and their families. "During their many years at White Earth," Sister Carol

34

Berg concluded, the pioneer "Benedictine missionaries grew to know and respect some aspects of Ojibway [Chippewa or Anishinaabe] culture, but their own goals, like those of most of their fellow Americans working with Indian people, were directed strongly toward change. Perhaps if they had been introduced to Indian traditional religion and culture, and if they had considered the idea of missionary adaptation to Indian culture as well as the ideals and aims of Indian mission work, the process of change might have been different for both the Ojibway and the missionaries."

Father Aloysius noted later, "We made no wholesale conversions among the Indians, such as we read of being made in Asia and elsewhere. Soul after soul had to be gained by hard fight, patience and prayer, and many of these were converted from their heathen view and practices only after years of hard work. . . . The largest number baptized by me on one day was seventy, and this after a preparation of one week with the help of four catechists."[32]

FINDING THE WORD FOR RELIGION

"American Indians lack a word to denote what we call religion," wrote Åke Hultkrantz in *The Religions of the American Indians*. "Of course, nothing else is to be expected in environments where religious attitudes and values permeate cultural life in its entirety and are not isolated from other cultural manifestations."[33]

Tribal cultures denote in their languages the distinctions between what is traditional or sacred and what is secular or profane. Stories, told in an oral tradition, are both sacred and secular; however, the stories that have been recorded, translated, and published as scripture, are impositions in tribal religious experiences. The formal descriptions of tribal events by outsiders, such as missionaries, explorers, and anthropologists, reveal more about the values of the post-colonial observers than the imagination of tribal people.

35

Paul Beaulieu, the government interpreter and one of the first farmers on the White Earth Reservation, told about his experiences with a *jessakkid*, a shaman or healer, who had performed at Leech Lake. Beaulieu, a Catholic crossblood, had little faith in the elusive powers of tribal shamans.

Walter James Hoffman, in "The Mide Wiwin; or 'Grand Medicine Society' of the Ojibwa,"[34] wrote that reports of the "wonderful performances" of a local shaman "had reached the agency, and as Beaulieu had no faith in jugglers, he offered to wager $100, a large sum, then and there, against goods of equal value, that the juggler could not perform satisfactorily one of the tricks of his repertoire." The shaman erected a lodge for the occasion. "The framework of vertical poles, inclined to the center, was filled in with interlaced twigs covered with blankets and birchbark from the ground to the top, leaving an upper orifice of about a foot in diameter for the ingress and egress of spirits and the objects to be mentioned, but not large enough for the passage of a man's body. At one side of the lower wrapping a flap was left for the entrance of the *jessakkid*.

"A committee of twelve was selected to see that no communication was possible between the *jessakkid* and confederates. These were reliable people, one of them the Episcopal clergyman of the reservation. The spectators were several hundred in number, but they stood off, not being allowed to approach.

"The *jessakkid* then removed his clothing, until nothing remained but the breechcloth. Beaulieu took a rope," which he selected for the purpose, Hoffman wrote, "and first tied and knotted one end about the juggler's ankles; his knees were then securely tied together, next the wrists, after which the arms were passed over the knees and a billet of wood passed through under the knees, thus securing and keeping the arms down motionless. The rope was then passed around his neck, again and again, each time

36

tied and knotted, so as to bring the face down upon the knees." A flat black stone from a river, the sacred spirit stone of the shaman, "was left lying upon his thighs.

"The *jessakkid* was then carried to the lodge and placed inside upon a mat on the ground, and the flap covering was restored so as to completely hide him from view.

"Immediately loud, thumping noises were heard, and the framework began to sway from side to side with great violence; whereupon the clergyman remarked that this was the work of the Evil One and 'it was no place for him,' so he left and did not see the end. After a few minutes of violent movements and swayings of the lodge accompanied by loud inarticulate noises, the motions gradually ceased when the voice of the juggler was heard, telling Beaulieu to go to the house of a friend, nearby, and get the rope.

"Now, Beaulieu, suspecting some joke was to be played upon him, directed the committee to be very careful not to permit anyone to approach while he went for the rope, which he found at the place indicated, still tied exactly as he had placed it about the neck and extremities of the *jessakkid*. He immediately returned, laid it down before the spectators, and requested of the *jessakkid* to be allowed to look at him, which was granted, but with the understanding that Beaulieu was not to touch him.

"When the covering was pulled aside, the *jessakkid* sat within the lodge, contentedly smoking his pipe, with no other object in sight than the black stone *manidoo*," or manitou, a spiritual stone. Beaulieu paid his wager of one hundred dollars.

Shamanism and tribal spiritual events were often explained in economic terms, the dominant metaphors of the dominant culture. Others have interpreted tribal religious events from secure carrels in libraries. Christopher Vecsey, for example, wrote in his dissertation, "Traditional Ojibwa Religion and Its Historical Changes," that the "Ojibwas have lost their trust in their aboriginal" *manidoog*, or man-

37

Anishinaabe ceremonial

itou, the spirits, "and in themselves. . . . They have changed many of their religious rituals and today hold very few shaking tent ceremonies . . . their traditional religion no longer exists. . . . They stand between their collapsed traditional religion and Christianity, embracing neither." Vecsey seems to perceive tribal cultures in a museum diorama; his monologue is with social science and not a discourse with tribal religious imagination.[35]

William Warren, the mixedblood historian, was more serious in his observations of religious tribal events. He wrote, in *History of the Ojibway Nation*, that certain rites had been held from the whites. Some tribal healers believed that death would come to those who revealed sacred rituals. "Missionaries, travelers, and transient sojourners amongst the Ojibways, who have witnessed the performances of the grand Me-da-we ceremonies," he wrote with reference to the Midewiwin, "have represented and

38

published that it is composed of foolish and unmeaning ceremonies. The writer begs leave to say that these superficial observers labor under a great mistake. The Indian has equal right . . . to say, on viewing the rites of the Catholic and other churches, that they consist of unmeaning and nonsensical ceremonies. There is much yet to be learned from the wild and apparently simple son of the forest, and the most which remains to be learned is to be derived from their religious beliefs."[36]

Harold Hickerson, on the other hand, wrote that "Chippewa culture is a shambles, so much have the people everywhere had to accommodate to the new conditions imposed by their relations" with the white world. Nowhere, he asserted, does the tribe depend upon goods of their own fashioning; much of the traditional material culture has been lost or "replaced and enriched by the introduction of mass-produced commodities from outside."[37]

WILD CONVERSION IN A THUNDERSTORM

George Copway, in *The Life, History, and Travels of Kah-ge-ga-gah-bowh,* revealed that his conversion took place when he was twelve years old. One of the first published tribal authors, he wrote that his mother had been bedridden with consumption for several months, and then "just before her death she prayed with her children, and advised us to be good Christians, to love Jesus, and meet her in heaven. She then sang her favorite hymn: *Jesis ish pe ming kah e zhod, Jesus, my all, to heaven is gone.*

"This was the first hymn she heard or learned; and it is on this account that I introduce and sing this sweet hymn whenever I lecture on the origin, history, traditions, migration, and customs, of the Ojebwa nation."

Copway remembered that sublime moment of his own conversion, which took place at a religious camp where he had gone with his father. There was a thunderstorm, he mentioned lightning and rain, and wrote, "My father held

39

me by the hand. . . . We had to walk thirty miles . . . in order to reach the place of destination. Multitudes of Indians, and a large concourse of whites from various places, were on the ground when we arrived. In the evening, one of the white preachers spoke . . . of the plain and good road to heaven; of the characters that were walking in it; he then spoke of the bad place. . . .

"I now began to feel as if I should die; *I felt very sick in my heart* . . . I was deeply distressed, and knew not the cause," he wrote. Then he knelt at the roots of a tree while his father prayed for him. The storm ended, and the frightened child recollected that he felt like a *"wounded bird,* fluttering for its life. . . .

"The small brilliant light came near to me, and fell upon my head, and then ran all over and through me, just as if water had been copiously poured out upon me . . . my head was in a puddle of water, in a small ditch. . . .

"I clapped my hands, and exclaimed in English, *Glory to Jesus.*" Copway wrote about the instant of his conversion, when "I looked around for my father, and saw him. I told him that I had found Jesus. He embraced and kissed me. . . . I felt as strong as a lion, yet as humble as a poor Indian boy saved by grace, by grace alone. . . ."[38]

Following his conversion in the woods, he studied with his father, attended numerous evangelical meetings, and in time he traveled to the east for more instruction and direction. Copway studied with white religious leaders, and returned to the woodland, to the tribal communities he knew as a child, with a new mission. He became a religious reformer with the single ambition to convert the tribes. He became a stranger in his own land, an estranged survivor on a familiar landscape.

"During my residence of six years among the pale faces," Copway wrote, "I have acquired a knowledge of men and things, much, very much more I have yet to learn, and it is my desire that my brethren in the far west may share with me my crust of information. . . . Education

40

and Christianity are to the Indian what wings are to the eagle; they elevate him; and these given to him by men of right views of existence enable him to rise above the soil of degradation, and hover about the high mounts of wisdom and truth."[39]

PEYOTE AND URBAN EVANGELISM

Mitchell Whiterabbit, the late minister in the United Church of Christ, and Iver Grover, leader in the American Evangelical Church, were inspired to serve the religious and social needs of tribal people in urban areas—the need for solace in the cities. These, and other ministries, became more critical as urban tribal populations increased.

The United States census in 1980 reported 35,016 Indians in Minnesota, according to the League of Women Voters in their publication *Indians in Minnesota.* "Minneapolis had the third highest percentage of Indian population" of all major cities in the United States. "Within Minneapolis, the Phillips neighborhood has by far the largest concentration of Indian population. It is sometimes called 'the largest reservation in the state.' In an area one and one-half miles square, 3,026 Indians were living in 1980." Minnesota had 2.6 percent of total national population of Indians, the twelfth largest in the country. "The Indian communities are certain that the 1980 census did not count all Indians in the state. . . . The director of the Indian Affairs Council estimated the state's Indian population at 45,000 in 1982."[40]

Mitchell Whiterabbit directed the Council of American Indian Ministry; he was one of the founders of the Native American Theological Association, an ecumenical coalition that encouraged tribal people to attend seminaries. Whiterabbit was a pastor at the Winnebago Indian Mission in Wisconsin, and during the Second World War he was the first Native American Indian chaplain in the navy.[41]

Iver Grover, in a testimonial, told how he "took part in all the religious ceremonies of my Indian people—the feast

41

offerings of wild rice and berries. . . . I had a sack full of idolatrous objects which I revered—skins of animals and birds and carved wooden images. For all those years I followed this form of false worship faithfully. . . . Since my conversion, God has called me to witness Him and to win souls for Christ among my own people—the Indian American. I preach in Chippewa and English."[42]

The Native American Church of North America is the most controversial and misunderstood of modern tribal religions; the members chew peyote, which contains the hallucinogen mescaline, to commune with their creator. The tribal use of peyote in religious practices has been protected in federal courts. In 1974 the United States Supreme Court declined to review a lower appeals court decision that the tribal ceremonies were permissible. That, however, has not settled the issue of peyote and religious freedom.

Judge Edwin Mechem, in a recent federal court decision, ruled that employers cannot refuse to hire people who use peyote as part of their religious practices. Wilbur Toledo, a member of the Native American Church, was not hired as a truck driver because he used a religious hallucinogen. "Church peyote users believe that peyote is a sacred and powerful plant," wrote Mechem. "Peyote is seen as a medicine, a protector and a teacher."

Emerson Jackson, chairman of the Native American Church, explained that peyote must be used in ceremonies. "It's like going to church, you have a Bible, you pray to God, to Jesus, but you cannot have the ceremony without that Bible. It's like the peyote," he told a newspaper reporter.[43]

Certain traditional tribal spiritual practices, such as herbal and symbolic healing, are culture specific, limited to one cultural experience. The sacramental use of peyote has been successful in the treatment of alcohol problems; the Native American Church, pantribal evangelical move-

Demonstration at the Bureau of Indian Affairs, Minneapolis, 1966

ments, herbal spiritualism, radical and other authoritarian ideologies have been operative methods of rehabilitation.

The Native American Church, the Sun Dance, and other tribal practices and ceremonies, have been enhanced by modern theological attention. Christian credence crossed with tribal traditions has become a new theology for tribal clerics. Virgil Foote, for instance, holds communion for an Episcopal congregation and practices the Sun Dance; he pierces his chest with skewers and offers the symbolic blood of Jesus Christ. "When I pray, I pray in Lakota and

English. Our people need to hear there is truth in both. I'm a Lakota; I'm a Christian. I'm one in the same. I pray to one God," he told a reporter for the *Minneapolis Star and Tribune.* "At the Sun Dance, if you are humble and put your whole self into it, you feel it down to the core of your being. You get in touch with your physical and spiritual self and respect the sacred in everything."

RELOCATION AND THE VANISHING TRADES

Lewis Meriam, in *The Problem of Indian Administration*, reported there were many mixedbloods in Minneapolis, St. Paul, Duluth, and Superior. In fact, one gets the impression that "most of the persons claiming to be Indians have but a slight degree of Indian blood. From 'lists of Indians' furnished by the several reservations, many were reached whose personal appearance indicated French or Scandinavian blood rather than Indian." Meriam estimated, in the twenties, there were about six hundred tribal people in Minneapolis and St. Paul.

"Inquiry into the reasons for migration from the reservation was almost invariably met with the answer, in one form or another, from every migrated Indian man questioned: 'No way to make a living on the reservation.' The alternative was starvation or pauperism," wrote Meriam.[44]

Tribal populations in these same urban areas have increased about forty times in the past generation; there are now more tribal people in cities than on reservations. Education, and the search for employment, motivated tribal people to move to urban areas; the reasons are similar to those given in the past but the historical circumstances were not the same; economic depressions and then the wars brought tribal people to the cities. Tribal women were needed in munitions factories; at the end of the war, their men returned with aspirations a reservation could not sustain. Later thousands of tribal people were relocated in cities to attend various trade schools; these new assimilation

44

programs, which provided initial subsistence stipends, trained most relocatees in the "vanishing trades," such as refrigeration repair.

"In what the Interior Department described at the time as 'the greatest exodus of Indians from reservations that has ever taken place,' some 25,000 Indians joined the armed forces and saw action in Europe and the Pacific. Some 40,000 quit the economic desert of the reservations for jobs in war industries. For many Indians, experiences in the factory or on the battlefront constituted their first real exposure to the larger American society."[45]

Paulette Fairbanks Molin, who was born on the White Earth Reservation, wrote that the 1950s "brought yet another attempt to abolish reservations. This time the idea was called 'termination.' The government wanted to end its legal ties with reservations and 'get out of the Indian business.' One way to do that, lawmakers decided, was to move Indians into cities, where the government would no longer be responsible for them." In 1952, the Bureau of Indian Affairs created a program called Indian Relocation Services.

"Although the war and relocation account for most of the Indian movement to urban areas, many Indian people moved for reasons of their own. Some hoped to find better living conditions. Others left reservations to attend school or join family members in the city. Indian children who were placed in non-Indian foster or adoptive homes grew up off the reservation. Other children were born and raised in cities by parents who had migrated" earlier.[46]

"The Pueblos, Navajos, and Apaches are among those who have retained a large measure of their tribal life, customs, and language, while the Chippewas, Klamaths, Omahas, Yakimas, Winnebagoes, and many of the Indians of Oklahoma, are among those who have discarded most of their primitive habits in favor of the typical manner of life of the surrounding white community," reported Meriam. Tribal people in the cities maintained "friendly relations with their white neighbors, but naturally their closer friendships are made with their former classmates in the Indian schools."[47]

Meanwhile, as urban populations increased, new leaders, some of them radical, expanded their demands for tribal services in cities; new organizations were established outside the direct control of reservation politics.

RADICAL FROWNS AND SECULAR VESTMENTS

Dennis Banks, on February 12, 1974, was dressed in secular vestments. He wore beads, bones, leathers, ribbons, and a wide cultural frown, for his appearance in court; he was on trial for alleged violations of federal laws in connection with the American Indian Movement occupation of Wounded Knee on the Pine Ridge Reservation in South Dakota.

Banks looked down that afternoon as he stood alone before twelve federal jurors; he seldom smiled. His focus shifted from table to chair, past the rims and rails in the courtroom, and then he raised his head and told the jurors in his opening statement that he was at Wounded Knee, as charged, and that he was "guilty of asking that the Senate investigate all the conditions that the federal government has imposed upon our people."

Banks, a crossblood from the Leech Lake Reservation and one of the founders of the American Indian Movement, was on trial with Russell Means, a crossblood from the Pine Ridge Reservation. Banks moved forward and told the jurors that he was a member of the traditional Oglala Sioux Sun Dance religion, which, he explained in a gentle voice, is a "very sacred religious event where men warriors offer themselves to the great spirit to seek a vision, that we have to go through it for four years and somewhere through those four years we will find that vision; that there must be fasting, that we must give up water, and that we must prove to mother earth and all the fe-

46

male objects of this planet, to all the female things, that we would like to share some of the pain. The men warriors would like to share some of the pain that our mothers, that our mothers had, when we were born."[48]

The Sun Dance is a ceremony in which vows are made in sacred preparation for a personal vision. Some participants in the ritual puncture the skin on their chest with wooden skewers that are tied to a sacred tree in the center of the dance circle. Those who seek a vision dance in the circle of the sun until the skewers are torn from the flesh.

"The piercing of the skin," Banks told the jurors that afternoon in federal court, "is a reminder to me that I truly owe myself to mother earth and to all the female things of this planet." The government prosecutors were charged with misconduct because they withheld information from the defense lawyers, and the charges against the two radicals in federal court were dropped.

The American Indian Movement was a radical urban organization whose members tried from time to time to return to reservations as warrior heroes. To some, the radicals are characters in dominant histories; to others the leaders are the freebooters of racism. The radical leaders have been paid well for their activities.

The American Indian Movement was established in a storefront on Franklin Avenue in Minneapolis about five years before the occupation of Wounded Knee. Banks, Clyde Bellecourt, and several others, organized a patrol to monitor the police on the urban reservation. When the patrol acquired mobile radio units in expensive automobiles, some of the members returned to the reservation.

Banks and Bellecourt remained in the organization and continued confrontation politics with the intellectual and legal assistance of dozens of romantic white radicals and liberals from the peace movement. Those tribal people who followed the ideologies of confrontation were in conflict at times with those who believed that negotiations made institutional changes possible. These differences in

47

ideologies and radical practices were emphasized in media coverage. Newspaper reports created the heroes of confrontation for an eager white audience, but those dedicated to negotiations were ignored.

The political ideologies of the radical tribal leaders are reactions to racism and cultural adversities; that much all tribal people have in common. The radical rhetoric of the leaders was not learned from traditional tribal people on reservations or in tribal communities. Some of the militant leaders were radicalized in prison, where they found white inmates eager to listen. The poses of tribal radicals seem to mimic the romantic pictorial photographs by Edward Curtis. The radicals never seemed to smile, there were no tricksters, no humor; an incautious throwback to the stoical tribal visage of slower camera shutters. The new radicals frown, even grimace at the cameras, and revise in first person pronouns the atrocities endured by tribal cultures for more than a century.

Some militants decorate themselves in pastiche pantribal vestments, pose as traditionalists, and announce their cultural pride in the romantic binaries of racial opposition. These radical emblems were not elected to speak for tribal people on reservations, nor were they appointed to represent the interests and political views of elected tribal officials. In response to this criticism several tribal radicals have returned to reservations. Vernon Bellecourt, also known as Wabuninini, a member of the American Indian Movement, returned to the White Earth Reservation where he was once elected a tribal representative.

Banks, however, has never faced tribal constituencies in an election. His influence is differential and media borne; he has carried numerous administrative titles in the past, but his power seems to be ideological, material, and institutional. He was chancellor of Daganawidah-Quetzalcoatl University, located near Davis, California, when Governor Jerry Brown denied his extradition to South Dakota. Banks had been convicted and was wanted on a fugitive warrant

48

in connection with a riot in Custer County, South Dakota; he returned to the state, surrendered, and served one year in prison.

Russell Means has been associated with the International Indian Treaty Council. In 1984, Larry Flynt, publisher of *Hustler*, named Means his presidential running mate. "Over the last few months, the Reagan Administration has found an unlikely supporter for its policies in Central America," James Holbrook wrote in *City Pages*. "After slipping into Nicaragua from Honduras and roaming through the jungles with armed bands of Indians . . . Russell Means is apparently convinced that the United States should send weapons to Miskito Indians who are trying to achieve independence from the Nicaraguan government."[49]

Clyde Bellecourt, one of the founders of the American Indian Movement and past chairman of the Little Earth United Tribes, a public housing project in Minneapolis, was arrested by drug agents; a federal grand jury indicted him on "nine separate counts of drug distribution including one count for conspiracy," according to a report in the *Minneapolis Star and Tribune*. "Bellecourt and six other men pleaded guilty to one count each of related drug distribution charges as part of a plea agreement setting five and seven year caps on their sentences."[50]

THE NAMES WERE NEVER THE SAME

The name of American Indian Movement leader Dennis Banks is familiar to tribal people in thousands of urban and reservation homes, not because the radical leader has visited tribal communities, but because he has been named in more newspaper stories, and pictured in more television reports, than any other tribal person in recent history.

Banks has used the media to his advantage, but he has also been a constant critic of newspaper reporters for their coverage of tribal issues. His motives in using the media

49

Associated Press

Dennis Banks talked to reporters at D-Q University, Davis, Calif.

Dennis Banks says he'll return to South Dakota

Associated Press

Pierre, S.D.
American Indian Movement (AIM) leader Dennis Banks has confirmed that he will go back to South Dakota, even though he faces a prison sentence on riot and assault convictions.

"I will be armed with whatever weapon — one of peace or one that will carry myself to the Great Spirit," Banks told Indians in Davis, Calif., on Tuesday. He said said that if blood should flow again "whether it be Indian blood or not, I will lead the charge."

He plans to return from California for a five-day prayer vigil at the Dakota AIM's Yellow Thunder Camp and marches to nearby Rapid City, S.D., to show support for the camp, AIM leader Russell Means said. The camp was set up 18 months ago on federal land to dramatize Indian claims to ownership of the Black Hills.

In South Dakota, Gov. Bill Janklow, who prosecuted Banks as state attorney general in 1975, said that Banks will be arrested "as soon as he steps into South Dakota."

Banks was convicted in 1975 on charges of rioting while armed with a dangerous weapon and assault with a dangerous weapon without intent to kill. He faces a maximum of 15 years in prison. The charges stemmed from a 1973 Indian rights demonstration at the Custer County Courthouse.

Banks fled to California before he could be sentenced and California Gov. Edmund Brown Jr. refused to sign extradition papers, saying he feared for Banks' life if he were returned. In response, Janklow instituted a policy of allowing accused criminals to avoid prosecution by moving to California.

may be challenged, but his general criticism of newspapers is based on good evidence. In spite of his disapproval of the media, the images of tribal people in local newspapers has expanded and improved in the past few decades.

Thirty years ago it was not uncommon to read about tribal people as if they were somnolent cultural artifacts or uncivilized pagans living on wilderness reservations. White people were most often consulted then as the authoritative sources of information about tribal cultures. But in the past decade the emphasis in newspaper reports has shifted from the patronizing views of white "experts" to tribal people as the authentic sources of information about themselves. As a result, the diversities of tribal cultures have been reported.

The shift from dominant white views to authentic experiences of tribal people corresponds to changes in public attitudes toward minority people in general. The romantic tales of tribal traditions or the denigrating preconceptions of reservation worldviews have given way to factual reports on such issues as industrial development or new programs in health and education. These observations are based on an examination of several hundred newspaper reports and editorial columns which were published in the *Minneapolis Star* and the *Minneapolis Tribune* in the past several decades.

Thirty years ago, for example, the *Minneapolis Tribune* published a series of romantic stories about tribal life on a reservation by a person named Deerskin. The stories revealed traditional experiences. The editors wrote that they had checked into the background of Deerskin and found him to be "eminently qualified to write about Indian tribal life." Don Foster, then the local director of the Bureau of Indian Affairs, commented in a letter to the editor that he thought the stories were accurate. "They will meet with great public interest, and we think they should be widely read." This would be a dubious endorsement in the tribal world. Helen Clapesattle, then editor of the University of

Five to challenge Jourdain for Red Lake chairmanship

By Jon Holten
Northern Minnesota Correspondent

Roger Jourdain faces five challengers in his campaign for reelection as tribal council chairman of the Red Lake Band of Chippewa Indians.

Meanwhile, Stephanie Hanson, an anti-Jourdain leader whose removal as treasurer three years ago sparked rioting and the takeover of the Red Lake Indian Reservation, is a candidate for her former office.

Her candidacy was in question until Thursday, when the tribal council reviewed the list of candidates and certified eligibility.

In March the council adopted election regulations that would have excluded Hanson as a candidate. But the federal Bureau of Indian Affairs (BIA) warned that it would not recognize results of the May 26 election if any candidates were eliminated by criteria the BIA judged in conflict with the tribal constitution.

In addition, the BIA will assign poll watchers to monitor the election. Dissidents complain that past elections have been unfair, particularly with regard to absentee ballots.

Jourdain, surrounded by controversy in recent years, has been chairman since a new tribal constitution was adopted in the late 1950s. His opponents include Nathan (Joe) Head, who was acting superintendent of the Red Lake Agency following the outbreak in 1979; Melvin Lawrence; Harold White Sr.; Phillip Johns, and Levi Johnson.

Don Cook, another of Jourdain's critics and a candidate for secretary, said the large number of candidates reflects dissatisfaction with Jourdain.

If no candidate receives a majority, the top two vote-getters will compete in a runoff election. Cook said some observers doubt that Jourdain has enough support to qualify for a run-

Roger Jourdain

Stephanie Hanson

off.

On May 18, 1979, the council, at Jourdain's direction, removed Hanson from office about a year after her election, alleging that she had violated the tribal constitution and been insubordinate.

The next day her husband, Harry Hanson Jr., leading a band of five armed men, broke into the reservation law enforcement center. They took three police officers hostage, demanding Jourdain's removal as chairman in exchange for their re-

lease.

In the next three days, $4 million in property was destroyed and two teen-age boys died in gunshot mishaps. Jourdain fled from the reservation as his home burned.

Harry Hanson is now serving an eight-year sentence in a federal prison.

Filing as Mrs. Harry S. Hanson Jr., Stephanie Hanson is running against acting treasurer Hollis Littlecreek, George Spears, James (Gus) Strong, Bobby Whitefeather and Harlan Beaulieu.

The tribal council, in what Cook interpreted as a two-pronged attempt to keep Hanson off the council, decreed on March 4 that anyone removed from the council "for any reason" and anyone whose spouse had been convicted of a felony was ineligible for candidacy.

However, at an April 3 meeting in Minneapolis, the tribal council was told that to impose requirements

Red Lake continued on page 4C

52

Minnesota Press, said that the "narrator's level of literacy, vocabulary, is obviously much higher than his description of himself and his way of life would lead one to expect."

Another example was the late Jay Edgerton's series of editorial columns for the *Minneapolis Star* about the Nett Lake Reservation. The columns implied a sense of cultural superiority. "Out of the hard rock of Spirit Island in Nett Lake a series of crude pictographs holds a special significance for these remote Chippewa Indians living in the deep north woods . . . For some Chippewa," Edgerton wrote, "especially the older ones, the pictographs are said to have a connection with their ancient tribal religion . . . with practices curiously like voodoo . . . which is having a revival among the Chippewa. More progressive Indians deny this."

In another report about the wild-rice harvest Edgerton wrote that "money will flow into the reservation again, and provident Indians will prepare for the year between harvests. Storerooms and freezers will be filled and old accounts settled. But for many more the harvest will mean a series of sprees, poverty, and even destitution."

Two decades later, in 1966, the *Minneapolis Tribune* reported on the emergence of "Indian Red Power." In the following three years there were hundreds of reports on urban tribal issues and numerous articles about Dane White and Thomas White Hawk. White committed suicide after being held six weeks in jail awaiting a juvenile court hearing. White Hawk was sentenced to death by electrocution in South Dakota for homicide; his sentence was commuted by the governor.

Twenty years ago national attention was focused on the problems of all minority people through the creation of federal poverty programs. Journalists were writing more about the issues of minority people because they had more knowledge of urban problems and were able to understand the language and experiences of urban tribal people better than those living on reservations.

53

At the same time that the number of newspaper reports about tribal people increased, newspapers began sampling public opinion about Indians. In 1965, the *Minneapolis Tribune* Minnesota Poll found that "six out of every ten persons in the survey contend that Indians on reservations do not have a reasonable standard of living." Sixty-two percent of those surveyed thought that tribal people have been treated with dishonor by the federal government in the past three centuries.

To some extent the results of surveys on public attitudes and the radical activities of urban tribal people helped journalists expand their views and write with more understanding about tribal values and cultures. Twenty years ago both the *Minneapolis Star* and the *Minneapolis Tribune* began to publish several series on tribal people. They included news reports and editorial articles. But the increased attention to tribal issues has not eased the criticism of the media.

Some radical critics believe that only tribal people are capable of reporting on tribal issues. The number of tribal people working in the media has increased in part because of several special training programs for minority journalists. At the same time that newspapers increased their coverage of tribal issues, urban and reservation, hundreds of small tribal newspapers and newsletters were published on reservations and in urban areas across the nation. Some of the best tribal newspapers were edited and published by crossbloods more than a century ago.

The Progress and later *The Tomahawk* were two newspapers published on the White Earth Reservation. The first issue of *The Progress* was dated March 25, 1886, and the second number was published six months later on October 8, 1887; the newspaper had been seized by federal agents because there were several articles critical of government policies. The district court defended the right to publish a newspaper on the reservation. In the first issue the editor wrote that "we may be called upon at times to criticize individuals and laws, but we shall aim to do so in a spirit of kindness and justice. Believing that the 'freedom of the press' will be guarded as sacredly by the government on this reservation as elsewhere."[51]

1989

NOTES

The concept of "hyperreality" is borrowed from *Travels in Hyperreality* by Umberto Eco. He writes that Americans live in a "more to come" consumer culture. "This is the reason for this journey into hyperreality, in search of instances where the American imagination demands the real thing and, to attain it, must fabricate the absolute fake; where the boundaries between game and illusion are blurred." Tribal people, in this sense, have been invented as "absolute fakes" in social science models, cinema, and popular media — consider "powwow" dancers at a shopping mall on the Fourth of July.

"In the humanization of animals," Eco writes, "is concealed one of the most clever resources of the Absolute Fake industry, and for this reason the Marinelands must be compared with the wax museums. . . . In the latter all is sign but aspires to seem reality." On the other hand, "In the Marinelands all is reality but aspires to appear sign." Tribal cultures are signs that aspire in social science dioramas to be hyperrealities; at the same time, and like the "humanization of animals," the real tribal cultures were colonized and "civilized" into signs. For instance, the organization "Indian Guides" has transvalued tribal cultures as signs — there is "more to come" in new racial hyperrealities.

Chippewa, Ojibwa, Anishinaabe, and orthographic variations of these words, are names for the same woodland tribal culture. *The American Heritage Dictionary of the English*

55

An alleged simulation by Senator Hubert Humphrey and Muriel "playing Indian" at a costume party, circa 1955

Language defines Ojibwa as a "tribe of Algonquian-speaking North American Indians inhabiting regions of the United States and Canada around Lake Superior. . . . Also called 'Chippewa,' 'Chippeway.' "

John Nichols, a linguist and editor with Earl Nyholm of

56

Dennis and Ellie Banks at their wedding in Mound, Minnesota, 1969

Ojibwewi-Ikidowinan: An Ojibwe Word Resource Book, writes that the "Ojibwe language is one language of a widespread family of North American Indian languages known as the Algonquian language family, one of many such families of languages. Ojibwe is spoken by perhaps forty-thousand to fifty-thousand people in the north-central part of the continent. Although the English name 'Chippewa' is commonly used both for the people and their ancestral language in Michigan, Minnesota, North Dakota, and Wisconsin, in the language itself the people are the *Anishinaabeg* and the language is called *Anishinaabemowin* or *Ojibwemowin.*"

1. Robert Rydell, *All the World's a Fair: Visions of Empire at American International Expositions, 1876–1916* (Chicago: The University of Chicago, 1984), 149.

2. Rydell, 162. McGee gained scientific credence from the contributions and advice of distinguished anthropologists such as

57

Franz Boas, Frederick Starr, and Aleš Hrdlička. Starr, a professor at the University of Chicago, lectured and arranged field research on tribal cultures at the exposition. Other anthropologists, including Clark Wissler, respected the racial theories demonstrated at the cultural exhibitions. These racist notions of "cephalization" are based on theories of an "upward movement" and a "gradual increase in the cranial capacity of different races." Moreover, McGee believed that "cheirization" or the "increase of manual dexterity along racial lines . . . is a matter of common observation that the white man can do more and better than the yellow, the yellow man more and better than the red or black." Rydell points out in a note, "As a consequence of cheirization and cephalization, the 'advance of culture' proceeded along lines of racial achievement."

3. Lewis Meriam, Institute for Government Research, *The Problem of Indian Administration* (Baltimore: Johns Hopkins University Press, 1928), 333.

4. *Investigation of the White Earth Reservation*, Committee on Expenditures in the Interior Department, House of Representatives (62nd Cong., 3rd sess., Report 1336, volume 1, 1913), 72–86.

5. Meriam, *The Problem of Indian Administration*, 471.

6. *Investigation of the White Earth Reservation*, 93–99.

7. *Minnesota Chippewa Tribal Government* (Cass Lake, Minn.: Minnesota Chippewa Tribe, 1978), 58.

8. *Minnesota Chippewa Tribal Government*, 79–80.

9. Meriam, *The Problem of Indian Administration*, 471.

10. *Investigation of the White Earth Reservation*, 139.

11. Meriam, *The Problem of Indian Administration*, 12.

12. *Investigation of the White Earth Reservation*, XVIII, 14.

13. *Investigation of the White Earth Reservation*, 731–32.

14. Gerald Vizenor, "Tribal Newspapers," *Minneapolis Tribune*, August 25, 1974.

15. Stephen Cornell, "The New Indian Politics," *Wilson Quarterly*, New Year's 1986, 114–15.

16. Vernon Bellecourt, "An Angry Response at White Earth: 'Our land Is Not for Sale,' " *Minneapolis Star and Tribune*, October 6, 1985.

17. Louise Erdrich, and Michael Dorris, "Who Owns the Land?" *New York Times Magazine*, September 4, 1988.

18. Gerald Vizenor, "Hunting and Fishing Agreement,"

Walker Pilot [Walker, Minn.], June 22, 1972; and "Treaties and Tribal Rights," *Minneapolis Tribune*, June 15, 1974.

19. Jim Parsons, "U.S. Suit Could Alter Indian Rights to Hunt in Northeast Minnesota," *Minneapolis Star and Tribune*, October 21, 1985, 4A.

20. Martha Thomas, "Sioux Chief Al White on Prairie Island's Bingo Jackpot," *City Pages* [Minneapolis, Minn.], November 13, 1985, 5.

21. Dave Anderson, "Tribe Sues to Oust Bingo Hall Company," *Minneapolis Star and Tribune*, February 10, 1985, 1B.

22. Jim Parsons, "Bingo Pact Paid N. Crooks Thousands," *Minneapolis Star and Tribune*, January 8, 1985, 1A.

23. Martha Thomas, "High Stakes Bingo: The Sioux Community at Prairie Island is Playing for Keeps," *Minnesota Monthly*, December 1985, 41–44, 106.

24. *New York Times*, "New Issues in Congress: Gambling and Indians," July 1, 1986.

25. Alvin Wilcox, *A Pioneer History of Becker County* (Saint Paul: Pioneer Press Company, 1907). Reprinted in Gerald Vizenor (ed.), *Escorts to White Earth, 1868 to 1968, 100 Year Reservation* (Minneapolis: Four Winds, 1968).

26. John Rogers, *Red World and White: Memories of a Chippewa Boyhood* (Norman, University of Oklahoma Press, 1957). First published as *A Chippewa Speaks*.

27. Gerald Vizenor, *The Everlasting Sky: New Voices from the People Named the Chippewa* (New York: Crowell-Collier Press, 1972), 34–38.

28. Meriam, *The Problem of Indian Administration*, 13, 14.

29. *Investigation of the White Earth Reservation*, 1221.

30. Sister Carol Berg, "Climbing Learners' Hill: Benedictines at White Earth, 1878–1945," unpublished dissertation, University of Minnesota, 1981.

31. *Investigation of the White Earth Reservation*, 1241–1261.

32. Sister Carol Berg, "Agents of Cultural Change: The Benedictines at White Earth," *Minnesota History*, Winter 1982, 158.

33. Åke Hultkrantz, *The Religions of the American Indians* (Berkeley: University of California Press, 1979).

34. Walter James Hoffman, "The Mide Wiwin; or 'Grand Medicine Society' of the Ojibwa," United States Bureau of Ethnology,

Seventh Annual Report 1885–86 (Washington, D.C.: Government Printing Office).

35. Christopher Vecsey, "Traditional Ojibwa Religion and Its Historical Changes," unpublished dissertation, Northwestern University, 1977.

36. William Whipple Warren, *History of the Ojibway Nation* (Minneapolis: Ross and Haines, 1957). First published by the Minnesota Historical Society, 1885.

37. Harold Hickerson, *The Chippewa and Their Neighbors: A Study in Ethnohistory* (New York: Holt, Rinehart & Winston, 1970).

38. George Copway [Kahgegagahbowh], *The Life, History, and Travels of Kah-ge-ga-gah-bowh* (Philadelphia: James Harmstead, 1847).

39. George Copway [Kahgegagahbowh], *The Traditional History and Characteristics of the Ojibway Nation* (London: Charles Gilpin, 1850).

40. Elizabeth Ebbott, *Indians in Minnesota* (Minneapolis: University of Minnesota Press, 1985), 40–44.

41. Roman Augustoviz, "Mitchell Whiterabbit, 70, United Church of Christ Minister, Dies," *Minneapolis Star and Tribune*, April 21, 1968, 12A.

42. Gerald Vizenor, *The Everlasting Sky*, 20.

43. Sue Major Holmes, "Indians' Peyote Use Continuing Source of Misunderstanding," *Albuquerque Journal*, April 20, 1986, C7.

44. Meriam, *The Problem of Indian Administration*, 727–28, 736.

45. Cornell, "New Indian Politics," 118–19.

46. Paulette Fairbanks Molin, "Places Where I've Lived," *Roots: On the Reservation*, Minnesota Historical Society, Spring 1986, 22-23.

47. Meriam, *The Problem of Indian Administration*, 705, 763.

48. United States District Court, *Testimony of Russell Means and Dennis Banks*, Transcript of Trial Proceedings before Federal Judge Fred Nichol. Tuesday, February 12, 1974, St. Paul, Minn., 3909–3977.

49. James Holbrook, "Little Rambo Man," *City Pages* [Minneapolis, Minn.], April 2, 1986, 3.

50. Kevin Diaz, "Bellecourt Pleads Guilty in Bargain for 7-Year Prison Term," *Minneapolis Star and Tribune*, April 4, 1986, 3B.

51. Gerald Vizenor, *The People Named the Chippewa: Narrative Histories* (Minneapolis: University of Minnesota Press, 1984), 78–97.

✝ Bone Courts: The Natural Rights of Tribal Bones

Ishi, the last survivor of his tribe, died in 1916 in a museum at the University of California. Alfred Kroeber was in New York at the time and wrote to the curator of the museum, "If there is any talk about the interests of science, say for me that science can go to hell.

"We propose to stand by our friends," the distinguished anthropologist continued. "Besides, I cannot believe that any scientific value is materially involved. We have hundreds of Indian skeletons that nobody ever comes to study. The prime interest in this case would be of a morbid romantic nature."[1]

Kroeber protected the remains of his tribal friend and, in his letter to the curator, anticipated by two generations the debate over the disinterment of aboriginal bones and the reburial of tribal remains. Three hundred thousand tribal bodies have been taken from their graves to museums and laboratories, asserted a tribal advocate, "If this would happen in any other segment of society there would be outrage. . . . Whether they were buried last year or thousands of years ago, they have the right to the sanctity of the grave."[2]

Suzan Shown Harjo argued that the number of tribal people alive today may be outnumbered by "our dead stored in museums, federal agencies, historical societies and private collections." Indians are "further dehumanized by being exhibited alongside the mastodons and dino-

62

saurs and other extinct creatures." Harjo, executive director of the National Congress of American Indians, wrote
for the *Los Angeles Times* that some of the skulls of her
Cheyenne relatives are in the Smithsonian Institution. "It
wasn't enough that these unarmed Cheyenne people were
mowed down by the Cavalry at the infamous Sand Creek
massacre; many were decapitated and their heads shipped
to Washington as freight." Later, some bodies were ex-
humed; imagine the reactions of grieving families, "finding their loved ones disinterred and headless."

This is a contentious discourse on the prima facie rights
of human remains, sovereign tribal bones, to be their own
narrators, and a modest proposal to establish a Bone
Court. This new forum would have federal judicial power
to hear and decide disputes over burial sites, research on
bones, reburial, and to protect the rights of tribal bones to
be represented in court.

The rights of bones are neither absolute nor abolished at
death; bone rights are abstract, secular, and understood
here in narrative and constitutional legal theories. The
rights of bones represented in federal court would be substantive and procedural; these rights are based on the
premise that human rights continue at death.

Most human remains were buried with ceremonial heed,
an implied communal continuation of human rights;
death, cremation, subaerial exposure, earth burial, and
other interments, are proper courses, not the termination
of human rights. The rights we hold over our bodies and
organs at death are the same rights we must hold over our
bones and ashes.[3] Brain death, or heart death, is not a constitutional divestment; death is not the absolute termination of human rights. In the Bone Court the last rites are
never the last words.

This proposal to hear bones is not an ontological argument to discover being, the soul, or to measure the dura-
tion of human consciousness; however, concern over the
evolution of the soul, and the spiritual return of souls, is

Traditional Anishinaabe grave houses near Lake Andrusia, Minnesota

pertinent in a wider discourse on tribal remains. "Conscious persons consist of body and soul," wrote Richard Swinburne in *The Evolution of the Soul,* but "humans cannot discover what else is needed to get souls to function again, unless they can discover the ultimate force behind nature itself."[4] Here, the proposal for bone rights is a postmodern language game with theories on narration and legal philosophies to direct the discourse. Narrative theories augment the proposition that bones have the right to be represented and heard in court; moreover, tribal bones would become their own narrators and confront their oppressors in a language game, in a legal forum—the proper person, mode, and perspective in narrative mediation.

THE NARRATIVE RIGHTS OF BONES

Franz Karl Stanzel, in his theoretical research on narrative structures, defines three fictional narrative mediations: the narrator belongs to the world in the story; the narrator conveys information; the narrator gives the reader or listener an external view. These three categories, person, mode, and perspective, are based on the idea of a mediator; in this discourse, tribal bones are mediators and narrators. Stanzel explains that "whenever something is reported, there is a mediator." He terms this phenomenon "mediacy," or the "generic characteristic which distinguishes narration from other forms of literary art."[5] Narrative theories are language games; here, bones are the "mediacy" with representation in court. Tribal bones as narrators could be considered the *real* authors of their time and place on the earth; the representation of their voices in a court would overturn the neocolonial perspectives, written and invented tribal cultures.

Roland Barthes, in *Image—Music—Text*, wrote that "writing is that neutral, composite, oblique space where our subject slips away, the negative where all identity is lost. . . . As soon as a fact is *narrated* no longer with a view to acting directly on reality but intransitively, that is to say, finally outside of any function other than that of the very practice of the symbol itself . . . the voice loses its origin, the author enters into his own death, writing begins. . . . Narrative is first and foremost a prodigious variety of genres, themselves distributed amongst different substances—as though any material would fit to receive man's stories."[6]

Tribal narratives are located in stones, trees, birds, water, bears, and tribal bones. The narrative perspective on tribal remains has been neocolonial; tribal bones held in linguistic servitude, measured and compared in autistic social science monologues. Tribal bones are liberated in this proposal, represented in court as narrators and mediators; manumission in postmodern language games. Social and moral contention arises not in tribal remains but in research demands, academic power, material possession, criminal and accidental exhumation. Archaeologists and anthropologists have assumed an absolute right to burial sites, an improper right to research tribal remains and narratives. Tribal bones must oppose science and narrative simulations; bones have a right to be represented and to have their interests heard and recorded in a federal Bone Court.

This modest proposal to hear the rights of tribal bones in a new federal court is based on the constitutional premise that Congress has the power to establish courts with plenary jurisdiction; and that federal judicial power is proper in cases that arise under constitutional definitions, such as human and civil rights, treaties, and tribal sovereignties. Human remains, tribal bones, have rights, human rights, protected by a creative and pragmatic interpretation of the Bill of Rights, which forbids the taking of life, liberty, or property, without due process of law. Tribal bones are sovereign, a moral measure of properties, and an agonistic continuation of narrative rights in a postmodern language game. Tribal remains would have the same rights to be represented in court as those human and civil rights provided in constitutional interpretations; moreover, bones are in human communion with the earth, a natural disposition, and cannot be taken for public use, such as archaeological research and museum servitude, without legal consideration and compensation.

The rights of tribal remains would abolish ownership claims on bones, those policies and provisions that sustain research, discoveries, and hidden treasures; bones are not properties in the same categories as precious stones and metals, or abandoned sea treasure.[7]

This proposal to establish bone rights in a new court does not rest on primitivism, naive religionism, or semantic binaries, engendered in the recent spiritual and institutional bone wars, but is based on secular, theoretical propositions, and legal philosophies. "The reliance on contradiction is the most familiar trait of dialectic," argues

66

Robert Cumming, "whether it be sophistic or Socratic,"[8] but the dialectic seems better suited to the criticism of social science methodologies and monologues than to an interpretation of the rights of human remains.

Ronald Dworkin asserts that even legal pragmatists argue that "judges must sometimes act *as if* people had legal rights, because acting that way will serve society better in the long run. The argument for this as-if strategy is straightforward enough: civilization is impossible unless the decisions of some well-defined person or group are accepted by everyone as setting public standards that will be enforced."[9] The pragmatists, it seems, would salute the proposition to establish a new court and to provide bones the right to be represented; bone rights would resolve the grievances and servitude of tribal remains. Legal pragmatists would liberate bones, and the courts, in this legal language game, would "act *as if*" tribal bones had rights to their own narratives.

THE COLOR OF TRIBAL BONES

Social scientists are loath to associate archaeologists with necrophilism, even in semiotic ironies; however, the distinctions between some methodologies and the peculiar practices of collecting aboriginal bones are blurred causeries in modern tribal consciousness. There is, to be sure, a color and culture variance in the collection of tribal bones; white bones are reburied, tribal bones are studied in racist institutions. The bone robber barons, as some archaeologists would be apprehended, are academic neocolonialists and racial technocrats who now seem to posture as liberal humanists, the institutional emblems distended in worldviews that deliver models and the hyperrealities of the "absolute fake."[10] These bone barons protect their "rights" to advance science and careers on the backs of tribal bones. The tribal dead become the academic chattel, the aboriginal bone slaves to advance archaeological technicism and the

Caucasian cranium in South Dakota

political power of institutional science. The methodologists, and liberal apologists, assume that tribal bones have no rights, that bones are the properties of an advanced civilization.

Thomas Rock, the fictional character in *The Doctor and the Devils*, a film scenario by Dylan Thomas, lectured to his students in an amphitheater, "Let no scruples stand in the way of the progress of medical science!" Rock was an anatomist, a remote trope to science in this discourse, but his dramatic monologue is borrowed as a moral lesson. "I stand before you gentlemen," lectured Rock, "a *material* man to whom the heart, for instance, is an elaborate physical organ and not the 'seat of love,' a man to whom the 'soul,' because it has not shape, does not exist. . . . Our aim forever must be the pursuit of the knowledge of Man

68

in his entirety. To study the flesh, the skin, the bones, the organs, the nerves of Man, is to equip our minds with a knowledge that will enable us to search *beyond* the body."[11] The real doctor behind this scenario purchased murder victims and bodies stolen from graves to continue his research.

Fifteen years ago a "bulldozer blade uncovered an unmarked cemetery" and overturned the basic assumptions and practices of archaeologists. "As the roadwork continued bits of tombstone and the bodies of twenty-seven people were uncovered," wrote Vine Deloria, Jr.[12] "One of the bodies had next to it several hundred glass beads. . . . This body was tentatively identified as the remains of an Indian girl. The remains of the twenty-six other bodies were reverently taken to the Glenwood Cemetery and reburied. The remains believed to be Indian had another destination." The state archaeologist "demanded that the bones be sent to him under the provisions of an Iowa law." Running Moccasins, a tribal woman, protested and "demanded that the bones be given proper burial. She discovered that the bones had been taken to Iowa City, where they were destined for space in a museum."

Duane Anderson, in his article "Reburial: Is It Reasonable?" wrote that the "incident brought to light the inadequacies of the Iowa legal code for dealing with such situations, and left archaeologists without a procedure for conducting investigations of aboriginal remains."[13] These bones bound to a museum resulted in state legislation to recover human remains, to establish a cemetery for aboriginal remains, and to measure responsibilities of state archaeologists.[14]

These reburial issues demonstrate the real need for a Bone Court; a new forum where the rights of human remains, and aboriginal bone narratives, would be represented. The Bone Court would establish a proper record of rights and narratives, and the measured interests of the various parties, state politicians, archaeologists, the public, tribal rights organizations, would be balanced with the rights of the bones.[15] The Bone Court decisions would occasion legal philosophies over research and reburial; the discourse would be based on the rights of tribal bones. These decisions would establish legal histories and anticipate research and contention over human remains. Reburial narratives are muddled in local politics when the prima facie rights of bones are determined in state or local governments. Bones have a right to be represented and heard in court; these rights, not the assumed rights of science, or the interests of politicians, must be the principle concern in court. Science and academic power would survive; bones would be represented and servitude to science would be broken.

In Iowa the issues were research and reburial, but bone rights and narratives were not represented in legislation. "Both scientists and Indians have encountered some difficulties with the new legislation," wrote Duane Anderson. "For archaeologists and physical anthropologists, two problems stand out. First, the intent of the law is to provide for investigation of only those cemetery areas threatened with destruction. . . . Their second difficulty with the law is its reburial requirements; no scientist likes to bury comparative research material."[16]

The rights of tribal bones to be represented in court are not based on religion or interpretations of the American Indian Religious Freedom Act. The rights of bones are abstract, secular, and substantive; religion would be a consideration in certain reburial issues argued in Bone Court, but the rights of bones to be represented in court are neither religious nor doctrinal. The rights of bones in this proposal would not violate the constitutional amendment restricting the "establishment of religion."[17]

The Smithsonian Institution has more than eighteen thousand tribal remains, the largest collection in the nation. Walter Echo-Hawk, attorney for the Native American Rights Fund, told *People* magazine, "If you desecrate a white grave, you wind up sitting in prison. But desecrate an Indian grave, and you get a Ph.D. The time has come for people to decide: Are we Indians part of this country's living culture, or are we just here to supply museums with dead bodies?" Stanford University, the University of Minnesota, and other universities have agreed to return their bone collections to representative tribes. The University of California at Berkeley, however, has not decided what to do with the ten thousand tribal bones in the Lowie Museum of Anthropology. Not all archaeologists agree with the decision to return tribal remains; critical scientific research is the most common argument against reburial.

"Scientists say that these deceased Indians are needed for research that someday could benefit the health and welfare of living Indans," wrote Suzan Shown Harjo for the *Los Angeles Times*. "But just how many dead Indians must they examine?"

STANDING IN THE BONE COURT

Human remains have rights and those rights should be honored as legal standing; bones, the continuation of human rights, would be saluted with the same legal standing in court as corporate bodies, ships at sea, church, state, and municipalities. These inanimate associations possess legal rights that oceans, red pine, owls, and rainbow trout are denied. The asseveration of insensate corporate bodies should include the natural and constitutional rights of bones in court; more than provisions for endangered species.

Christopher Stone, in his legal thesis, *Should Trees Have Standing? Toward Legal Rights for Natural Objects*, proposed that "we recognize legal rights of forests, oceans, rivers, and other so-called 'natural objects' in the environment—indeed, of the natural environment as a whole. As strange as such a notion may sound, it is neither fanciful nor without considerable operational significance,"[18] he continued. "It is not inevitable, nor is it wise, that natural objects

71

should have no rights to seek redress in their own behalf. It is no answer to say that streams and forests cannot have standing because streams and forests cannot speak. Corporations cannot speak either, nor can states, estates, infants, incompetents, municipalities or universities. Lawyers speak for them, as they customarily do for the ordinary citizen who has legal problems."[19]

THE LEGAL VEIL OF IGNORANCE

"Justice is the first virtue of social institutions," John Rawls asserted in *A Theory of Justice*, "as truth is of systems of thought. A theory however elegant and economical must be rejected if it is untrue; likewise laws and institutions no matter how efficient and well-arranged must be reformed or abolished if they are unjust."[20]

Roger Finzel, counsel for American Indians Against Desecration, pointed out that tribal organizations have demanded the "reburial of the three hundred thousand to six hundred thousand remains of ancestors in museums," laboratories, and those bones held at universities.[21] These, and other recorded reburial issues, demand professional reformation and the abolition of research on remains that denies the rights of tribal bones.

The Bone Court, however, would not abolish the academic attention to tribal remains; rather, archaeologists, osteologists, anthropologists, and others would answer to the rights of tribal bones; the rights and interests of bones would be represented and narrated in court.

Rawls argues, "Each person possesses an inviolability founded on justice that even the welfare of society as a whole cannot override." Here, in this discourse, bones hold the continuance of human rights, and, to include the argument above, human remains possess "an inviolability founded on justice" that cannot be reversed. "For this reason justice denies that the loss of freedom for some is made right by a greater good shared by others. It does not allow

72

that the sacrifices imposed on a few are outweighed by the larger sum of advantages enjoyed by many."[22] Clearly the power of academic institutions and the freedom demanded by archaeologists and anthropologists to conduct their research has been the loss of tribal rights, and the rights of human remains. The proposed Bone Court would not abolish research on tribal bones, but the rights of human remains would be represented; the injustices, not freedom, would be denied. Tribal bones would cease to be the neocolonial research chattel of the social sciences.

Concurrence, and association, is significant in scientific research, but methodologies are mere monologues. The representation of human remains is inviolable and justice is possible in a new court where the narratives of tribal bones are heard and recorded in more than monologic methodologies; these rights would enrich social science research and unburden tribal culture and language games. Rawls asserted that the "circumstances of justice may be described as the normal conditions under which human cooperation is both possible and necessary."[23] The Bone Court would provide a practical forum for an association between tribal bones, their narratives, and the demands of science.

The rights of tribal bones, however, will not be discovered in conservative semantic theories that establish legal criteria. The legal realist movement, for instance, "insisted on the proposition that legal rules cannot guide courts to definite results in particular cases and demanded that legal scholarship recognize the social forces influencing legal change."[24] These forces, in the proposition for the rights of bones, include the critical issue of "standing," and, as Justice William O. Douglas reasoned, would allow "environmental issues to be litigated before federal agencies or federal courts in the name of the inanimate object."[25]

The theoretical proposition that bones have legal rights, and the proposal to establish a federal forum to hear bone narratives, is based on the concept that law is interpretive, and that justice "is a matter of the right outcome of the political system."[26] Ronald Dworkin argues, "Fairness is a matter of the right structure for that system, the structure that distributes influence over political decisions in the right way. Procedural due process is a matter of the right procedures for enforcing rules and regulations the system has produced."[27] Political positions, public policies, limited legislation, social values, and religious consciousness have issued from the controversies over the exhumation of tribal remains and the demands for reburial.[28] Some rules and regulations have been published on these issues; now, what must follow is the due process of bones, the procedural rights to be represented, the right to *voice* a narrative in a new federal court.

Dworkin, in *Taking Rights Seriously*, reasoned that "constitutional law can make no genuine advance until it isolates the problem of rights against the state and makes that problem part of its own agenda. That argues for a fusion of constitutional law and moral theory, a connection that, incredibly, has yet to take place. It is perfectly understandable that lawyers dread contamination with moral philosophy, and particularly with those philosophers who talk about rights, because the spooky overtones of that concept threaten the graveyard of reason."[29]

Indeed, the idea of bone rights and narrative representation threatens the "graveyard of reason" in archaeology, anthropology, and other social science monologues.

BONES AND LANGUAGE GAMES

"Arguments of principle are arguments intended to establish an individual right; arguments of policy are arguments intended to establish a collective goal," argues Ronald Dworkin. "Principles are propositions that describe rights; policies are propositions that describe goals."[30] The proposition that bones should be represented in court is a right, a principle of justice based on human rights; however, tribal bones are dominated by academic policies and must oppose the goals of institutions. Tribal bones must counter institutional power to be represented and heard in their own narratives, in their own legal language game.

The power of social science methodologies is intractable because that power, reduced to goals, is located in institutions; academic power has prevailed in structural opposition and metonymic binaries; tribal narratives, popular memories, and political resistance have been reduced to models and dialectics. Alan Sheridan, in *Michel Foucault: The Will to Truth,* construes that "power and knowledge are two sides of the same process. Knowledge cannot be neutral, pure. All knowledge is political not because it may have political consequences or be politically useful, but because knowledge has its conditions of possibility in power relations."[31]

Cultural *anthropologies* and *archaeologies,* for example, are not discourse but monologues with science and power; moreover, social science languages subdue tribal rights and imagination. These *anthropologies* and *archaeologies* are neocolonial tropes to power; causal methodologies, reductive expiries, but not an agonistic discourse on *anthropos* or humans and their *real* narrative remains. Those who reduced tribal cultures to models, and invented the tribes in dioramas, imposed dominant material worldviews in their research on ceremonies and tribal remains. Now, the tribal survivors are summoned to the universities and museums, roused to be proud, cited to abide by the monologues, the dubious splendors of neocolonial tropes on tribal cultures, invented narratives, and aboriginal remains.

Roy Wagner argues that "anthropology exists through the idea of culture," which is a monologue with science. "The study of culture *is* culture . . . The study of culture is in fact *our* culture; it operates through our forms, creates in our terms, borrows our words and concepts for its meanings, and re-creates us through our efforts." The dominant culture "is a vast accumulation of material and spiritual

75

achievements and resources stemming from the conquest of nature and necessary to the continuance of this effort."[32]

George Marcus and Michael Fischer, in *Anthropology as Cultural Critique*, explain that what "has propelled many modern anthropologists into the field and motivated resultant ethnographic accounts is a desire to enlighten their readers about other ways of life, but often with the aim of disturbing their cultural self-satisfaction." In their descriptions of other cultures, "ethnographers have simultaneously had a marginal or hidden agenda of critique of their own culture, namely, the bourgeois, middle-class life of mass liberal societies, which industrial capitalism has produced."[33]

Paul Feyerabend, on the other hand, argues that when some anthropologists "collected and systematized" tribal cultures, the scientific emphasis was on the "psychological meaning, the social functions, the existential temper of a culture," while the "ontological implications" were disregarded. Feyerabend contends that, to the anthropologists who transformed tribal cultures, the "oracles, rain dances, the treatment of mind and body, *express* the needs of the members of a society, they *function* as a social glue, they *reveal* basic structures of the relations between man and man and man and nature but without an accompanying *knowledge* of distant events, rain, mind, body. Such interpretations were hardly ever the result of critical thought— most of the time they were simply a consequence of popular antimetaphysical tendencies combined with a firm belief in the excellence . . . of science."[34]

James Clifford and George Marcus, in the introduction to *Writing Culture: The Poetics and Politics of Ethnography*, warrant that ethnographic truths are "inherently *partial*— committed and incomplete. This point is now widely asserted—and resisted at strategic points by those who fear the collapse of clear standards of verification. But once accepted and built into ethnographic art, a rigorous sense of partiality can be a source of representational tact. . . .

76

Ethnographic work has indeed been enmeshed in a world of enduring and changing power inequalities, and it continues to be implicated. It enacts power relations. But its function within these relations is complex, often ambivalent, potentially counter-hegemonic."[35]

Manfred Stanley, in *The Technological Conscience*, a study of "linguistic technicism—the misuse of scientific and technological vocabularies with regard to human activities," argues that technicism is a special case of "cultural imperialism,"[36] He explains that his "course is not revolution against science. The enemy, rather, is our universal complicity in the degradation of linguistic discipline." Stanley outlines a "modern scientific world view" as materialistic and nihilistic; he asserts that "knowledge based upon sensuous relations of human beings to a perceived object world is downgraded in favor of knowledge conceived in terms of conceptual operations performed upon the world."[37]

Tribal bones and those who assert their relations with tribal remains, must oppose those social science "conceptual operations" on tribal cultures and narratives. The rights of bones, legal practices, and narratives are argumentative; science has no absolute rights to objects, methods, narratives. Tribal bones have earned the right to their own popular memories, to their own narrative properties; bones have earned the rights to be represented and heard in court.

Rights, arguments, narratives are discourse, not isolated monologues. The rights of bones to be represented are not semantic, positivist, or religious, but a secular, theoretical, and agonistic interpretation of legal propositions.[38] To overbear tribal narratives, to oppose discourse on bone rights, and to reduce arguments to a religious or radical performance, as the social sciences have done, could "demonize science and technology to a point of some great religious convulsion of primitivist simplification."[39]

Clifford Geertz, in "Blurred Genres: The Refiguration of Social Thought," concludes that the "relation between thought and action in social life can no more be conceived of in terms of wisdom than it can in terms of expertise. How is it to be conceived, how the games, dramas, or texts which we do not just invent or witness but live, have the consequence they do remains very far from clear. It will take the wariest of wary reasonings, on all sides of all divides, to get it clear."[40]

First, however, we must establish the sides, the forums, the narratives, modes, and perspectives in this cultural discourse, and these postmodern language games. The Bone Court is the best place to begin, where tribal bones are the narrators, where tribal bones have the legal right to be represented. There are no better operative tropes in these cultural language games than the narrative rights of tribal bones; the genres, but not the tribal bones and our rights, are blurred.

1986, 1989

NOTES

I proposed the Bone Court, and the rights of bones to be represented, at the School of American Research in Santa Fe, New Mexico. The response from other resident scholars, archaeologists and anthropologists, was tolerant; the idea invited some humor as critical abatement, but a discourse never matured at the seminars.

1. Theodora Kroeber, *Ishi in Two Worlds* (Berkeley: University of California Press, 1961), 234. Ishi was cremated and his remains "placed in a niche at Mount Olivet Cemetery. Pope and Waterman decided and I agreed," wrote the museum curator to Alfred Kroeber, "that a small black Pueblo jar would be far more appropriate than one of the bronze or onyx urns." The inscription

reads: *Ishi, the last Yana Indian, 1916.* "The funeral was private and no flowers were brought."

2. *New York Times,* "MX Cable Gives Air Force and Sioux a Bond," Thursday, November 15, 1984. Jan Hammil, a Mescalero Apache from New Mexico, directs American Indians Against Desecration. She said, "What we're interested in is respect for the dead because for us it's just another step in life."

3. Effie Bendann, *Death Customs: The Analytical Study of Burial Rites* (New York: Knopf, 1930), 45-46, 268–83. See also Robert Chapman, Ian Kinnes, and Klavs Randsborg (eds.), *The Archaeology of Death* (Cambridge: Cambridge University Press, 1981).

4. Richard Swinburne, *The Evolution of the Soul* (Oxford: Clarendon Press, 1986), 176, 311.

5. Franz Karl Stanzel, *A Theory of Narrative* (Cambridge: Cambridge University Press, 1984), xi, 4.

6. Roland Barthes, "Introduction to the Structural Analysis of Narratives," and "The Death of the Author," in *Image—Music—Text* (New York: Hill & Wang, 1977), 79, 142.

7. *Twentieth Judicial District Court,* Parish of West Feliciana, State of Louisiana, Suit Number 5,552, March 18, 1985. Human remains, however, are viewed in terms of property rights or in some cases as religious issues. In the Louisiana decision the court pointed out that a *"treasure* is a thing hidden or buried in the earth, on which no one can prove his property, and which is discovered by chance." This provision "requiring discovery *by chance* admits to no misunderstanding. Its intent is to deny ownership to one who goes on the property of another with reasonable knowledge that he will discover something of value on that property." The court decided that ownership of "discovered" artifacts should be awarded to the Tunica-Biloxi Tribe. "Its principal concern is that of title to the burial grounds which was not put at issue in these proceedings."

8. Robert Denoon Cumming, *Starting Point: An Introduction to the Dialectic of Existence* (Chicago: University of Chicago Press, 1979), 186.

9. Ronald Dworkin, *Law's Empire* (Cambridge, Mass.: Harvard University Press, 1986), 152–53.

10. Umberto Eco, *Travels in Hyperreality* (San Diego: Harcourt, Brace, Jovanovich, 1986), 3–58. Eco writes that Americans live in a "more to come" consumer culture. "This is the reason for this

79

journey into hyperreality, in search of instances where the American imagination demands the real thing and, to attain it, must fabricate the absolute fake." Tribal cultures, in this sense, have been invented as "absolute fakes" in social science models, cinema, and popular media.

11. Dylan Thomas, *The Doctor and the Devils* (London: Dent, 1953), 10. Donald Taylor (he commissioned Dylan Thomas to write the film scenario) wrote that the *real* doctor who practiced in the last century had an "abiding passion" for ethnography and lectured to "invited audiences, using for demonstration purposes a group of North American Indians who were appearing in a circus" in England.

12. Vine Deloria, Jr., *God Is Red* (New York: Grosset & Dunlap, 1973), 32, 33, 66.

13. Duane Anderson, "Reburial: Is It Reasonable?" *Archaeology*, 38 (September/October 1985), 48.

14. Ibid., 49.

15. Logan Slagle pointed out that in some cases a skeleton would invite a "competency hearing" to determine "standing" and how many actual bones were present to be represented. Slagle is a legal scholar and tribal advocate.

16. Anderson, "Reburial," 49.

17. Ellen M. W. Sewell, "The Indian Religious Freedom Act," *Arizona Law Review*, 25 (1983), 429–72. Sewell wrote that the "American Indian Religious Freedom Act intends extensive protections of Indian traditional practices, whether or not those practices would necessarily be protected by the free exercise clause, as judicially interpreted, and that the Act's protections are not prohibited by the establishment clause."

"The American Indian Religious Freedom Act, passed with almost no opposition," Sewell continued, "was signed into law by President Jimmy Carter in August 1978. The Law is unusually general and cryptic. It states it is the 'policy of the United States to protect and preserve for American Indians their inherent right of freedom to believe, express, and exercise the traditional religions. . . . ' The statute specifically protects three aspects of religious practice: 'access to sites, use and possession of sacred objects, and the freedom to worship through ceremonies and traditional rites.' "

For a more general discussion see Robert Michaelsen, "Civil Rights, Indian Rites," *Society*, 21 (May/June 1984); reprinted in Roger Nichols (ed.) *The American Indian: Past and Present*, 3rd ed. (New York: Knopf, 1986).

18. Christopher Stone, *Should Trees Have Standing? Toward Legal Rights for Natural Objects* (New York: Avon, 1975), 25, 26 (Southern California Law Review, 1972).

19. Ibid., 40, 41.

20. John Rawls, *A Theory of Justice* (Cambridge, Mass.: Harvard University Press, 1971), 3.

21. Roger Finzel, "Indian Burial Site Issues," unpublished outline presented at *Indian Law Training Conference*, University of California, Berkeley, July 1985.

22. Rawls, *Theory of Justice*, 4.

23. Ibid., 126.

24. *Harvard Law Review*, " 'Round and 'Round the Bramble Bush: From Legal Realism to Critical Legal Scholarship," 95 (May 1982), 1669–1690.

25. Justice William O. Douglas, quoted in Stone, *Should Trees Have Standing?* 50.

26. Dworkin, *Law's Empire*, 404.

27. Ibid., *Law's Empire*, 404, 405.

28. *New York Times*, "Smithsonian in Dispute over Indian Skeletons," February 14, 1986. "Officials of the Smithsonian Institution's Museum of Natural History" said "they would turn over to recognized tribal leaders Indian skeletons that have a 'clear biological or cultural link' to modern-day tribal units," the article reported. "But the museum officials estimated . . . that this description would apply to fewer than 10 percent of the Smithsonian's collection of 14,000 Indian skeletons, since most of the remains are of undetermined prehistoric origin. The Indian organizations want all the remains returned to Indians for reburial, citing religious reasons."

29. Ronald Dworkin, *Taking Rights Seriously* (Cambridge, Mass.: Harvard University Press, 1977), 149. Walter Berns, "Equally Endowed with Rights," in Frank Lucash (ed.), *Justice and Equality Here and Now* (Ithaca, N.Y.: Cornell University Press, 1986), asserts that "Dworkin recognizes that there can be no constitutional law independent of philosophy but he maintains that

until recently there has been no philosophy—or, at least, no *good* philosophy—to which constitutional law can be attached."

30. Dworkin, *Taking Rights Seriously*, 90.

31. Alan Sheridan, *Michel Foucault: The Will to Truth* (London: Tavistock, 1980), 220.

32. Roy Wagner, *The Invention of Culture* (Chicago: University of Chicago Press, 1981).

33. George Marcus and Michael M. J. Fischer, *Anthropology as Cultural Critique: An Experimental Moment in the Human Sciences* (Chicago: University of Chicago Press, 1986), 111.

34. Paul Feyeraband, *Science in a Free Society* (London: Verso, 1978), 77.

35. James Clifford and George Marcus (eds.), *Writing Culture: The Poetics and Politics of Ethnography* (Berkeley: University of California Press, 1986), 7, 9. (A School of American Research Advanced Seminar, Santa Fe, New Mexico, April 1984.)

36. Manfred Stanley, *The Technological Conscience: Survival and Dignity in an Age of Expertise* (Chicago: University of Chicago Press, 1978), xii, 14.

37. Ibid., 23, 142.

38. Dworkin, *Law's Empire*, 33–37.

39. Stanley, *Technological Conscience*, 16.

40. Clifford Geertz, "Blurred Genres: The Refiguration of Social Thought," *American Scholar*, 49 (Spring 1980), 179.

✛ Socioacupuncture:
Mythic Reversals and
the Striptease in Four Scenes

*There's a battle for and around history going on at
this very moment . . . The intension is to
programme, to stifle what I've called 'popular
memory'; and also to propose and impose on people
a framework in which to interpret the present.*

MICHEL FOUCAULT
Interview in *Cahiers du Cinema*

SCENE ONE: RELEASE FROM CAPTURED IMAGES

Roland Barthes shows that the striptease is a contradiction;
at the final moment of nakedness a "woman is desexual-
ized." He writes in his book *Mythologies* that the spectacle
is based on the "pretence of fear, as if eroticism here went
no further than a sort of delicious terror, whose ritual signs
have only to be announced to evoke at once the idea of sex
and its conjuration."

Tribal cultures are colonized in a reversal of the striptease. Familiar tribal images are patches on the "pretence
of fear," and there is a sense of "delicious terror" in the
structural opposition of savagism and civilization found in
the cinema and in the literature of romantic captivities.
Plains tepees, and the signs of moccasins, canoes, feathers,
leathers, arrowheads, numerous museum artifacts, con-
jure the cultural rituals of the traditional tribal past, but the

83

pleasures of the tribal striptease are denied, data bound, stopped in emulsion, colonized in print to resolve the insecurities and inhibitions of the dominant culture.

The striptease is a familiar expression of theatrical independence and social titillation. In the scenes and voices here that delicious dance is a metaphor and in the metaphor are mythic strategies for survival.

The striptease is the prime form of socioacupuncture, a therapeutic tease and technique that is accomplished through tribal trickeries and mythic satire, eternal contradictions that release the ritual terror in captured images.

Ishi, for example, lived alone with one name, loose change, and a business suit in a corner of an institution, the perfect tribal ornament. The anthropologists at the museumscape declared his private time a public venture; the survivor was collared for a place in an academic diorama until he danced in a striptease.

The inventions and historical plunders of tribal cultures by colonists, corporations, academic culture cultists, with their missions, reservations, deceptions, museum durance, have inhibited the sovereign striptease; racism and linear methods of perception have denied a theater for tribal events in mythic time.

SCENE TWO: EUPHEMISMS FOR LINGUISTIC COLONIZATION

Edward Curtis possessed romantic and stoical images of tribal people in his photographs. Posed and decorated in traditional vestments and costumes, his pictorial tribes are secular reversals of a ritual striptease, frozen faces on a calendar of arrogant discoveries, a solemn ethnocentric appeal for recognition of his own insecurities; his retouched emulsion images are based on the "pretence of fear."

Curtis could have vanished in his own culture, which he strove to understand through tribal civilizations, if tribal people appeared in his soft focus photographs as assimilated: perched at pianos, dressed in machine stitched clothes, or writing letters to corrupt government agents.

Tribal cultures have been transformed in photographic images from mythic time into museum commodities. "Photography evades us," writes Roland Barthes in *Camera Lucida*. "Photography transformed subject into object, and even, one might say, into a museum object."

Photography is a social rite that turns the past into a "consumable object," argues Susan Sontag in her book *On Photography*, "a defence against anxiety, and a tool of power." One cannot possess realities, but one can possess images, and "photographs are a way of imprisoning reality. . . . The primitive notion of the efficacy of images presumes that images possess the qualities of real things, but our inclination is to attribute to real things the qualities of image."

Curtis retouched tribal images; he, or his darkroom assistants, removed hats, labels, suspenders, parasols, from photographic prints. In one photograph entitled "In a Piegan Lodge" the image of an alarm clock was removed from the original negative.

Christopher Lyman, in his recent book *The Vanishing Race and Other Illusions*, reveals that the image of a clock, which appeared in a box between two tribal men, was removed from the gravure print published in the multivolume *The North American Indian* by Edward Curtis.

Curtis invented and then possessed tribal images while at the same time he denied the tribal people in one photograph the simple instrument of chronological time. The photographer and the clock, at last, appear more interesting now than the two tribal men posed with their ubiquitous peacepipes. Curtis paid some tribal people to pose for photographs; he sold their images and lectured on their culture to raise cash to continue his travels to tribal communities. He traveled with his camera to capture the neonoble tribes, to preserve metasavages in the ethnographic present as consumable objects of the past.

Lyman writes that the "removal of unwanted detail was certainly not the only end toward which Curtis employed retouching. When it came to pictorialist aesthetics, he was dedicated in his pursuit of dramatic effect."

Photographs are ambiguous according to the novelist and art critic John Berger. "A photograph arrests the flow of time in which the event photographed once existed," he writes in *Another Way of Telling*. "All photographs are of the past, yet in them an instant of the past is arrested so that, unlike a lived past, it can never lead to the present. Every photograph presents us with two messages: a message concerning the event photographed and another concerning a shock of discontinuity." Photographs of tribal people, therefore, are not connections to the traditional past; these images are discontinuous artifacts in a colonial road show.

The inventions of the tribes and denials of the striptease, however, are not limited to emulsion images. Jingoists, historians, anthropologists, mythologists, and various culture cultists have hatched and possessed distorted images of tribal cultures. Conference programs and the rich gossip at dinner parties continue to focus on the most recent adventures in tribal commodities. This obsession with the tribal past is not an innocent collection of arrowheads, not a crude map of public camp sites in sacred places, but rather a statement of academic power and control over tribal images, an excess of facts, data, narrative interviews, template discoveries. Academic evidence is a euphemism for linguistic colonization of oral traditions and popular memories.

SCENE THREE: METASAVAGES IN PERFECT OPPOSITION

Encyclopaedia Britannica has sponsored the creation of a dozen tribal manikins, dressed in traditional vestments for promotional exhibition at various shopping centers.

The sculpted figures, named for Black Hawk, Pontiac, Cochise, Massasoit, and other tribal leaders from the footnotes of dominant cultural histories, stand like specters from the tribal past in a secular reversal of the striptease. What is most unusual about this exhibition of anatomical artifacts is not that tribal leaders are invented and possessed as objects in a diorama to promote the sale of books, but that few of the tribal names celebrated in plastic casts are entered in the reference books published by the sponsor of the manikins.

"The Indian leaders whose likenesses appear in this exhibition represent every major region of the country and span more than four centuries of history," the editors write in the illustrated catalogue that is sold to promote their reference books. "Some were great military leaders who fought valiantly to defend their lands. Others were statesmen, diplomats, scholars, and spiritual leaders." Nine manikins, however, are feathered and the same number are praised as warriors. Black Hawk, the catalogue reveals, "established his reputation as a warrior early in life. He wounded an enemy of his tribe at the age of fifteen and took his first scalp the same year." Three invented tribal images bear rifles; but only Massasoit, the manikin who associated with the colonists, is dressed in a breechcloth and holds a short bow. In addition to those mentioned, the other plastic manikins are named Joseph, Cornplanter, Powhatan, Red Cloud, Sequoyah, Tecumseh, Wovoka, and Sacagawea, the one female tribal figure in the collection.

The editors of the catalogue and the sculptors of the manikins consulted with "scholars in the fields of Indian history, anthropology, and ethnology," and point out that the tribal biographies in the catalogue are the "product of hundreds of hours of research involving scores of sources of information." Such claims seem ironic, even deceptive, because the sponsors were not able to consult entries in the

87

Encyclopaedia Britannica for most of the tribal names in the promotion catalogue.

The manikin of Wovoka, spiritual founder of the Ghost Dance religion, was created from photographs, while the other manikins, for the most part, were invented as neo-nobles and metasavages from historical descriptions and from portraits painted by Charles Bird King. "It seems odd," the editors of the catalogue write, "that Wovoka is shown dressed in white man's clothes, but this is the costume he typically wore as did many other Indians." The other manikins in this cultural contradiction, however, are dressed in what appear to be romantic variations of tribal vestments, evidence of the denials of the striptease.

The sources of visual information, portraits, and historical descriptions, that the sculptors used to cast the manikins are colonial inventions, museum bound. Portrait painters, photographers, explorers, traders, and politicians have, with few exceptions, created a metasavage in perfect racist opposition to the theologies of the dominant culture. The editors and research consultants, even the witnesses at the shopping centers, might vanish if these manikins were embodied in mythic time and participated in a striptease: the structural distances captured in plastic would dissolve in a delicious dance.

SCENE FOUR: EVELYBODY IS HOPPY IN MYTHIC TIME

Tune Browne, crossblood tribal trickster from a woodland reservation, and the inspiration behind socioacupuncture, never wore beads or feathers or a wristwatch; he never paid much attention to time or to his image until he became an independent candidate for alderman.

Tune captured his own electronic and emulsion image when he first saw his outsized face and eruptive nostrils on television and in newspaper photographs. He improved his pose from week to week, one image to the next; he

SOCIOACUPUNCTURE

cocked his cheeks high at a traditional angle to mimic the old photographs, bought a watch, and dressed in leathers, beads, bits and pieces at first, and then in six months he appeared on election eve in braids and feathers, a proud reversal of the striptease. He seldom responded to abstract questions about economies; and in spite of his captured image, he found himself in the oral tradition from time to time. It happened when he removed his watch: he told stories then, myths and metaphors unfurled like blue herons in flight at dusk. Linear time seemed to vanish when he removed his watch.

Tune lost the election, he even lost the urban tribal vote, but he had earned the distinction of being the first tribal person to enter the aldermanic race. Pictures of him in feathers and braids appeared months later in editorial articles, dubious footnotes to a loser, which he soon recognized as a captured image, his image, from the past.

"Who *was* that stranger in the image?" he asked in a rhetorical pose at the first international conference on socioacupuncture and tribal identities at the University of California at Berkeley. Tune was dressed in leather and beads for the conference, redundant beside his photographic image on the right side of the screen behind the podium. "A dreamer who lost his soul for a time and found his families in still photographs," he said as he projected a second photograph on the left side of the screen.

Tune moves in mythic time, an unusual dreamer who tells that he shaves with crows and drives behind bears to the cedar treelines near the cities, hunkers with beaver over breakfast, and walks backward under fluorescent lights and in institutions without windows. When he cannot see a tree he looses four white faces from his memories, an urban revision of the Ghost Dance.

Tune stands on stage, the lead speaker on tribal identities in the modern world, between two photographic images. On the right is his captured image in braids, sitting on the ground in a tepee with several peacepipes and an

89

alarm clock. The photograph projected on the left side of the screen is "In a Piegan Lodge" by Edward Curtis.

"See here," Tune said as he pointed to the images, "Curtis has removed the clock, colonized the culture games and denied us our time in the world. . . . Christopher Lyman wrote that the clock could have been a medal, a peace medal, but the box is too thick and besides, we *wore* medals then, never museum boxed medals for a posed picture.

"Curtis paid us for the poses; it was hot then, but he wanted us to wear leathers to create the appearance of a traditional scene, his idea of the past. . . . Curtis stood alone behind his camera, we pitied him there, he seemed lost, separated from his shadow, a desperate man who paid tribal people to become the images in his captured families. We never saw the photographs then and never thought that it would make a difference in the world of dreams, that we would become *his* images."

Tune pushed the podium aside and measured the captured images on the screen with his outstretched hands; from heads to hands he moved his fingers in shadow gestures over the screen. "But it did make a difference, we were caught dead in camera time, extinct in photographs, and now in search of our past and common memories we walk right back into these photographs, we become the invented images as this one did during the aldermanic election, to validate those who invented us on negatives."

He lowered his arms, spread his stout fingers like birds in flight and released several feathers from his vest. The lights were dim, the audience in the conference center was silent. Crows called in the distance, an otter slid down a river bank and snapped back in mythic time as a crossblood trickster on a high wire between the woodland and the cities.

"Socioacupuncture is our means of survival on the wire, our striptease in mythic satire," he said in a deep voice as he untied the ties of the costumes in captured images, unhooked the hooks to museum commodities, and bead over bead he performed a slow striptease, a ritual contradiction between two frozen photographic images from the time bound past.

"Not satire as shame," Tune explained to the tribal people at the conference, "not social ridicule as a form of social control," he continued as he dropped his bone choker to the floor, "but satire from magical connections with the oral tradition. . . . Robert Elliott writes about a 'mystical ethos' in satire, from ritual dances and tribal trickeries. Mythic satire, not as a moral lesson, but a dream voice out of time like a striptease in the middle of the word wars."

Tune removed his beaded leather vest and dropped it to the floor of the stage. His hands danced as he continued his lecture stories on the ethos of ritual striptease.

"Socioacupuncture reverses the documents, deflates data, dissolves historical time, releases the pressure in captured images, and exposes the pale inventors of the tribes. Lyman tells us that Curtis set out to construct a 'photographic monument to a vanishing race.' Not so, it was the photographer who would have vanished without our images to take as captured families.

"On the frontier white settlers were offered free guns with the purchase of sewing machines," Tune announced to the conference participants as he untied his mocassins. "The tribes were offered free clocks with a peace medal and a reservation. . . . Curtis stole our alarm clocks and we missed the plane and lost the election dressed in leather and feathers."

"Take it off," someone yelled from the audience.

"Give him time," someone responded.

"Roy Wagner must have stopped the clocks for a time when he wrote *The Invention of Culture*," Tune said as he kicked his pinched moccasins with the floral bead patterns into the audience and gestured, at the same time, toward his image on the screen to the right. "He wrote that 'the study of culture is in fact *our* culture,' the dominant culture

91

is what he means here, and 'it operates through our forms, creates in our terms, borrows our words and concepts for its meanings, and re-creates us through our efforts. . . . By applying universal theories naively to the study of cultures we invent those cultures as stubborn and inviolable individualities. Each failure motivates a greater collectivizing effort.'

"We lost the election in leathers and feathers, failed and fixed in histories, but through mythic satire we reverse the inventions, and during our ritual striptease the inventors vanish."

"Take it off," the tribal audience chanted again and again as Tune unbuttoned his shirt and unbraided his hair and shivered between the captured images at his sides.

"Wagner tells how Ishi, the last survivor of the Yahi tribe in California, 'brought the world into the museum,' where we lived and worked after our capture," Tune confessed as he threw his shirt and the ribbons from his braids to the audience. "In good weather anthropologists and others would take the two of us from the museum back to the hills where we would demonstrate how to survive with a small bow and wooden arrows. He was the 'ideal museum specimen. . . . Ishi accomplished the metaphorization of life into culture that defines much of anthropological understanding,' Wagner wrote."

"Take it off."

"Take it off."

"Take it off."

"Take it off."

"Tune is the name and the end of the captured game," he chanted as he combed his hair free from braids, and then he untied the beaded belt that held his leather trousers erect, "the end of the captured game."

Tune turned the projectors off and the captured images died when he dropped his trousers in a sovereign striptease. The audience burst into wild cheers and peels of animal laughter in the dim light, even the cats and crows called from the crowd. Tune listened to the birds over the trees and when he removed his wristwatch the dichotomies of past and present dissolved one last time. The inventors and colonialists vanished with the striptease, even those whose ideas he had quoted seem to vanish like petals on a pasture rose. The conference on socioacupuncture was silent.

Tune turned toward the trees in mythic time and told how he and Ishi lived together and worked at the museum to protect the anthropologist, for a time, from vanishing. Then, last summer, "the anthropologists were secure enough in their own culture to recommend that we receive honorary degrees from the University of California at Berkeley."

Tune paused in silence to celebrate the trees in his vision. Then he told stories about the graduation ceremonies in the redwoods: "Morning ghosts ride with our dreams over the tribal stories from the past, dark waves, slow waves, water demons under our ocean skin waves, trickeries and turtle memories under the stone waves, under the word gates, through the earth where we hold our origins with the trees and the wind, creation myths with ocean roots. . . . The ghosts dance roundabout in our dreams, clouds dance and burn free in the rituals of the morning sun.

"College degrees are degrees in words, with special awards for sentence structure, uniforms in the word wars, which is not much better than being elected to the plastic flower growers association hall of fame, but we must not pluck the carrier pigeons with the documents too soon because the academics might vanish."

Silence.

Gregory Bateson writes in his book *Mind and Nature* that in the affairs of living "there are typically two energetic systems in interdependence: One is the system that uses its energy to open and close the faucet or gate or relay; the other is the system whose energy 'flows through' the fau-

93

cet or gate when it is open." Photographers and colonists are the faucets, historians hold the word gates, and we are the energies of the tribes that run like dreams in a dance with the morning sun over wet meadows.

Ghosts hover in the tall redwoods roundabout the outdoor amphitheater in the Mather Redwood Grove. Animals and birds soar through the treescapes, dream beasts browse over the mountains. Tune remembers the flood and calls the crows back from the cities.

"The imagination is always aware of the present" wrote Mary Warnock in her book *Imagination*. "Neither understanding alone nor sensation alone can do the work of imagination, nor can they be conceived to come together without imagination. . . . Only imagination is in this sense creative; only it makes pictures of things." We remembered, "pictures are imagination not photographs."

Alfred Kroeber, Thomas Waterman, Edward Sapir, the linguist, and Phoebe Apperson Hearst, Regent of the University of California, and Robert Sproul and Benjamin Ide Wheeler, were all there for the graduation ceremonies, roundabout in the redwood trees, soaring out of time and place in magical flight.

"The University of California strives not to isolate academic ideas, races and nations, on our campus as single population groups. This is not a place of racial separations," asserted Provost Pontius Booker as he pinched the skin under his chin. "Our academic communities are based on trust, research, instruction, fair examinations, and, of course, on excellence. . . .

"This afternoon we are privileged to announce that our very own Ishi, and Tune Browne, will receive honorary Doctor of Philosophy degrees here at the University of California, where these two instinctive native scholars have lived in a museum. . . . It is a distinct pleasure to announce these degrees and to introduce Alfred Kroeber, the famous anthropologist who worked with these two proud and unusual natives."

94

Kroeber shuffled on stage close to the microphone, leaned over and spoke in a gentle but distant voice: Ishi was the "most patient man I ever knew. I mean he had mastered the philosophy of patience. . . . "

Saxton Pope, our medical doctor and master of bows and arrows, was not present for the graduation but he wrote the following to be read at the ceremonies: Ishi "looked upon us as sophisticated children—smart, but not wise. We knew many things, and much that is false. He knew nature, which is always true. . . . His soul was that of a child, his mind that of a philosopher."

Phoebe Apperson Hearst came down to the microphone from the right rim of the amphitheater to decorate us with colorful sashes and to present our degrees. "Doctor Ishi Ishi, Doctor Tune Browne, you are both intuitive scholars, we have all agreed." Doctor Kroeber has recorded the first words that Ishi spoke in English. . . . We are, at last, pleased to imitate this fine man on this special occasion, is *evelybody hoppy?*

"The transvaluation of roles that turns the despised and oppressed into symbols of salvation and rebirth is nothing new in the history of human culture," writes Robert Bellah, a sociologist from the University of California at Berkeley, in his book *The Broken Covenant*. "But when it occurs, it is an indication of new cultural directions, perhaps of a deep cultural revolution."

We danced roundabout on the stage of the amphitheater dressed in our breechcloths and academic sashes with all the animals and ghosts under the redwood trees; a striptease, deep in a cultural revolution.

The fogdogs laughed and barked from the rim.

"*Evelybody hoppy?*" asked Doctor Ishi.

"Time now for a word striptease," someone chanted.

"Take it off."

"Silence. . . . "

"We are what we imagine," wrote N. Scott Momaday, the Kiowa novelist. "Our very existence consists in our

95

imagination of ourselves. . . . The greatest tragedy that can
befall us is to go unimagined."

"Evelybody hoppy?" asked Doctor Tune Browne.

1987

REFERENCES

Barthes, Roland. *Camera Lucida: Reflections on Photographs* (New
York: Hill & Wang, 1981).

Barthes, Roland. *Mythologies* (New York: Hill & Wang, 1972).

Bateson, Gregory. *Mind and Nature* (New York: Dutton, 1979).

Bellah, Robert. *The Broken Covenant: American Civil Religion in Time
of Trial* (New York: Pantheon Books, 1975).

Berger, John, and Jean Mohr. *Another Way of Telling* (New York:
Pantheon Books, 1982).

Boesen, Victor, and Florence Curtis Graybill. *Edward S. Curtis:
Photographer of the North American Indian* (New York: Dodd,
Mead, 1977).

Cahiers du Cinema, "Anti-Retro," July-August 1974, number
251–52. "Film and Popular Memory," an interview with Michel
Foucault translated by Martin Jordin, *Radical Philosophy* (London), 11, (1975), 24–29.

Davidson, James West, and Mark Hamilton Lytle. *After the Fact:
The Art of Historical Detection.* Chapter 5, "The 'Noble Savage'
and the Artist's Canvas," 113–38 (New York: Knopf, 1982).

Drinnon, Richard. *Facing West: The Metaphysics of Indian-Hating
and Empire-Building* (Minneapolis: University of Minnesota
Press, 1980).

Elliott, Robert. *The Power of Satire: Magic, Ritual, Art* (Princeton,
N.J.: Princeton University Press, 1960).

Encyclopaedia Britannica, Great American Indian Leaders (1980).

Fromm, Erich. *On Disobedience* (New York: Seabury Press, 1981).

Hawks, Terence. *Structuralism and Semiotics* (Berkeley: University
of California Press, 1977).

Kroeber, Theodora. *Ishi in Two Worlds* (Berkeley: University of
California Press, 1963).

Lyman, Christopher. *The Vanishing Race and Other Illusions: Photographs of Indians by Edward S. Curtis* (New York: Pantheon

Books, in association with the Smithsonian Institution Press, 1982).

Momaday, N. Scott. *House Made of Dawn* (New York: Harper & Row, 1968).

Momaday, N. Scott. *The Way to Rainy Mountain* (Albuquerque: University of New Mexico Press, 1969).

Pope, Saxton Temple. *Hunting with the Bow and Arrow* (San Francisco: James H. Barry, 1923).

Sontag, Susan. *On Photography* (New York: Farrar, Straus & Giroux, 1977).

Vizenor, Gerald. "The Psychotaxidermist." In Jean Ervin (ed.), *The Minnesota Experience* (Minneapolis: Adams Press, 1979), 220–28.

Vizenor, Gerald. *Earthdivers: Tribal Narratives on Mixed Descent* (University of Minnesota Press, 1981).

Wagner, Roy. *The Invention of Culture* (Chicago: University of Chicago Press, 1981).

Warnock, Mary. *Imagination* (Berkeley: University of California Press, 1976).

PART 2
CAPITAL PUNISHMENT

<u>Notes Pertaining to my case!</u>

Dr. Rehan said that I knew I couldn't use liquor as an excuse for what had happened. He also had wished me luck with my case.

During the whole time I was at Vermillion, I felt that somebody should pay for what had happened to Mr. Yeads. Naturally, as I was the person who held the rifle, I felt that I should pay equally for the death of Mr. Yeads. I disregarded the circumstances of the crime completely. I knew I wasn't the same person that went into the Yeads home. I made mention of this fact to Judge Bandy, specifically.

Then when the circumstances at Vermillion, that is, my discussion with Lee about the trial, came up, I just gave up any and all hope. From then forward I didn't care what happened to me.

I had been engaged to O.M.B. but broke the engagement because she had spent a night with someone and didn't bother to hide it when she came to visit me later. Personally, I think she did it merely for the soul purpose of having me break the engagement. My conclusions for such were because of her actions while we were talking.

Because I was supposed to become married to her the following summer (1967) I wanted to have "my cake and eat it too." It can't be done! I never really considered the outcome of my

✝ Thomas White Hawk

MURDER ON GOOD FRIDAY

It was a warm spring afternoon; southern winds blew the paper and dirt against the buildings along Main Street. School boys were banging in and out of the Monogram News Shop. James Yeado closed his store a little after five o'clock, Thursday, March 23, 1967, double checked the door, and went home for dinner. That evening he and his wife Dorthea attended a special Lenten service at St. Agnes Catholic Church. The next day was Good Friday and a close friend was stopping by for lunch.

For thirty years James A. Yeado was a jeweler in Vermillion. He was born under the sign of Virgo on September 14, 1904, in LeRoy, North Dakota. He married Dorthea McMahan on August 31, 1931, at Bird Island, Minnesota. The Yeados lived in Hector, Minnesota for a brief time, and in 1937 they moved to Vermillion. They lived at 315 South University for twenty-six years, raised two children, and shared the responsibilities of their church and community. James Yeado kept a garden and he was a member of the Fraternal Order of Eagles and the Vermillion Chamber of Commerce. His many friends remember his unassuming friendly manner, his gentle smile and quiet sense of humor.

The Yeado Jewelry Store was located on Main Street. In January 1967 James Yeado sold an engagement ring to

101

Thomas James White Hawk, who was a freshman premedical student at the University of South Dakota. Yeado had sold a good many engagement rings to University students, but this one was different. He knew them both. They were Indians. He often talked to Dorothy McBride over coffee at the cafe where she worked as a waitress. Thomas White Hawk had planned to marry her late in the summer.

Thomas White Hawk picked up his girl friend after work. He was driving her car. They had planned to spend the evening together, but they argued and he took her home. He was driving through town listening to the radio. The weather would be warm tomorrow. He was looking for William Winford Stands. They had made plans during the day to spend the evening together.

Tom found Willy walking downtown. They decided to buy some beer. Four quarts. They stashed the beer in an abandoned house on the north side of town. Later that evening Tom returned the car to his girl friend. He walked back to Julian Hall where he lived at the University. Stands lived in the same dormitory. They were up late talking, planning, talking; time would be difficult to remember. Plans would be difficult to remember.

Before dawn on Good Friday, Thomas White Hawk and William Stands walked to the abandoned house and picked up the four quarts of beer they had stashed. It was warm.Tom had his rifle. His guardian had delivered it on Wednesday. He could not keep it in the dormitory. It would be difficult to remember why they had planned to target practice so early in the morning. Time was compressed. It started and stopped. They walked across town and south on University Street toward the Yeado home. It was quiet. Foggy. They could hear the traffic light changing. It was too quiet to talk. With little Willy following, Tom walked through the yard to the side entrance on the north side of the Yeado home. They whispered. Tom opened the storm door slowly. With the barrel of his rifle

Vermillion, South Dakota, 1968

he broke a small glass pane on the inside door, reached in, turned the key, unlocked the door, and stepped in. It was still dark. White Hawk whispered for little Willy to follow him in. They walked through the kitchen into the living room and sat down. The house smelled clean. The Yeados were still sleeping.

James Yeado was a member of the Knights of Columbus. Following the Lenten service Thursday night, he stayed for a meeting at the church. After watching the late news, he locked the doors, and retired to his bedroom upstairs . . . Dorthea awakened early, looked at the clock on her cedar chest and went back to sleep. White Hawk and little Willy were waiting downstairs.

Thomas White Hawk loaded about fourteen cartridges into his pump action Winchester .22 magnum rifle. The stairs creaked as he walked. Bathroom on the left. Dorthea on the right. He walked into James Yeado's bedroom.

Dorthea Yeado was awakened by her husband screaming. She went to his bedroom and saw him on the floor waving his arms and legs in space. She did not hear a gun shot. She did not see blood. White Hawk forced her back

103

into her bedroom and tied her to the bed with nylon stockings and covered her head with a pillow case. She remained there all day. It was Good Friday. She heard the telephone ring four or five times, the noon sirens, and the sound of the toilet flushing.

Clay County Sheriff Arnold Nelson had been trying all week to find time to get his hair cut before Easter Sunday. He was in his car when he received the call to proceed to the Yeado home. He talked to the neighbors. Friends were called. The Yeados had not been seen all day. Nelson went to the side entrance and noticed the broken window in the door. The storm door was locked. He pried it open and found the inside door locked. He reached through and opened the inside door with a skeleton key. He saw blood spots down the stairs and on the basement floor a body covered with bedding and a blood soaked braided rug. He stood in the hallway. Someone was walking upstairs. He waited for help. A neighbor observed the drapes moving and a short time later Dorthea Yeado came out the front door dressed in a dark pink house coat. She tried to say something and went back into the house. She came out a second time and was quickly escorted to a police car. "They took Jim," she said. She told the police that there was an Indian in the house.

More police had arrived. Sheriff Nelson entered the Yeado home again with his deputy, Leonard Andera. They searched the basement and first floor. No one there. They edged up the stairs. The house was warm. There was no one under the bed. Sheriff Nelson moved into the bedroom slowly and saw a pile of clothing on the floor in the closet. He reached in and grabbed. Under the clothing was a Dakota Indian. He came out without a struggle. In handcuffs, as he was leaving the Yeado home, where he had been for almost twelve hours, he said, "I didn't pull the trigger." Outside someone in the crowd gasped, "Oh my God, it's Tommy White Hawk."

104

Thomas James White Hawk in Sioux Falls, South Dakota

The bullet wound punctured James Yeado's chest and ruptured the lobe of the lung causing massive internal bleeding. The wound in the right lower chest had not punctured the abdominal cavity . . . Two slugs from a Winchester magnum were found by police. One in White Hawk's pocket along with two empty cartridges when he was arrested. He could not remember how they got there. The other slug was found lodged in the box spring of James Yeado's bed.

White Hawk was taken to the Clay County jail. He immediately gave a confession to Sheriff Nelson. Clay County States Attorney Charles Wolsky was there. A few hours later State Agent Patterson arrived with a tape recorder and advised White Hawk on his constitutional rights. White Hawk knew only one attorney, Lee McCahren, who had represented him a few months before in U. S. District Court on a charge of auto theft. Enter Lee McCahren, attorney at law less than one year.

The following day the police sent several friends of the Yeados to the house to clean up the blood and look for clues.

William Winford Stands was seen by his roommate in Julian Hall about ten o'clock in the morning on Good Friday. He was arrested on the Rosebud Reservation, held in Mission, and returned to Vermillion the next day. In his possession was a gold diamond ring belonging to the deceased James Yeado. In his dormitory the Sheriff found a black key case taken from the Yeado home. He was charged with murder and locked up in the Clay County jail next to Thomas White Hawk.

The emotional intensities and vengeance grew. The *Vermillion Plain Talk* ran the headlines "James Yeado Apparent Murder Victim." The news reports to follow were reasonable and factual but the editorials were strained. There were organized conversations about getting those *injuns*. A close friend of the Yeados said: "We almost solved the whole thing . . . when I think about what we could have

106

done . . . we talked about getting them." *Vermillion Plain Talk* publisher Charles Bellman was quoted in the *Minneapolis Tribune:* "Right after the crime . . . the reaction was quite violent. If White Hawk had been available, he might have been lynched." It would have been easy to shoot White Hawk and Stands through the windows in the jail. Sheriff Nelson finally convinced the County Commissioners to fix the windows. They were replaced with concrete and glass blocks. States Attorney Charles Wolsky moved to have the prisoners held in the State Penitentiary for greater safety. The motion was denied.

THE HEARING

The preliminary hearing was held on Thursday, March 30, 1967, before the Honorable Judge Phillips B. Crew in Municipal Court, Vermillion, South Dakota. Lee McCahren was appointed by the court as defense counsel for Thomas White Hawk. McCahren made a motion asking for a psychological examination. "There is no sense in having a preliminary hearing if he is unable to understand the primary concerns. . ."

Prosecutor Charles Wolsky objected. He argued that there was a "proper time when medical examinations should be made . . . it is for the State to show that a crime has been committed, and that the individual accused did commit the crime."

The Court denied the motion and proceeded with the preliminary hearing allowing defense counsel to remake the motion at a different time. McCahren objected. In his affidavit he wrote: ". . . I have reason to believe that the defendant may not be capable of comprehending the nature of the court proceedings with which he is faced."

At the preliminary hearing in Vermillion, Dorthea Yeado testified that she was awakened in the morning by the sound of her husband screaming. She said she got up and ran into his bedroom and observed a "man wrestling with

107

Prosecutor Charles Wolsky

my husband on the floor." In Court she identified Thomas James White Hawk as that man.

WOLSKY: ". . . what did you do?"
YEADO: "I screamed."
WOLSKY: "What did you observe or did you hear anything at that time?"
YEADO: "Yes. He hollered for Willie to bring the gun."
WOLSKY: "Did you observe anyone else in the house?"
YEADO: "Well, my husband, myself, and this man (White Hawk) and then Willie came up the stairs at that time."
WOLSKY: "Did he have the gun?"
YEADO: "Yes."

Dorthea Yeado testified that White Hawk took her into her room, blindfolded her, and questioned her about the combination to the safe in the jewelry store.

WOLSKY: "Did you inquire about your husband?"
YEADO: "Yes."
WOLSKY: "Were you informed that he was alive?"
YEADO: "Yes, but they said he had been shot but he was still alive."
WOLSKY: "At any time were you physically harmed in any way, other than being gagged and bound?"
YEADO: "Yes."
WOLSKY: "What was that?"
YEADO: "Raped."

In cross examination Lee McCahren asked her if she saw anyone shoot her husband. She replied that she did not, but testified that she saw the gun held against his side.

MCCAHREN: "You were blindfolded and then you had a pillowcase over your head all day, is that correct . . . So that you saw nothing that transpired?"
YEADO: "Well, I could see when he came into the room."

109

McCahren questioned Dorthea Yeado eleven times during the preliminary hearing. Sheriff Arnold Nelson testified that he arrested White Hawk in a bedroom closet in the Yeado home. Myron Iverson, mortician and Clay County Coroner, described the wounds on the body of James Yeado.

IVERSON: "There were two bullet holes piercing the body."

WOLSKY: "Were there any other wounds?"

IVERSON: "There was a laceration in the skull, or the head right where the hairline meets the forehead."

MCCAHREN: "Did you make any determination as to the time of death?"

IVERSON: "As close as I could assume it would have been."

MCCAHREN: "Was that a few hours after six-thirty?"

IVERSON: "He had been dead for several hours when we arrived."

MCCAHREN: "When you say a few hours after six-thirty, what do you mean?"

WOLSKY: "This calls for a medical expert and this is not the purpose of the County Coroner being here."

MCCAHREN: "The County Coroner filled out the death certificate."

IVERSON: "I didn't put any time exactly on the death certificate."

MCCAHREN: "Had the body been dead for some time?"

IVERSON: "Yes, it had been dead for some hours."

MCCAHREN: "Can you make any closer determination of the actual time of death?"

IVERSON: "No."

WOLSKY: "I have no further questions . . . The State rests."

MCCAHREN: "I have *no defense*, Your Honor. I do have a motion to make, though."

110

JUDGE CREW: "What I intend to do is reserve the ruling pending the findings, and outcome of the examination. Mr. Wolsky is going to call Yankton State Hospital and see if we can get Mr. White Hawk examined this afternoon by Doctor Behan and hold the rest of this session this afternoon . . ."

Thomas White Hawk was taken to Yankton State Hospital and examined for about an hour and found competent to stand trial. Superintendent Lawrence G. Behan, M.D., writes about the examination: "There is little evidence of anxiety or depression, and little show of feelings of guilt . . . His judgment regarding society is poor, but there is no evidence that he has ever had a psychotic episode. *Impression: Sociopathic Personality Disturbance, Antisocial Reaction.*" White Hawk was returned to Vermillion.

Lee McCahren made a routine motion for dismissal: "All the testimony indicated there was a struggle between the defendant and the decedant . . . She was blindfolded during the ordeal and could not for this reason identify the alleged person."

The motion for dismissal was routinely denied and White Hawk was bound over to Circuit Court on both counts charged in the information: Murder and Rape.

LITTLE TOM WHITE HAWK

Dorothy McLean married Calvin Edward White Hawk when he came home from World War II. There were six White Hawk children. The oldest child, Thomas James, was born on the Rosebud Reservation, April 30, 1948.

The family home was near Wood, South Dakota. For a brief time the family lived in Chicago and in Winner, South Dakota. Thomas James was ten years old when his mother died. He had been sent away to boarding school at Rosebud. Friends have told him that his mother died in childbirth, but he has dreams that she died some other way.

111

In the autumn of 1959 Calvin Edward White Hawk died from injuries received in an automobile accident on the reservation. He missed a curve on a dirt road near Mosher, rolled over, walked three miles for help, but died a few days later.

Of the five other White Hawk children, two live with an Episcopal vicar in Texas and two live with a foster farm family near Mission. One lives with a family near Clearfield, South Dakota. His brothers and sisters were placed in foster homes. He was sent to live with relatives in Winner. He learned not to show his pain and fear and loneliness. He was a Dakota Indian. Memories were altered and combined with dreams. Years later a teacher said of him: "He had difficulty compromising."

Tom attended elementary school in Wood and Winner, South Dakota. During the summer of 1960 he was sent to the Bishop Hare School in Mission. John Artichoker was the headmaster of the school at the time, and bachelor Philip Zoubek, former production engineer at Minneapolis Honeywell, was counselor and Bishop Hare handyman. John and Emily Artichoker became mother and father to every boy at the school. Emily remembers the first time she saw Tommy: "Poor little soul, he was so lonely and so strong, he walked up the road to the school and all he had with him was a change of clothes in a little brown paper sack . . . He became our son." Handyman Philip Zoubek became the self-appointed guardian. He needed Tom as a son. He took the boy fishing, swimming, riding, hunting, camping, and taught him things about the world that he would be expected to know on his way to the top. Zoubek had great ambitions for this little Indian boy. It would take the old ingredients of hard work and discipline. For Tom it was a fantasy. He knew he was different by the way he thought people looked at him. He learned to read facial expressions and he learned to do things in a different way. He would return one day and they would all honor him for his differences and accomplishments.

112

Thomas James White Hawk lived at Bishop Hare in an Episcopal Christian environment for three years, while he attended the Todd County public schools. He entered in the seventh grade and completed the ninth grade at Todd, before guardian Zoubek took him to Faribault, Minnesota. In the autumn of 1963, White Hawk moved from an Indian Christian environment to Shattuck School and a Christian military environment.

At Todd County public schools Thomas White Hawk was an Indian. He lived with Indians and expressed his internal feelings with Indians. He was their rhythm, their psyche, but some people told him that he was different. He was a good student and a member of the football, basketball, and track teams. He took up pole vaulting at Todd in the seventh grade.

He was just beginning to play good football; the coach at Todd said, "He held back, sometimes he was afraid he might get hurt." With the exception of Philip Zoubek, the counselors and teachers at Bishop Hare and Todd School were reluctant to see Tom leave for Shattuck. He better understood his identity and material and space in the world at Bishop Hare. The guidance counselor at Todd said: "He could have had a better life here . . . we knew it was wrong to let him leave." But he would succeed and the change would leave him with his uniform and bangles of acceptance and stomach trouble. The ambitious guardians of the *Indian problem* hovered over this exceptional Indian. They wanted him to go all the way. The dominant way. His guardians would teach him that he was entitled to many things. And he would acquire the ingravescent fear of failure in the dominant society. Thomas White Hawk would become a white man and fulfill their ambition. A cultural schizophrenic. He would become their beauty mark.

"My name is Thomas James White Hawk," he wrote when he was twelve years old. "I was born at Rosebud, South Dakota, April 30, 1948. I live at Mission, South Dakota at the present time.

113

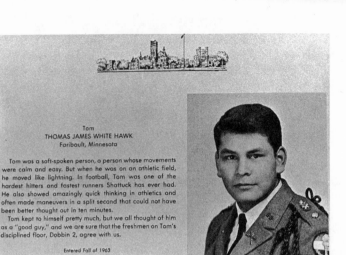

Tom
THOMAS JAMES WHITE HAWK
Faribault, Minnesota

Tom was a soft-spoken person, a person whose movements were calm and easy. But when he was on an athletic field, he moved like lightning. In football, Tom was one of the hardest hitters and fastest runners Shattuck has ever had. He also showed amazingly quick thinking in athletics and often made maneuvers in a split second that could not have been better thought out in ten minutes.

Tom kept to himself pretty much, but we all thought of him as a "good guy," and we are sure that the freshmen on Tom's disciplined floor, Dobbin 2, agree with us.

Entered Fall of 1963
Second Lieutenant 4; Platoon Leader 4; Corporal 2; Sergeant 3; Private First Class 2; Track 2,3,4; Football 2,3,4; Basketball 3,4; Acolyte 2,4; Band 2,3,4; Floor Officer 4; "S" Club 2,3,4; M.I.S.L. Conference 3; Track Captain 4; Hunting Club.

"My father's name is Calvin Edward White Hawk but he is deceased, so at the present time my guardian's name is Mr. John Artichoker. He works as a principal at Bishop Hare School, Mission, South Dakota. My mother's name was Dorothy McLean. She is deceased too. My present mother's name is Mrs. John Artichoker.

"There are six in our family. I'm the oldest one. Five are younger than I. I can speak Sioux and English. I had mumps when I was nine years old.

"The most pleasant experience was learning how to ride a bicycle. The storekeeper caught me swiping a candy bar when I was six years old and that was unpleasant.

"When I grow up, I'd like to be a 'doctor.' "

At Shattuck School White Hawk was named the *Cat*. It took special courage for a smaller boy to even say the name. The more daring called him the *Tomahawk*. He was quiet and quick and methodical on the playing field. The

114

football coach at Shattuck said Tom was a loner and in his last year, after that head injury, "he let small things bother him . . . his temper was too quick . . . he complained about his headaches." One of his teachers put it this way: "Tom was the way an Indian should be, he was the person you would like an Indian to be."

Oliver Towne Columnist Gareth Hiebert wrote in the *St. Paul Pioneer Press*, Sunday, June 13, 1965, about an *INDIAN BOY EQUAL TO CHALLENGE* surging "toward the pole vault pit at John Marshall Stadium in Rochester, Minnesota . . . Suddenly his feet left the ground as mighty hands swung his body upward on the pole. For just an instant did his eyes see the bar, silhouetted against the sky . . . Cheers went up . . . Tom White Hawk of Shattuck had cleared the bar at 13 feet, 7⅞ inches—setting an official Minnesota state high school record and establishing a new mark at Shattuck. Minnesota could be proud of him, Shattuck and Shads everywhere could bust their buttons with pride. And so, too, could the legions of ancestors who belonged to the Dakota . . . In the mind of Thomas White Hawk, descended from a long line of chiefs, orphaned three years ago, eldest of six brothers and sisters, clearing that bar in a spectacular pole vault meant more than merely establishing a record. It was like clearing an important hurdle in life . . . *Phil Zoubek* . . . dormitory counselor at St. James, one-time production engineer who left the treadmill to follow his heart, is Tom's guardian and *a lot more*. Each of these two men is half of a warm human adventure . . . Phil had gone through Central high school and was graduated as a mechanical engineer from the University of Minnesota in 1943. The possibility of Phil and a little Indian boy named Tom White Hawk ever meeting was as remote as plucking a falling star. While Phil was working his way ahead at Minneapolis Honeywell, Tom was going to Rosebud mission school . . . But even then Tom had a dream of becoming somebody—on the athletic grounds and later life. He wanted to be a doctor and he still

does. But not even his wildest dream ever took him to the
playing fields of Shattuck, training ground for so many
military leaders in five wars and business executives
throughout its history . . . Then, in 1958, Phil Zoubek decided he'd had enough of the pressures of the treadmill
. . . got a job as boy's adviser and maintenance man at the
Bishop Hare school near the Rosebud reservation. That
same year, Tom White Hawk transferred from Rosebud to
Hare school . . . Phil Zoubek got to thinking. He wanted
Tom to go to Shattuck. And he wanted Tom to be as a son
. . ."

Thomas James White Hawk had given up his right to cry
and he was giving up his freedom to dream. His unconscious was a burden of the past. When he walked alone he
was bird and animal. He was one soul but he found himself in a prison of agreements with the burdens of opportunity and the false promises of success. He was becoming
a white Indian. The youthful passion to know himself was
displaced and consumed by his need to be successful in
things that other people planned for him. He was dissoci-
ated from himself by his own greed for acceptance. He was
among strangers. He watched himself respond. In a dream
he saw the evangels of controlled words placed around
him like empty boxes. He understood the exploitations of
other men better than he understood himself. His unconscious was his *winter count*. He would have trouble in the
spring.

THE ARRAIGNMENT

The matter came before First Circuit Judge James R. Bandy
on May 5, 1967, in Vermillion. Additional information was
filed charging White Hawk with two counts of murder and
rape in the first degree. The preliminary information
charged murder *with premeditation;* the amended complaint
alleged the felony murder charge. In South Dakota there is

116

Circuit Judge James Bandy, Armour, South Dakota, 1968

only one degree of murder. White Hawk was charged with
two counts of murder, but the charges in the information
became confused and misunderstood.

Arraignment proceedings took place on July 14, 1967, in
the Clay County Court House.

JUDGE BANDY: "Now, upon the advice of your counsel,
you may have twenty-four hours in which to plead to
the charges made against you . . . If I have not over-
looked it, I think that I have advised him of all his constitutional rights. Can you think of any others, Mr.
McCahren?"

117

MCCAHREN: "No, Your Honor . . . I have one objection. I would move that the Information be set aside since this charges more than one crime. The element of *premeditation* is included in this, which was *not* included in the crime with which he has been held to answer in the Municipal Court. There he was merely charged with murder in the commission of a felony. Here there is the additional element of *premeditated design* . . . In addition, there is no statutory reference to any crime which has been committed; and, this being a code-pleading State, I feel there should be a statutory reference."

JUDGE BANDY: "I disagree with that. I think it is a very, *very poor pleading* to charge violation of a specific statute. You are supposed to charge what is in the statute . . . I am at this moment uncertain as to the procedure of this matter."

Clay County States Attorney Charles Wolsky proceeded with the arraignment on the second charge in the Information—rape in the first degree. Lee McCahren objected, asking for the Court to rule first on the Information for murder.

MCCAHREN: ". . . we would ask that a ruling be made on the first Information before we plead to the second Information . . ."

JUDGE BANDY: "If the Court has to rule right now, the Court will rule that, without any prejudice, and with the right to file a new Information, that your motion to dismiss the arraignment on the murder charge be granted . . . The Court is complying with his request. Now he has got the ball."

The arraignment proceedings were continued a week later. Judge Bandy stated for the record: "At the prior hearing here, objection was made to the arraignment charging the defendant, White Hawk, with the crime of murder; and, the Court, believing that such Information might be

118

duplicitious *(sic)*, sustained the motion to set aside the Information. The defendant at that time was thereafter arraigned upon a charge of rape and through his counsel, requested that he be permitted to withhold his pleas to such charge until formal arraignment had been made and a plea taken upon the charge of murder. New Information on the murder charge was read omitting the *premeditated* element of the previous charge . . . the defendant did wilfully, unlawfully, and feloniously, *without any design to effect death*, did shoot and kill and murder James Yeado with a rifle while the said defendant was engaged in the commission of a felony . . ."

JUDGE BANDY: "Let the record show that counsel is entitled—or, the defendant, rather, is entitled to twenty-four hours in which to plead . . . the Court now asks counsel for the defense whether the defendant is ready to plead at this time?"

MCCAHREN: "He is, Your Honor."

JUDGE BANDY: "Will you stand up, please . . . the Court states to you at this time the offense with which you are charged is what is known as a capital offense and carries with it, in the event of your conviction upon trial, or in the event of a plea of guilty, a possible electrocution death penalty. Now, that might be taken in the *sense* that, if you were to at this time enter a plea of guilty to the charge, it would be *in my sole discretion* as to whether to impose the death penalty or up to life imprisonment. In the event that you do stand trial before a jury, and a jury shall find you guilty as charged, and shall additionally recommend the death penalty, it would then be in the discretion of the Trial Judge as to whether to impose the death penalty or not. I make this full explanation *not expecting you to enter a plea of guilty* but so that you will fully understand what is involved in this matter . . . how do you at this time plead, guilty or not guilty?"

119

WHITE HAWK: *"I plead not guilty . . . And not guilty by reason of insanity."*

JUDGE BANDY: ". . . the States Attorney is now directed to prepare and submit to this Court an Order for psychiatric examination of the defendant. That will be at the State Hospital at Yankton, and the Order will provide not only that he be examined psychiatrically as to his sanity *at the time of the commission of the offense* but also that he be examined as to his capacity under what we call the Magenton rule (sic), to stand trial."

The matter of arraignment came before Judge Bandy again on October 27, 1967. It is difficult to believe that if the Court was not clear about the counts of murder in the Information—with or without premeditated design—the defendant White Hawk was superior to the Court in understanding the arraignment proceedings. He began to feel that they wanted him to change his plea and leave something in confusion to bargain with if he did. The speedy trial continued in Vermillion. In Judge Bandy's absence the defendant was arraigned before Judge Puckett at the opening of the fall term of the Circuit Court, but the entering of a plea was deferred until Judge Bandy returned from his honeymoon.

MCCAHREN: ". . . I would like to make a motion . . . it is the defendant's contention that the Information should be set aside, and he so moves to set aside the Information, in that it charges a crime with which he has not had preliminary examination. This is, in effect, the same crime charged as was charged by another Information in that it contains the allegation that this was *premeditated design* and without a justifiable or excusable cause; and, under the appropriate Code citation . . ."

JUDGE BANDY: "Motion is denied."

MCCAHREN: ". . . I wanted to wait until I had a ruling on this, in order to determine whether I would . . . orally state that the defendant intends to demur on the

Attorney Lee McCahren

grounds that the Count One of the Information does not conform to the title on pleadings of the South Dakota Code . . .''

JUDGE BANDY: "You have made a record of his demurrer which will be put in writing. The demurrer is overruled . . . Is the defendant now ready to plead?"

MCCAHREN: "We are ready, Your Honor."

WHITE HAWK: "I plead not guilty . . . by reason of insanity."

JAIL TIME

Taxpayer A. H. Lathrop had just sent off a letter to the editor of the *Vermillion Plain Talk*, commenting on the poor street lighting on Linden Avenue. It was November and the first snow had fallen. William Winford Stands and Thomas James White Hawk had been awaiting trial in Clay

121

County jail since Good Friday. White Hawk had been thinking about changing his plea. It had been more than seven months since he was arrested. He was tired of talking about it to so many people who didn't understand. He exercised daily, painted pictures for the sheriff and friends, wrote, studied electronics, and took notes from an abnormal psychology book a friend had given him.

Dorothy McBride told him she was planning to marry another man. His stomach ulcer bothered him. He was talkative and nervous. He could still feel that numbness and tingling nerves where he had an appendectomy. The scar was pink. Six days chained to a bed in the hospital . . . *Killer rapist Indian* . . . So much time to think. There were so many people involved. It burdened him to think about all the people who would be called into court.

His regular visitors in jail were the Episcopal vicar, Douglas Hiza, and his wife Jeb. She was a good cook and her husband loved to talk like a close friend. He could tell them some things about his past but he was still cautious. He was sensitive to the feelings about him in Vermillion. Before they replaced the windows in the jail, he could see several times a day, a man standing in the Meisenholder Motors lot watching the jail. He was always watching when someone went in or out. The Hizas visited often. Escaping. He knew he would never get out of town alive. He put his mind to it several times, but he wanted to live. He began to listen. Was the psychiatrist honest . . . Even his dreams became a prison. He remembered him saying that he didn't have much of a chance in court. He would be better off making some kind of plea bargain with the judge and prosecutor. He had to do something. He would testify for the State at Stands' trial in Yankton and change his plea.

Philip Zoubek visited when he could . . . *how could you do this to me after all I've done for you* . . . but Zoubek was so controlled and disinterested. He was worried about delivering the gun two days before Good Friday. Time was compressed. It started and stopped. Dreams.

THE TRIAL

There was standing room only in the Douglas County Court House in Armour, South Dakota, on November 13, 1967. It was the first day of trial for Thomas James White Hawk. The jury was drawn and present. The charges in the Information had been settled for the day on *three* counts of murder including the *premeditated design.* Everyone had made it to court. Judge Bandy was sitting between a picture of General Pershing and the Declaration of Independence. The court reporter had been practicing his speed for two weeks. Judge Bandy was quick and in complete control of his First Circuit power: ". . . This Court now states for the record that it has no doubt whatever of the mental and emotional capacity and ability of the defendant to stand trial at this time upon the counts of murder pending against him."

Things went badly for the spectators. Right off Lee McCahren indicated that White Hawk wanted to have a conference with the Judge in his chambers. He announced his decision to withdraw his prior insanity plea. McCahren was ready: " . . . I would ask, if his pleas are withdrawn that one count of murder be submitted to him . . ." And Judge Bandy was ready: "Very well. I am agreeing with you that what we have before us are charges containing three different ways in which murder can be committed. I rather think that the Court would have no objection to the States Attorney choosing one count, arraigning him on that and taking a plea . . . but I will say for the record that we are going back in the court room, Mr. White Hawk, and I am going to interrogate you *extensively,* in open court, so that I and everyone else, whoever reads this record in the future, is going to know that you do precisely what you

123

want to do and not what anyone else, you might subsequently think, has talked you into."

Meanwhile back in the court room, the spectators were whispering about the weather, the offense, and a loose piece of ceiling tile hanging over the jury box. The door opened near Pershing's picture and the whispering stopped. The confusion surrounding the charges against White Hawk in the Information would finally be settled.

JUDGE BANDY: "Mr. White Hawk, if I should speak too low a tone of voice, or mumble, so that you do not hear anything I say, stop me, because I want this to be completely and fully understood by you . . . Now, it seems completely innate (sic) at this time to go back and advise you as to your constitutional rights, but I am going to do it. There is present a jury selected from among people in Douglas County, to which county the trial to the accusations against you was moved upon your request. So, you are going to have a speedy trial. That would be commencing this day . . . You have been supplied with counsel, at the expense of Clay County . . . Mr. McCahren, by the Court's observation has stood at your side at all times. I am going to ask this direct question at this time: Do you have any objection at all to the way in which Mr. McCahren have served you as counsel?"

WHITE HAWK: "No. Your Honor, I don't."

JUDGE BANDY: "You feel that he has done as well for you as *anyone* could, is that correct, or am I putting words in your mouth?"

WHITE HAWK: "No, you are not putting words in my mouth. I feel he is quite competent."

JUDGE BANDY: "You are entitled, at the expense of Clay County, to have the Sheriff go out and serve what we call a subpoena upon any person that you think might be able to testify in your favor, in the event that this Court should *refuse to permit you to withdraw your plea*. That would require that witness to come in and testify under

124

oath and be subjected to cross examination. No witness may testify against you at this time unless that witness comes into open court, confronts you face to face, while testifying, and submits to cross examination at the hands of either yourself or your counsel . . . Under the law of this State, if you stand trial and the jury recommends the death penalty, the Trial Judge may, in his *discretion*, impose it. If they do not, the Trial Judge may not impose it. If, at this time, you withdraw your pleas of not guilty and not guilty by reason of insanity and enter a plea of guilty, it is then in my *uncontrolled discretion (sic)* to impose either a death sentence or a life imprisonment sentence, and I want it to be distinctly and clearly understood that, in the event that you enter a plea of guilty, I am not now and I have not committed myself as to the penalty which is to be imposed. Do you understand that?"

WHITE HAWK: "Yes, I do."

JUDGE BANDY: "Now, I am going to ask you this question, which relates in a manner to a confession, but that is what you would be making if at this time you were to enter a plea of guilty; you would be confessing the entire crime; Do you claim that the Sheriff, the States Attorney, your counsel, your spiritual advisor or me or anyone else has made any threat or promise to you which causes you to at this time move to withdraw your pleas?"

WHITE HAWK: "The only influence is myself."

JUDGE BANDY: "In other words, you have thought this thing out for your own self, is that correct?"

WHITE HAWK: "Yes, it is."

JUDGE BANDY: "I am not trying to put words in your mouth; I am trying to find out whether this momentous decision on your part is your own, made solely by yourself and not by anyone else."

WHITE HAWK: "I have thought it out. I have thought it out myself."

125

JUDGE BANDY: "And this is your own conclusion of what you feel that you should do and want to do, is that it?"

WHITE HAWK: "Well, Your Honor, *feeling and wanting to do is two different things.*"

JUDGE BANDY: "Well, that is rather an abstract statement. You care to elaborate on it? I want to be completely fair to you, young man. I don't want you to carry in your mind the idea that anything is being done to cause you to give up a right that you have of a trial before a jury . . . I know that what you feel you are doing this time is making a clean breast of the situation. You propose, I *would assume,* to throw yourself upon the mercy of the Court, and you are hopeful that a clean breast of the situation will cause the Court to look with some leniency upon the punishment imposed. *I think that those are the thoughts that are going through your mind,* is that correct?"

WHITE HAWK: *"No, they aren't."*

JUDGE BANDY: "They are not?"

WHITE HAWK: "That wasn't any ground for my decision at all."

JUDGE BANDY: "Well, do you care—*I am not compelling you to state the ground for your decision.*"

WHITE HAWK: "That is why I haven't elaborated on *feeling* and *wanting.*"

JUDGE BANDY: *"In other words,* you just don't care to state the ground, is that it; it is personal to you?"

WHITE HAWK: "Yes, it is."

JUDGE BANDY: "Well, it is not as the result of any external pressure, is it by anyone else?"

WHITE HAWK: "No. I said that before."

JUDGE BANDY: "Very *well permission is granted* and in each of the counts now pending before this Court, the pleas of not guilty and not guilty by reason of insanity may be considered to be withdrawn. Mr. States Attorney, you may rearraign the defendant."

126

Prosecutor Charles Wolsky read the new Information . . .
with malice aforethought.

JUDGE BANDY: "The Court accepts the plea of guilty of
the charge of murder as orally made by the defendant at
this time. I correctly understood you to say *guilty* did I?"

WHITE HAWK: "Yes, you did."

JUDGE BANDY: "Very well. Upon such plea *the defendant
is convicted of the offense of premediated murder* as charged in
the Information upon which he has now been arraigned
. . . Mr. McCahren, the States Attorney has indicated
that he desires an opportunity to offer testimony in aggravation, and, of course, you have a like right to offer
testimony in mitigation . . . he would like a day certain
fixed at Vermillion, for the convenience of witnesses . . .
I may say for the record, that I am going to inquire of the
defendant as to his version of the circumstances under
which the statements were made to the officers, and he
may have that in mind, and we'll try to make a full
record of that . . ."

"Well, I'll be damned," a red faced farmer said on his
way out of the court room, "He must want to die in a
hurry." Judge Bandy returned to his office, took off his
robe, and wondered what White Hawk meant by *feeling*
and *wanting*. The radiators clanked in the empty court
room.

THE HEAD INJURY

Sixteen stitches closed the laceration. White Hawk was in-
jured during a track meet at the University of Minnesota
on April 11, 1964. He was hit in the head by a shot put
causing a large laceration in the right parietal region of his
scalp. After the accident Tom complained about nervousness, dizziness, and visual disorders. His teachers at Shattuck noticed a marked change in his behavior. He was irri-
table, quarrelsome, and moody. "He let small things
bother him," the athletic coach said, "he wanted to be left

alone." The hospital record lists more than a dozen visits to the infirmary: *Having trouble with eye sight . . . dizzy at times . . . see neurologist . . . headache . . .feels nervous . . . talked at length about headaches and being dizzy . . . talked about headaches . . . phenobarbital before meals . . . headaches . . .*

Phenobarbital was frequently prescribed. Tom complained frequently to his friends, particularly to his roommate at Shattuck, William Mahojah, about severe headaches, dizziness and brief blackouts. He was concerned that nothing could be done about his complaints. Dr. C. W. Rumpf, physician to Shattuck School, writes: "He apparently made a satisfactory recovery from the immediate injury, but complained of dizziness, headache, and spells of momentary unconsciousness from time to time. The dizziness gradually became less, but the headaches persisted. He became very nervous and apprehensive. Neurological examination did not reveal any localization of any abnormality. When he left school in June 1966, he still complained of headaches and nervousness." None of this information was presented to the court. Attorney Lee McCahren did not communicate with Dr. Rumpf about White Hawk's medical history at Shattuck School.

Thomas White Hawk graduated from Shattuck School in June 1966. He lived in California for the summer 1966, working and living with a fellow student from Shattuck. He returned in the fall to the University of South Dakota as a freshman student in pre-medicine. He had applied to the University of Minnesota, was accepted on a track scholarship, but reasoned that he would be more adequate in a smaller college for the first two years. He was on full scholarship at the University of South Dakota. He shared a room with three other students in Julian Hall. He was doing average work for a freshman. He failed chemistry. He wanted to get married. He thought about being a doctor.

During the 1966 Thanksgiving vacation, he had a quarrel with his girl friend and decided to go to Minneapolis with friends from the university. While he was there he hot wired a car in Minnetonka and drove it back to Vermillion. A few days later he was involved in a minor accident in Vermillion and a police report revealed the car was stolen. White Hawk was arrested on auto theft and released on bail. Lee McCahren, who had been in practice about six months, was appointed defense counsel for White Hawk, in Municipal Court. He arranged for a dismissal of the charges in Minnesota and South Dakota and argued the matter in U.S. District Court in January 1967, three months before Good Friday. White Hawk was placed on probation for two years. The pre-sentence investigation revealed no previous criminal record, no aberrant behavior, and no conflicts with authorities. He was well accepted. Handsome. Pleasant. Verbal. A most unusual Indian. White Hawk was a beauty mark. White Indian.

THE PSYCHIATRISTS

Testimony to hear aggravation and mitigation: Vermillion, November 16, 1967. There was very little mitigation. Twenty-seven year old Charles Wolsky, Clay County States Attorney, called six witnesses. This was his first important trial. He had been in practice (admitted to the bar July 1966) and States Attorney for less than a year, when the crime occurred. The FBI flew out three expert witnesses for the trial and Wolsky was determined to use them. Many people in Vermillion were holding him responsible for getting White Hawk into the electric chair. He believes that capital punishment is a deterrent. On the other hand, sixty-eight year old First Circuit Judge James R. Bandy has been practicing law since he graduated from the University of South Dakota Law School in 1922, and is for the record *opposed* to capital punishment.

Charles Wolsky called his first witness. Dr. J. D. Mahoney from Council Bluffs, Iowa.

WOLSKY: "On or about the 13th of September, 1967, did

129

you examine one Thomas James White Hawk in Clay County, South Dakota?"

MAHONEY: "Downstairs in the Sheriff's Office."

WOLSKY: "Generally, what kind of an examination did you give Mr. White Hawk on the date just described?"

MAHONEY: "The usual psychiatric examination, which consists of a discussion— his discussion of the reason for my examining him, and, in addition to that, to go into his developmental background, his life, up to the point of this examination and a discussion of this, sometimes general, sometimes specific."

WOLSKY: "Was one of the purposes of your examination to make a determination as to whether Mr. White Hawk knew right from wrong in terms of this so-called Mc-Naughton Rule?"

MAHONEY: "Yes, to see whether, I presume, whether, under the McNaughton Rule, he knew the difference between right and wrong, whether he could—was competent to stand trial, to confer with his attorney, et cetera."

WOLSKY: "Did you have also a purpose to determine whether there was, in fact, any type of personality disorder which made itself apparent in Mr. White Hawk?"

MAHONEY: "Well, in the course of examination, to attempt to fit—attempt to see in which *category the individual might best fit,* yes, this is the purpose—what we refer to as a differential diagnosis, to see, if the individual is a psychotic, into what category he might best fit."

WOLSKY: "As a result of your examination, were you able to determine or form an opinion, based upon reasonable medical certainty, whether Mr. White Hawk had any type of personality disorder whatsoever?"

MAHONEY: "Yes . . . we describe this as a personality disorder, and I felt, in this particular situation, that this is further described as a personality disorder, *passive-aggressive type.* In the diagnostic categories, from a psychiatric standpoint, this is a personality which indicates a pattern of behavior; that these individuals fit into a

130

rather structured kind of personality make-up; that they do not have the flexibility of reacting to various stresses, whatever they might be, or to things which the individual might interpret as stress; that they seem to follow a definite pattern of behavior in reacting to stress, to eliminate or to minimize the anxiety which might be created within them . . . realizing that the two terms are definitely contradictory, that is, the passive-aggressive part of this, we feel that these individuals, in the passitivity . . . have a tendency to be dependent, dependent in a sense that they feel that other people should do everything for them, that this has nothing to do really with our social standards or *our cultural norms* . . . The aggressive part of this means that, if things do not turn out the way they think they should, then they are more or less entitled to accomplish these ends . . . regardless of whatever means they might have to use . . ."

WOLSKY: "Assuming then that Mr. White Hawk has this disorder, do you have a prognosis as to whether, with treatment, this disorder could be *effectively cured* or adjusted, making Mr. White Hawk conform to ordinary norms?"

MAHONEY: "I have an opinion of this . . . based on experience in treating individuals previously, and ordinarily the treatment is quite prolonged. We usually think of it in terms of one, two, three years of individual psychotherapy, and even then sometimes you don't get very good results . . . it has been pretty well accepted that the personality patterns have a rather *poor prognosis* in treatment."

MCCAHREN: "How long did you examine the defendant?"

MAHONEY: "Probably a total of about three hours, a couple of hours before lunch, possibly forty-five minutes to an hour after lunch."

MCCAHREN: "How long do you normally devote to an examination of this type?"

131

MAHONEY: "Approximately an hour."

MCCAHREN: "Does your original impression ever change?"

MAHONEY: "Oh, sure."

MCCAHREN: "In order for your impression to change, you would have to have further consultation, is that true?"

MAHONEY: "Yes . . . you find out something that might alter your original opinion . . ."

MCCAHREN: "Did your opinion coincide with the opinion at the Yankton State Hospital?"

MAHONEY: "In essence, yes."

MCCAHREN: "How did it differ? You stated *in essence.*"

MAHONEY: "Well, really it didn't."

MCCAHREN: "Have you encountered passive-aggressive personalities in your private practice?"

MAHONEY: "Probably every day of the week."

MCCAHREN: "Have you ever made an error in your diagnosis, from your original diagnosis, where you changed it?"

MAHONEY: "Oh, certainly. I *am entitled to my percentage.*"

MCCAHREN: "You would agree that psychiatry is an art then, not a science?"

MAHONEY: "Oh, no. No. I think it is a—I think it depends on the training, the empathy that you have with the patient, your own desire to work at this thing . . ."

In his two page written report, Mahoney goes into past medical history, "There is nothing significant with the possible exception of the head injury in which he was accidentally struck on the head by a shot during a field trial." This "possible exception" was not discussed in court. Mahoney writes: "He and a friend of his began to plan to rob Mr. Yeado and they discussed this rather objectively. They felt that probably the simplest way would be to somehow get him to come to the store and give them some money. He wanted to use this money to buy things for his girlfriend

132

with the idea of marrying her . . . He feels basically that he is entitled to things."

Doctor George William Knabe, Jr., testified for the State as the pathologist who performed the autopsy on the body of James Yeado. He described the wounds he observed: "There was a bullet wound, entrance-type wound, which was on the left upper anterior chest . . . There was also a second bullet wound, of an entrance type, in the upper abdomen or lower part of the right chest and anterior laterally. There were also, on the posterior aspect, or the back of the body, two exit wounds . . . There were other wounds. There was a lacerated wound of a curved nature on the right frontal or anterior aspect of the scalp, which extended to the bone . . . The first one was approximately two and a half inches in dimension. The second one was also curved, deep, and on the left back of the scalp, posterior aspect of the scalp, and was approximately two inches in length and extended to the bone . . ."

Lee McCahren called one witness for the defense. He was Richard B. Leander, a neuropsychiatrist from Sioux Falls, South Dakota, who had examined White Hawk eight months after the offense. Time and memory.

MCCAHREN: "What was your medical—what was your clinical evaluation that you arrived at, with reasonable medical certainty, as to your examination of the defendant?"

LEANDER: "I suppose the wide category would be that of a personality disorder; specifically, in my mind, a sociopathic personality disturbance. There is, in the background, considerable *psychoneurotic elements,* and there is also some *schizophrenic elements . . .*"

MCCAHREN: "What is a personality disorder, as you define it?"

LEANDER: "It is a character disorder, a disorder of behavior, which could occur *in any of us,* and it results from the situation in which we are raised, the things that happen

133

to us, how we are taught to accept or not to accept stresses and strains in our everyday activities, has to do a lot with the people we live with and the people who basically form us in the first few years of our life."

MCCAHREN: "Now, you stated there were psychoneurotic shades in your diagnosis. Could you explain that, please?"

LEANDER: "A psychoneurotic is an individual who may have obvious anxiety or hidden anxieties that force him to impulsively or compulsively act in certain situations or have certain fears or phobias or likes and dislikes that are normally not found in the normal individual, and this, again, is the result of *environmental contacts.*"

MCCAHREN: "You stated that he had a sociopathic personality. Could you explain that, please?"

LEANDER: "Seemingly not being able to learn from experience, actually, is the biggest factor in this man's case. He does not seem to—or let's put it this way: He seems to repeat his mistakes as he goes on through the years."

MCCAHREN: "Would you state that, in your medical opinion, he is mentally ill?"

LEANDER: "There are two schools of thought on this, at the present time, in terms of these personality disorders. He is especially the sociopath. One group would like to probably put them in a criminal classification of insanity, and, the rest of us, who feel that they are distorted and warped and yet are competent and responsible for their actions."

MCCAHREN: "And with which theory do you agree?"

LEANDER: "I think I am riding the rail at the present time."

Neither James D. Mahoney nor Richard B. Leander had clinical experience with Indian people. There was no discussion of cultural schizophrenia. Dr. Leander worked in the Naval Prison System for more than seven years. He admits seven years experience working with sociopathic and psychoneurotic personalities.

MCCAHREN: "What has your experience been?"

LEANDER: "My experience with this type of personality has been that if you can act as a conscience for them and keep control over them, they will behave fairly well, but, if they get away from their conscience, they are in trouble again."

MCCAHREN: "Are you saying that, in a confined environment, they might perform and function favorably?"

LEANDER: "These individuals usually, in confinement, do very well for the simple reason that this is *uncomfortable* for them, and this type of personality does not like to be uncomfortable, so that they perform as a model prisoner for the most part. It is the psychoneurotic in the prison system that gets into trouble."

MCCAHREN: "Now, you stated that his reactions to stress and strain were abnormal, is that correct?"

LEANDER: ". . . they are abnormal in terms of how he or I would react in a similar situation. For instance, the weirdest part of this situation with Mr. White Hawk is the fact that he is seemingly—when something could have been done, in this situation, was unable to move in the direction of doing the right thing and just waited it out until the wrong thing occurred, which, I suppose, in the minds of everyone of us that have seen this—seen him, has raised the question of, well, what went on in this interval of time as far as his mental capacities were concerned. Was he actually functioning as a competent individual or was he functioning as an incompetent individual over that particular period of time?"

MCCAHREN: "Would the personality defect have contributed to this failure to act?"

LEANDER: "Very much so. This is typically the *personality of the Mafia* and the rest of the people in this country today; they function purely on the basis of what is good for

135

the whole of us and the whole of us being antisocial individuals.''

MCCAHREN: "With a sociopathic personality, is there any flexibility in their reaction to stress?"

LEANDER: "I believe there is, although the tendency of most of these individuals will be one of what is more comfortable for me at this particular time; and, secondly, it depends, also, on the amount of passive-aggressive behavior that these individuals have as an undercurrent, which I think many times people use as a diagnosis rather than going on to make a sociopathic diagnosis."

MCCAHREN: "Now, you stated that you, as well as everyone else, is interested in what went on during this interval of time."

LEANDER: "This would be what I would like to know. I don't think we ever will know, because, apparently, in trying to get this out of Mr. White Hawk, you don't get consistent stories; you get a vague type of reproduction of what was going on, something like you would expect to get from an individual who had been quite intoxicated the night before and can't quite remember what he was doing and yet trying to tell you what he did."

Lee McCahren moved that the Court authorize a pre-sentence report by the Board of Pardons and Paroles. White Hawk made this request and Judge Bandy after questioning him approved the motion. "The defendant is remanded to the custody of the Sheriff of Clay County . . . pending the receipt and consideration of the report, at which time this Court will fix a time and place for the imposition of sentence."

THE STANDS TRIAL

His attorney advised him against it but White Hawk was determined to testify as a rebuttal witness for the State in the trial of William Winford Stands. The trial was held in Yankton, South Dakota, on December 6, 1967. White Hawk

136

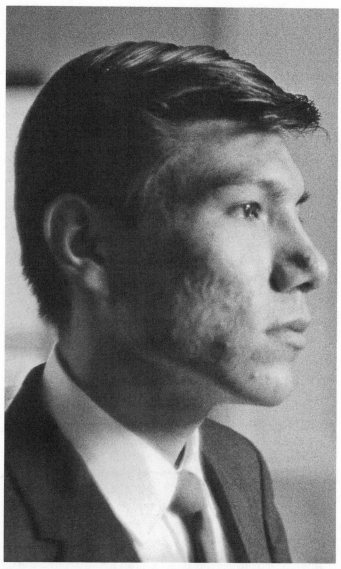

William Stands at his trial in Armour, South Dakota, 1968

probably had at least two reasons for testifying: he wanted to participate before sentencing Judge James Bandy; and he may have believed that he could learn something about the crime he had committed eight months before. Whatever the reason, it was an unwise thing to do while he was awaiting sentence. He came before the same judge and was questioned by the same prosecutor. The last thing he may have anticipated was his encounter with Ramon Roubideaux, William Stands' attorney. Roubideaux is a Dakota; he was born on the Rosebud Reservation and graduated from George Washington University Law School.

White Hawk had agreed to testify against his accomplice, an Indian, and found himself face to face under cross-examination with another Indian. The spectators were impressed.

Ramon Roubideaux requested a conference with the Court. In chambers Roubideaux said: ". . . I have learned that they intend to put Thomas White Hawk on as a witness, who has pleaded guilty to premeditated murder . . . we intend to question the witness concerning his awareness of whether or not the penalty for premeditated is . . . death by the electric chair or life imprisonment, in the discretion of the Court . . ." Judge Bandy had second thoughts and expressed his concern: "Now, at this moment, I will say to you quite frankly that I am vacillating as to whether defense counsel may be permitted to state the penalty for murder to this jury in the question . . ." A formula for discussing the death sentence was worked out between the prosecution, the defense and the judge. The trial was on again. C. E. Light assisted Charles Wolsky in the prosecution. White Hawk took the stand. He was asked if he had seen William Stands on March 24, 1967.

WHITE HAWK: "Yes, I did . . . we were together downtown at—from eleven o'clock until about twelve-thirty, then went back to school."

LIGHT: "What had you been doing downtown previous to that time?"

WHITE HAWK: "Well, I had finished the date with my girl friend, and went down to a bar and had a few drinks and met Bill, and then we went down, had some drinks together, and then I bought some beer and we hid it at a house . . . It was on the north side of town, an old abandoned house, and then went back to the dorm from there."

LIGHT: "Was there anything else hidden there at the house?"

WHITE HAWK: "Yes, the rifle."

LIGHT: "After you arrived back at the dormitory, about twelve-thirty, did you and Mr. Stands have a conversation?"

WHITE HAWK: "The only conversation, as such, was that we had been in the dormitory together, so we would leave together . . . to go to the house to get the beer and the rifle . . . we discussed the taking (sic) Mr. Yeado down to the jewelry store; and, while we were talking, I made sure that he would come on his own will, that I didn't drag him into it; and, once we started, he would be in it just as much as I would."

LIGHT: "When did you first start talking about taking Mr. Yeado down to the jewelry store?"

WHITE HAWK: "Wednesday afternoon is when I remember . . ."

LIGHT: "Did Mr. Stands know that there was a rifle there."

WHITE HAWK: "No, he didn't."

LIGHT: "How much of the beer did you consume before you arrived at the Yeado home?"

WHITE HAWK: "We consumed it all . . . we split the . . . bottles, and I drank both of mine and drank one of his and the majority of the other one . . ."

LIGHT: ". . . when you arrived at the Yeado house, what did you do?"

139

WHITE HAWK: "Well, we were outside on the lawn, and we discussed whether we should go through with it or not, because it was starting to get light . . . I broke the window and we went in."

LIGHT: "During the time you were upstairs, was Mr. Yeado shot?"

WHITE HAWK: "Yes, he was."

LIGHT: "How many times was he shot?"

WHITE HAWK: "He was shot twice."

LIGHT: "Was Mr. Stands present in the house at this time?"

WHITE HAWK: "Yes, he was in the house."

LIGHT: "Was he on the second floor at or about the time Mr. Yeado was shot?"

WHITE HAWK: "I am sure he was there when Mr. Yeado was shot the second time, but I don't know if he was or not for the first shot."

LIGHT: "From the time you two entered the house, until Mr. Stands left the house, had you ever attempted to compel him to stay in the house . . ."

WHITE HAWK: "I suggested it was light out and that there were people outside. That is why I didn't leave."

LIGHT: "Did you attempt to keep him in the house?"

WHITE HAWK: "Not by force, no."

LIGHT: "If Mr. Stands had refused to go with you, would this incident with Mr. Yeado ever have occurred?"

WHITE HAWK: "It wouldn't have, as far as I can see."

LIGHT: "In other words, you would not have gone into the house on your own?"

WHITE HAWK: "No, I wouldn't have."

ROUBIDEAUX: "So you're Thomas White Hawk?"

WHITE HAWK: "Yes, I am."

ROUBIDEAUX: "How old are you?"

WHITE HAWK: "Nineteen years old."

ROUBIDEAUX: "Are you aware, Mr. White Hawk, that the penalty for premeditated murder, in South Dakota,

Attorney Ramon Roubideaux

is death by the electric chair or life imprisonment, in the
discretion of the Trial Judge . . ."

WHITE HAWK: "I am aware of that."

ROUBIDEAUX: ". . . I believe that, without the knowledge of your attorney, Mr. McCahren, that you had
some conversations with one or more of the prosecutors,
prior to your testifying here today . . . and where did
these conversations take place?"

WHITE HAWK: "Clay County Jail."

ROUBIDEAUX: "And I believe it is a fact, is it not, Mr. *Yellow* Hawk, that you informed them, did you not—

JUDGE BANDY: "We moved in somebody else here. We
got Mr. *Yellow* Hawk in."

ROUBIDEAUX: "Oh, Mr. White Hawk."

WHITE HAWK: "I'm not yellow."

ROUBIDEAUX: "What's that?"

WHITE HAWK: "I'm not yellow."

ROUBIDEAUX: "You want to go into that, Mr. White Hawk?"

JUDGE BANDY: "Counsel!"

ROUBIDEAUX: "Is it a fact, Mr. White Hawk, that you do not expect to gain any favor whatsoever by your testimony here?"

WHITE HAWK: "Specifically not from the *attorneys*, no."

ROUBIDEAUX: "You do expect to gain some favor from His Honor?"

WHITE HAWK: "None."

Roubideaux continued his cross examination about the confession White Hawk gave to the Sheriff on the night he was arrested. White Hawk denied that it was his idea alone to enter the Yeado home. He was questioned about the shots.

ROUBIDEAUX: ". . . The first shot he was laying on the bed?"

WHITE HAWK: "Semi-laying. He wasn't exactly laying down, no."

ROUBIDEAUX: "What was he doing?"

WHITE HAWK: "Well, I was trying to take the rifle away from him."

ROUBIDEAUX: "Oh, now you—you say that it was self-defense, or that this shot was accidental?"

WHITE HAWK: "I am not saying it was self-defense, no."

ROUBIDEAUX: "As a matter of fact, you deliberately shot Mr. Yeado, didn't you, sir?"

WHITE HAWK: "No, I didn't."

ROUBIDEAUX: "You plead guilty to premeditated murder, did you not?"

WHITE HAWK: "Yes, I did."

142

ROUBIDEAUX: "And you are trying to say, are you, that the shooting of Mr. Yeado was accidental?"

WHITE HAWK: "I am not trying to say that; that is what I *do* say."

ROUBIDEAUX: "And are you also trying to say, Mr. White Hawk, that if Willy Stands had not accompanied you, that you never would have carried out this cold-blooded murder?"

WHITE HAWK: "I hadn't planned any murder, premeditated, cold-blooded, or anything."

ROUBIDEAUX: "When you talked to Sheriff Nelson, did he make any promises or inducements to you, if you would help out in this case?"

WHITE HAWK: "The only thing I can find out of helping, as you say, is for *clarification on my part.*"

Judge Bandy declared a mistrial at Yankton. Stands was released on bond and a second trial for murder was scheduled for March 18, 1968, in Armour, South Dakota. White Hawk did not testify in the second trial. He was in solitary confinement at the State Penitentiary in Sioux Falls, awaiting the death sentence. William Stands was acquitted at his second trial in Armour. The jury deliberated for more than twelve hours. Stands was served a warrant for burglary and grand larceny, arrested in the court room, hand-cuffed after being on bond, and taken back to Clay County jail. Ramon Roubideaux accepted his client's plea of guilty to the grand larceny charge. The other charges were dismissed.

THE SENTENCE

It was cold. The room was dry. Time was compressed. Thomas James White Hawk was dreaming. His mother and father visited him in his cell the night before. They didn't speak. His mother was crying. She was forgiven. He followed them out until they disappeared. He loved and hated his father. He remembered wanting to kill him when

143

he was very young. Vermillion. Afternoon. January 15, 1967. Sentencing. "The time has now been reached for the imposition of sentence, but, before so doing, I inquire, and you will get your advice from your counsel, as to whether you have any legal cause or reason to show why the sentence and judgment of this Court should not at this time be imposed."

MCCAHREN: "The defendant informs me, he doesn't understand the question, Your Honor."

JUDGE BANDY: "Well, that is probably up to you to explain that. There are certain legal grounds that would constitute a defense to a conviction that may even be raised at this late date, and, if you have any of those to state at this time, this is your opportunity to do so. You will probably have to rely upon your counsel's advice as to that . . . This question I am asking you is not what you referred to the other day as your allocution. When you have answered the question I have now asked, that will be the next question of you."

WHITE HAWK: "Your Honor, I don't find any legal reasons for delay of imposition of sentence." . . . *my mother and father are dead* . . .

JUDGE BANDY: "I will say this to you . . . if you were *not* represented by counsel, I would probably say I would break this question down into three parts" . . . *Your Excellency: Pursuant to the requirements . . . I have imposed a sentence of death upon Thomas James White Hawk* . . . "I would say, Do you claim that, at the time you committed this act, you were insane to the point where you couldn't distinguish between right and wrong and didn't know the wrongfulness of the act in which you were engaged." . . . *He has at all times declined to make any statement to the Court* . . . "The next thing I would say, is, Do you claim that, at this moment, you are insane to the point where you don't comprehend and know what is going on around you?" . . . *I believe the precise cause of*

144

death was internal bleeding from the chest wound . . . "and, thirdly, I would say, Do you claim that, up to this moment, you have been judicially punished for the offense you have admitted you committed?" . . . *he savagely beat him about the head with an iron skillet . . .* "those are not all of them, but those are the primary and principal ones. I am not attempting to advise you, your counsel does that, but that is what we are talking about." . . *Neither of them wore masks or other disguise. The only possible hope of avoiding detection and identification lay in killing both Mr. and Mrs. Yeado . . .* "Now, you are *not* raising any of those issues or any others that you know of, at this time, is that correct?"

WHITE HAWK: "What do you mean by judicially punished?"

JUDGE BANDY: "Ask your counsel." . . . *it was his fixed intention to kill both of these people and for that reason do not accept his claim that the gun was accidentaly discharged while wrestling with Yeado . . .*

MCCAHREN: "He has been advised, Your Honor, as to the definition of *judicially punished.*"

JUDGE BANDY: "Is there legal cause or reason to show at this time?"

WHITE HAWK: "No. No, Your Honor."

JUDGE BANDY: "Very well, Will you please stand up." . . . *this is the most atrocious crime that has ever been committed in the State and seemed to me to fall within the intent of the legislature in reinstating capital punishment . . . Most respectfully . . .* "Mr. White Hawk . . . is there anything you wish to say? . . . You are not compelled to make any statement whatever. You may, if you desire."

WHITE HAWK: ". . . I would like to say a few words . . . First of all, the acquisition of the weapons and named subsequent events, took place in the homicide of Mr. Yeado, was purely accidental; and, by *accidental,* I mean Mr. Zoubek, my guardian, had no foresight or knowledge beforehand of what I had intended to do." . . . *my*

145

stomach hurts . . . I can speak Sioux and English . . . we were in Colorado . . . "At least, as to what I had intended to do, that was just—well, Your Honor, actually, when I first started contemplating acquiring money for myself was taking Mr. Yeado down to the jewelry store." . . . *headaches . . . I had mumps when I was nine years old . . .* "but I had not contemplated using any weapons or anything else, except mere force, I suppose, and that leads to the death of Mr. Yeado" . . . *My mother's name was Dorothy McLean. She is deceased too . . .* "as I say, and I was intoxicated at the time; but, from what I remember, Mr. Yeado was *accidentally* shot." . . . *Dizziness. The combination . . . I saw myself there . . .* "Now, you said something about my not knowing right from wrong at the time of the crime, alleged crime. Well, I have to admit, at the time, I see myself lacking completely in judgment at that time." . . . *How could I dislike someone I didn't know . . . He was so controlled . . .* "As witnessed by you, in my statement at the beginning of this allocution and at the trial, William Stands' trial, I didn't know whether to get help for Mr. Yeado. I thought I did, but didn't pursue it.". . . *I read the paper and it would disappear . . . I would disappear . . .* "Your Honor, there are some things which I don't remember, which happened that date, and I have been asking around, as much as possible, as to what did happen. I have even asked Bill, but there are many things which I don't know what happened that day.". . . *I saw myself . . . nothing moved . . . I wanted the darkness . . .* "I thought, when I went to Yankton, that I would find out somehow, but I didn't. Your Honor, you have my report, I believe, pre-sentence report, there, and due to my diagnosed personality disorder, I don't know what to say anymore." . . . *When I grow up, I'd like to be a doctor.* . . . "I might say, there was one strike against me because of that. This is all I have to say, Your Honor."

JUDGE BANDY: "In a matter of this gravity, it would ordinarily and normally be the procedure of the Sentencing Judge to assign and explain his reasons for the sentence which he imposes. We have a situation that makes it different. Your confederate, William Stands, is yet to be tried. Any remarks that I might make at this time would be in the public domain and would probably be publicized, and I, therefore, am going to utterly refrain from any remarks that I might make which would be even considered to be in justification of the sentence that I feel is to be imposed in this case. It is the sentence and judgement of this Court, and it is ordered and adjudged, that, by reason of your conviction of the crime of murder of James Yeado, you, Thomas James White Hawk, suffer death by electrocution, and may God have mercy upon your soul."

THE AFTERMATH

On January 17, 1968, members of several Indian organizations in Minneapolis met at a press conference to protest the scheduled execution of Thomas White Hawk. "We are not here today to judge or condone but to strongly protest capital punishment for an Indian person in one of the strongest anti-Indian states in the country," a representative of the Indian Advancement Association said. At the University of South Dakota, the Dean of the Law School was critical of the press conference in Minneapolis. He said: "To emphasize racism or prejudice will only reinforce the attitudes that exist already toward capital punishment."

The Minnesota Civil Liberties Union was in contact with the national office. A press release followed: ". . . the national legal staff of the ACLU in New York has offered to provide legal representation in the matter of the execution of Thomas White Hawk in South Dakota . . . " Vermillionites reacted with suspicion. Many believe that the American Civil Liberties Union is a communist organization working to free all criminals so they can destroy the old

American way. The Clay County Sheriff was pressured to dismiss his deputy because he once was an ACLU member. Vermillion Episcopal vicar Douglas Hiza has been carrying on an active campaign for the abolition of capital punishment. His greatest problem is finding people to discuss the issue. It seems that those people vaguely supporting capital punishment are willing to discuss the abolition of the death penalty only after White Hawk is executed. Director of Student Affairs, Robert Adams, and other University of South Dakota faculty members, signed a letter opposing capital punishment. Adams said, "My opposition to the death penalty is a matter of civilization . . . wrongs are not solved by retribution . . . Our letter was an attempt to put a building block in the foundation of a modern civilized society." The letter was sent to State Representative Donald Osheim, who had prepared a bill to repeal capital punishment in South Dakota. The bill was defeated by a vote of 44 to 28 on February 1, 1968, in the House of Representatives.

Lee McCahren considered the ACLU offer of assistance. He was not certain which direction his appeal would take. He was either unable or unwilling to effectively argue the insanity defense. McCahren arranged for psychologist Jacob Stein to examine White Hawk. Stein's observations were not made available to the court. He reported: "Both parents contributed to the tension and bitterness that prevailed in the home . . . the picture of a disturbed familial environment . . . The boy's feeling of isolation and abandonment was further reinforced by his attending the reservation boarding school. In some respects . . . his responses can be related to his segregated childhood . . . paranoid trends appear to be in evidence especially in his close personal relationships . . . He sees himself as a peculiar individual conforming to societal mores and folkways at his convenience. This defiance of societal rules appears to be related to the patient's intense and overwhelming

148

Attorney Douglas Hall

feelings of loneliness and abandonment. Because of his inadequate feelings, he tries to compensate in athletic events
. . . Another aspect of the patient's personality disturbance
appears to be his ambivalence concerning his psychosexual
development . . . " A perceptive report but no discussion
of White Hawk's Indian identity. There is no information
in any of the psychological reports about White Hawk's
problems of unconscious and conscious links of identity,
dissociation, and cultural schizophrenia. White Hawk has

149

an Indian unconscious and a white man's conscious mind
. . . His behavior was controlled by pale greed and the social narcissism and violence of the dominant society.

Before McCahren could make up his mind about what
approach he would take on appeal, White Hawk, who had
often expressed his dissatisfaction with his court appointed
attorney, retained Douglas Hall, a Minneapolis attorney
with extensive trial experience in criminal cases. Hall is a
board member of the Minnesota Civil Liberties Union.

Judge Bandy runs a good courtroom, but beyond eye-
shot of the bench he talks in perplexing idioms. He states
for the record that he is *opposed* to capital punishment.
When he was questioned about his bewildering position at
the Stands trial in Armour, he said off the record: "I did *not*
sentence White Hawk to capital punishment . . . His prognosis was very negative . . . little chance for rehabilitation
. . . *I am removing him from the world . . .*" Respecting his
reputation for fairness in other matters and his willingness
to talk about the death penalty, his capricious power and
moral reasoning over life and death is frightening and demands strong criticism and human control. The Judge illustrated his strange reasoning with personal metaphors
about war, punishment and deterrence, and the criminal
mind. By acknowledging and accepting the negative prognosis report on White Hawk and the inadequate treatment
available in correctional institutions. he justified his decision to remove Thomas James White Hawk from the world.

Judge Bandy concludes in his letter to Governor Boe:
". . . less than a year before White Hawk had stolen an automobile and made no attempt at its concealment. He was
apprehended, pleaded guilty and was placed on probation
in U.S. District Court. It may be that he continued to be
careless as to the consequences of crime or it may be that
he learned from that experience to leave fewer tracks. I
fully believe that it was his fixed intention to kill both of
these people and for that reason do not accept his claim
that the gun was accidentally discharged . . . It is my un-

150

derstanding that, subsequent to entering a plea of guilty he had a conversation with the Sheriff of Clay County relating to what he had in mind and his plans. Because I did not wish to be in any manner influenced by his hearsay I have avoided discussing this conversation with the Sheriff. Imposition of this sentence has been most *odious* to me. However, insofar as I know, this is the most *atrocious* crime that has ever been committed in the State and seemed to me to fall within the intent of the Legislature in reinstating capital punishment. I will cooperate to the fullest extent in any investigation you desire to make. Most respectfully . . ."

It is doubtful that the Legislature intended capital punishment to be carried out only in cases where individual value judgments of "atrocious" crimes, were made. James Yeado's death was tragic, but it is difficult to believe that it was the "most atrocious crime that has ever been committed in the State." While White Hawk was awaiting trial, a white man in Rapid City walked into a court room, shot and killed his wife and her attorney, and wounded the judge. He was not sentenced to capital punishment.

Judge Bandy has a good reputation in South Dakota. He is most respected by trial attorneys for his fair attention to court procedure and knowledge of the law. He runs a tight courtroom. It is unconscionable that he found it so difficult to carefully consider the insanity defense. Measured against his own good reputation, Judge Bandy did not show his judicial fairness in understanding the White Hawk case. He reflected his majority community feeling when he imposed the uncivilized sentence of death. "There is little justice for the Indian," John Artichoker said, "We have been slow in defending ourselves . . . We are Indians at the mercy of ourselves." Christian rhythm. Judicial rhythm. South Dakota. May God have mercy upon your soul.

1968

151

✝ Commutation of Death

Thomas James White Hawk was shaving when the Governor of South Dakota announced the commutation of *his* sentence from death in the electric chair to life imprisonment. When he finished shaving, he smiled easily—after almost two years of isolation on death row at the South Dakota State Penitentiary. White Hawk wiped his face, hung up the towel and wrote the following letter to a friend:

I shall live . . . the world is full of surprises, wonderful ones and not so wonderful ones. But when a man is told that he will not be executed, there is no more wonderful gift; the gift of life . . .

With that romantic phrase, the plains story of the handsome *dakota* college youth who murdered a jeweler and raped the jeweler's wife should be concluded. But the story will not end because White Hawk has become a symbol of the conflicts and injustice of many *dakota* people living in a white-dominated state. And the dominant white people on the plains will not forget the savage demon who twice raped a white woman while her husband was dying of gunshot wounds in the next room.

"This act was one of the most brutal, dastardly crimes in the history of South Dakota," Governor Frank Farrar told spectators and newsmen at a press conference at the state capitol. "In a majority of nations in the world, the criminal would have received, long ago, the death sentence," the

152

Governor Frank Farrar, Pierre, South Dakota, 1969

Governor continued. "But the compassion, maturity, and guarantees under the freedoms we enjoy in America have allowed several avenues of appeal from the death sentence for Mr. White Hawk."

In the past, had those same "guarantees under the freedoms we enjoy" existed for the *dakota* people, history would show cavalry soldiers sentenced for wearing on their hats the severed genitals of *dakota* women and for the distribution of smallpox-infected blankets to the shivering tribes.

History may be dismissed, but if equal justice existed today for the *dakota*, white rancher Baxter Berry would not have been acquitted for the shooting death of Norman

153

White Hawk at Shattuck School,
Faribault, Minnesota, 1964

Guardian Philip Zoubek, 1959

Little Brave, who was unarmed at the time of his death. An assistant state attorney general sharing in the prosecution of Berry told the all-white jury that "the fact that Norman Little Brave was an Indian doesn't have a thing to do with this trial. I hope you can keep that out of your heart, and out of your soul, too."

Defense counsel for the white rancher argued that the whole controversy over the death of Little Brave was inspired by "people back east who don't know anything about Indians." The many people in South Dakota who wanted to smell the flesh of White Hawk burning in the electric chair also argued that the whole controversy over his life was inspired by eastern liberals from Minnesota and elsewhere who knew nothing about the problems of Indians.

154

The South Dakota Board of Pardons and Paroles recommended in a written report to the Governor that no further commutations be made in the future. Without the possibility of parole, White Hawk faces a natural death sentence in the state penitentiary. This special sentence without parole probably never has been offered a white man with a life sentence.

The next effort on behalf of White Hawk is to find a competent psychiatrist to work with him until the psychiatrist, White Hawk and the society have a better understanding of the disintegration of the *dakota* identity in the Christian world.

1970

PART 3
AMERICAN INDIAN MOVEMENT

✛ Confrontation Heroes

Eight years ago Dennis Banks, dressed in a dark suit, white shirt and narrow necktie, strode into the office of the director of the American Indian Employment Center and told him to stop picketing the Bureau of Indian Affairs.

"Demonstrations are not the Indian way," Banks said then, wagging his finger. The director of the center had organized a peaceful demonstration in front of the Minneapolis area office of the Bureau of Indian Affairs, demanding equal services for urban tribal people.

Since then Banks and hundreds of young adventurers have trouped across the country from Plymouth Rock to Alcatraz, dressed in century-old tribal vestments, demanding recognition of treaty rights, equal justice and sovereignty. The occupation of Wounded Knee may be the last symbolic act for the aging militant leaders.

The American Indian Movement is an urban revolutionary movement whose members have in recent years tried to return to the reservations as the warrior heroes of tribal people. To some, they are the heroes of contemporary history—but to others they are the freebooters of racism.

As in many new radical movements, the organizers first met in a store front in the midst of urban poverty. Banks, Clyde Bellecourt, Harold Goodsky, George Mitchell and others organized a patrol to monitor the activities of police officers in Minneapolis. The copwatch program grew from foot soldiers to mobile units in luxury automobiles. The is-

sue was police harassment—which is still a good issue—
but the method of trailing police cars in expensive convert-
ibles became an extravagant parody.

The symbols were oppression and poverty, the press
was good, and the guilt money came rolling in from church
groups, but the organizers of the movement began arguing
about philosophy and objectives. Mitchell dedicated himself to serving young people, Goodsky took a paying job in
corrections and others continued working in education
and social services.

Banks and Bellecourt remained to carry on a movement
of confrontation politics with the intellectual and legal assistance of dozens of romantic white radicals and liberals.
Those who followed the ideologies of confrontation were
in conflict with those who believed that confrontation
should lead to negotiation and institutional changes.

A.I.M. in the late 1960's became a symbolic confrontation group. The confrontation idiom means punching out
the symbolic adversary of racism and oppression at the
front door, with the press present, and walking out the
back door. The negotiation idiom means punching out the
adversary at the front door with the press present, but
waiting around for an invitation to return and grind out
some changes.

The problem in the differences of approach was not only
political ideology, but the response of the press. Journalists
seldom reported what happened beyond the symbolic
punch-out at the front door. The press presented the heroes of confrontation, but not of negotiation. Mitchell,
Goodsky and others are still serving and negotiating;
Banks, Bellecourt and others have pulled off the best symbolic press confrontations of the year at Custer and
Wounded Knee.

Behind the scenes, tribal people have been arguing
about the use of violence as a means of change. Some say
that violence has only polarized the dominant white soci-

160

Dennis Banks, right, at a ceremonial

ety and strained interpersonal relationships. Other tribal people argue that violence has made the job of moderates working within the system much easier. White people listen better after violence.

A.I.M. has been punching away at the issues of legal and economic injustices, but so have many educators and lawyers and politicians and writers. The grim statistics of life expectancy and infant mortality and unemployment on reservations have been recorded everywhere. The problem is not one of information, but rather a way to bring about institutional changes that will free tribal people from poverty and cultural invalidation.

Consider these changes through education: Four hundred tribal people have earned high-school equivalency certificates on three reservations in Minnesota in the past three years. Many have gone on to college and have found better-paying jobs. Six hundred tribal people are attending colleges in Minnesota compared with fewer than a hundred 15 years ago.

Consider these changes through the law: There are legal-services programs on most reservations, and hundreds of tribal people are studying in law schools across the country. There have been several successful treaty-law arguments in federal and state courts, including the hunting and fishing suit won by the Leech Lake Reservation.

Consider these changes through economic development: The Red Lake Reservation has a home-construction business and a new vocational school. The Leech Lake Reservation has a market and service station and a camping-and-recreation complex.

There are thousands of other examples of changes in education and economic development that have taken place on other reservations in the past few years. There have been failures, too, but every reservation is realizing a new consciousness of change.

Now consider the changes through violence and radical-ideologies: Last year at Cass Lake the leaders of A.I.M. were critical of elected tribal officials for negotiating a legal agreement with the state over the hunting and fishing rights won through a federal court decision. The agreement, ratified by the state legislature, will bring half-a-million dollars a year to the reservation. Many militants stated then that they had come to Cass Lake to die for tribal people. The issue was won through the courts, and suicide was not necessary. It was the first time the Movement had taken up the use of firearms.

162

Clyde Bellecourt, left, at a demonstration

During the occupation of the offices of the Bureau of Indian Affairs in Washington, radical leaders demanded another investigation and reorganization of the paternalistic bureaucracy that has controlled the lives of tribal people on reservations for more than a century. The militants had a powerful position from which to negotiate their demands: It was an election year and scores of congressional liberals were sympathetic. But rather than negotiate the demands, the leaders of A.I.M. accepted more than $60,000 to leave the building and the city. They left with hush money.

The leaders were at Wounded Knee voicing the very same demands that they sold out in Washington. While militant leaders are demanding an investigation of alleged

163

corruption of elected tribal officials, there should also be an investigation of where the hush money went.

A.I.M. has raised good issues through the press, but it has never followed through to negotiate. At Custer the militants drew national attention to the wrongful death of Wesley Bad Heart Bull. They said the white man who stabbed Bad Heart Bull should be charged with murder. The fire in the courthouse was a violent stunt that detracted from the issue of legal injustices.

In Rapid City, leaders of the Movement demanded sweeping changes in government, law enforcement and education, and many city officials were anxious to negotiate—but the seriousness of the issues was deflated when businessmen reported widespread shoplifting. While young adventurers following the excitement of the Movement were sleeping on the floor in a church dormitory, at least two dozen leaders stayed at a downtown motel for two weeks without paying the rent.

It would be witless to expect a revolutionary tribal group of true-believers to be rational and law-abiding toward white people, but the problems of racism and social and economic injustice are still so great that no one has the social or political right to play around with the expectations of tribal people.

The militant leaders are dedicated men who have given many years of their lives to a cause, but it takes more than a rifle and the symbolic willingness to die to bring about institutional changes that will benefit tribal people.

Where people have lived without justice there has been violence. Tribal people have lived for centuries without justice. The violence of the American Indian Movement is the problem of the white-dominant society. It is not the problem of tribal people; white people have created the need for violence. Yesterday was a good day to negotiate because tomorrow may be a new confrontation.

1973

164

✝ The Death of Bad Heart Bull

Killing Indians was once sanctioned by the military of this nation. Who can forget the slaughter of tribal people at Mystic River, and Sand Creek, and Wounded Knee in South Dakota.

"We had sufficient light from the word of God for our proceedings," said John Underhill at Mystic River.

"The only good Indians I ever saw were dead," said General Philip Sheridan at Fort Cob.

"I have come to kill Indians, and believe it is right and honorable to use any means under God's heaven to kill Indians," said Colonel John Chivington at Sand Creek.

Killing Indians in South Dakota today is not sanctioned, but it is seldom viewed as murder.

For example, Darld Schmitz admitted stabbing Wesley Bad Heart Bull in front of a cowboy bar at Buffalo Gap. Bad Heart Bull is dead. Schmitz is free.

Leaders of the American Indian Movement brought the incident to national attention by fire-bombing the historic Custer County Court House.

There were at least a dozen people in front of the bar when Bad Heart Bull stumbled in the street with blood throbbing from a wound in his chest. What each witness saw and remembers will be argued and settled by white people. Tribal people have few reasons to trust the courts and white juries.

165

Custer County attorney Hobart Gates agreed to second-degree manslaughter charges after considering information from only two witnesses. They were Schmitz, who was arrested about four hours after the death of Bad Heart Bull, and Schmitz's friend, Harold Wheeler Jr.

Schmitz said he left the bar at closing time and saw Bad Heart Bull standing in the street hitting a man later identified as Mad Dog.

"He knocked the guy down and kept hitting him with a chain," Schmitz stated. He went over with his friend Wheeler to help Mad Dog. "I told Bad Heart Bull to drop the chain . . .

"Then he attacked me," Schmitz said. "I had drawn my knife . . . I thought I could scare him off . . . when he swung at my head with the chain and lunged at me, I ducked and stabbed at him with my knife."

Other witnesses said that after Bad Heart Bull was stabbed he stumbled forward in the street saying: "I am bleeding, let me at him." His mother Sarah Bad Heart Bull and several friends took him to the hospital. The car stalled on the way.

Robert High Eagle was there. He said he remembers seeing Schmitz walking out of the bar and saying, "I want to kill an Indian."

Wheeler said that he and Schmitz came out of the bar together. "We got in the car and started to leave and a fight started . . . Darld got out of the car and he went over there. I think to break up the fight. I walked over to the guy that was laying on the ground and rolled him over to see how he was hurt. His face was bleeding.

"Some guy fired a gun in the air a couple of times. My back was turned to Darld and the fellow with the chain," Wheeler stated the morning after the incident. "We got back in the car and left . . . Darld told me on the way . . . that he had stabbed this fellow. We left the two girls off . . . and returned to Custer."

Frances Means said the fight started when a "white man who was about to drive off got out of his car and said he could whip any Indian there. He threw off his coat and Wesley and him started fighting. After knocking down this white man, Wesley backed up to a car and turned around and this guy Darld Schmitz stabbed him in the chest in the heart."

The woman who had accompanied Schmitz to the cowboy bar said she saw the fight with Mad Dog and "jumped out of the car and ran up and grabbed Wesley 'cause I knew I could stop it . . .

"But every time I went up there to grab him somebody would grab me and pull me away," she stated. "When I turned around somebody had grabbed Wesley because somebody had stuck a knife in him."

She said she did not know who had stabbed Bad Heart Bull. She thought Schmitz was in the car during the fight "except for when he grabbed me."

Eddie Clifford was with Bad Heart Bull the night he was stabbed at Buffalo Gap. He said a man "come out of the bar, opened up the knife, stood there looking at us and put it back in his pocket."

Clifford stated that the man with the knife walked over to a car with several other white men. Then Bad Heart Bull "called them and told them to stop because they left some beer . . . he was going to ask them if they wanted it back."

Then Mad Dog jumped out of the car and said he could fight any Indian there. Bad Heart Bull struck him with a chain and then "someone took a shot in the air and said to hold it down . . . it was some big cowboy dude, man, he was standing right outside of his car," Clifford stated.

"Then I heard someone say, 'He's got a knife,' and it kind of hit me that I seen this guy pull a knife out . . . so I went running over to Sarah Bad Heart Bull, her car, to see if she had a weapon in the car, you know, if I had to get into it I had to try to defend myself, but she didn't have none so I run back over to see what was happening and they said they have stabbed him . . ."

The official police report indicated that Schmitz was arrested on a charge of second-degree manslaughter about four hours after the incident. The arresting officer reported that he asked Schmitz for the knife. "It was a jackknife with what appeared to be dried blood on the large blade." Schmitz signed a statement and was released on bail about three hours after his arrest.

There are obvious differences in what the witnesses saw and heard. It is not clear whether Schmitz left the car first to help Mad Dog, or if he went for Bad Heart Bull. There is no proof that Schmitz was in danger or that the fight was his in the first place. Several witnesses said they were holding Bad Heart Bull from fighting. It may not have been necessary to stab Bad Heart Bull in the chest to keep him from Mad Dog, who, according to Wheeler, was already on the ground.

Had the police officer or county attorney conducted a proper investigation—they questioned only Schmitz and his friend Wheeler—more serious charges might have been justified. The county attorney, however, knows how difficult it is to convict a white man of murder when the dead man is an Indian.

1973

✛ Bandits in Rapid City

The American Indian Movement could not survive as a revolutionary tribal caravan without the affinity of lawyers and the press and the sympathy of the church.

Last month national television crews followed the revolutionary group to Custer, South Dakota, and were on hand to cover the burning of the county courthouse.

Thirty-eight people were arrested on charges of riot and arson. Ramon Roubideaux, a successful criminal attorney and member of the Rosebud Sioux Tribe, agreed to represent those arrested.

About a hundred young adventurers moved uninvited into a dormitory at the Mother Butler Center in Rapid City. The center is owned by the Catholic Church.

Without the press the death of Wesley Bad Heart Bull and the fires at Custer would have been less dramatic; without an attorney many people might still be in jail awaiting trial, and without the church there would be few places to stay. Most tribal people in Rapid City were not interested in taking a militant home for the night.

Many white residents of Rapid City responded to the presence of the young adventurers with a lump in the throat, a grimace on the face and one hand on a gun. The city had not yet recovered from a terrible flood and the arrival of A.I.M. was very bad timing.

But a few sensitive white people took the presence of

169

young militants as a challenge to right a few wrongs. Most
government officials were open for negotiation.

"I think you have a good message for this country,"
Mayor Donald Barnett said. The mayor seemed to be impressed by the intense dedication of the leaders of the
Movement until he received the criminal files on the militants and discovered they were armed and staying in mo-
tels without paying the bills.

"Are these men serious civil-rights workers, or are they
a bunch of bandits?" Barnett asked during an interview.
"People working for civil rights do not carry guns. I have
seen the records on these men, and you can't sit and negotiate with a man who has a gun."

Comparing militant tribal leaders to the black civil-rights
movement, Barnett said: "Martin Luther King was a man
of peace. He was never armed."

Two dozen members of A.I.M. stayed in a downtown
motel in Rapid City for two weeks. They were evicted by
the police and left a bill of about $2,500 unpaid. No one
was arrested, but police confiscated many weapons, including firearms.

"Now, I am no melodramatic martyr," the mayor said,
"nor the great white hope, but I believe in communications
and working things out through negotiations . . . I could
have done two things: violate their constitutional rights
and jail every one of the militants, or try to negotiate."

And the mayor did his best to negotiate. He called and
attended meeting after meeting. City officials were open
and anxious to negotiate changes, but militant leaders
changed the course of the arguments and demands from
day to day in an effort to maintain a position of confrontation and confusion.

The mayor and city council members moved to adopt a
new ordinance establishing a racial conciliation board with
investigative powers.

"We were making progress on the resolution," the
mayor said, "when at a meeting of council members and

170

militant leaders Vernon Bellecourt changed the demands and told white people to get out of the Black Hills . . . He was serious!

"Sure, I told him . . . I looked at my watch. Let me see, I said, give me about two hours to pack some things up before I leave," the mayor recalled. "But they left, in anger! How can you talk to someone who responds like that? The war is over, and it happened everywhere in history. We won and you lost. There is no changing that and we are not leaving."

But the symbolic war is real to the believers, and tribal people will not accept the loss.

There were many reports of shoplifting in supermarkets by young followers of the Movement. They were living at the Mother Butler Center with no money and no food. Rapid City merchants seemed to agree that it would cost less to put up with shoplifting than to make a legal complaint and suffer possible property damage.

Two weeks later the young adventurers moved to the Pine Ridge Reservation and Wounded Knee. They left the center damaged. Railings were removed and cut for weapons; doors were damaged and locks were broken. Supplies were destroyed, and the new carpets on the first floor were stained and burned from cigarettes.

"It is a simple thing to decry the acts of violence we have witnessed during this past week," said Bishop Harold Dimmerling of the diocese of Rapid City in a prepared statement. "It is no simple thing to decry the ills which have led to this present state. The inequities of our judicial system, the growing cancer of racial prejudice in each of us . . . and a long list of past grievances give birth to what occurred . . ."

Tribal people amount to about ten percent of the Rapid City population. One is a policeman. Less than four percent of the city employees are minority people, with less than one percent being tribal people. The city hires blacks and other minority people before tribal people. Half of all

171

Dennis Banks

the arrests in Rapid City last year were tribal people arrested for public drunkenness.

There are no special programs in the public schools for over one-thousand tribal children. One percent of the teachers are tribal people.

In the fifties most tribal people living in Rapid City lived in tents until the city moved them two miles out of town to a housing project with no water or sewer. Now there are about three-hundred children living in a new housing project next to the old one, which is about two miles from the nearest elementary school. Under state law, transportation is provided only for students living more than two and one-half miles from the nearest public school. To the

172

tribal people, their problems so often seem to be planned by racists.

Rapid City for most tribal people is a tough place to find a white friend. The problems are great, the money is short—South Dakota has no individual state income tax, and schools must depend on property taxes—but there are people in the professions and government who have the integrity to support changes.

While Dennis Banks was lecturing about racism and explaining his sacred religious connections with mother earth, the white and tribal leaders of Rapid City were sorting out the facts and issues from the symbols.

"If we can hang together, we can become a political power," said Reverend William O'Connell of Our Lady of Perpetual Help Cathedral in Rapid City. "The American Indian Movement did in two weeks what we could not have done in two years."

At the same time the new racial conciliation board was negotiating in Rapid City, Banks was riding a horse around Wounded Knee for photographers.

1973

✛ Good Little Indians

For six years the American Indian Movement has been demanding that white people change. In the process, the excitement of radical tribal ideologies has changed the consciousness of a few tribal people.

"We have been good little Indians too long, and I plan to dedicate the rest of my life to changing things for my people," said Ramon Roubideaux, a dauntless tribal attorney and one of the negotiators for members of the American Indian Movement while they were in South Dakota.

Changes in racial consciousness are often either symbolic or on a personal level, but for Roubideaux the changes will be through the courts. He represented people charged with arson and riot in connection with the firebombing of the Custer County Court House. White people who have found racial comfort in the assimilated moderation of professional men like Roubideaux may be looking for new tribal friends.

While many tribal people have been culturally overwhelmed by white racism, Roubideaux, an exception in any culture, has taken racism with levity and legal reasoning.

Telling personal stories with dramatic pleasure, he said that when he was first elected county attorney at Fort Pierre, he returned home and found a bucket of cow guts on the front steps. Many white people categorize tribal people as gut eaters.

"They tasted good," he said he told his adversaries. For the next sixteen years, as part-time county attorney and practicing private attorney, he argued his way through the courts and built a reputation as one of the best criminal attorneys in South Dakota. Juries and judges have acquitted half of more than two dozen people he represented on murder charges. Charges were reduced on the remaining half of those charged with murder.

For many years Roubideaux seemed to have forgotten that his tribal name was Brave Eagle and that he was a member of the Rosebud Sioux Tribe living in a racist state. Born at the Rosebud Indian Hospital, he attended several mission schools and completed a commercial business course before military service as a commissioned officer.

Twenty-nine years ago, in full military uniform, Roubideaux, a young officer and decorated war hero, was evicted from a dance hall in Edgemont, South Dakota because he was an Indian.

He vowed then to become a lawyer, he said, because he could not hire an attorney to prosecute the dance-hall manager. Six years later he received his law degree from George Washington University and began practice in South Dakota.

He wore expensive clothes, drove a luxury automobile, played golf and bridge with white friends and seemed to thrive on the humor and respect of white people in high places. But something happened to the gallant lawyer with the dark skin.

Roubideaux criticized the state parole board for detaining tribal people longer than white people in correctional institutions. He said at a corrections conference that the judicial system is racist and archaic, and he applauded the actions of the American Indian Movement: "I don't blame the militant because it's the only way to get attention."

"I have changed," Roubideaux said in an interview. "I have been treated well by white people, and for awhile I thought that was true for most Indians.

"But in the past few weeks, I have seen some people who I once thought were my friends turn into white savages. You know, sometimes I think white people are still playing out the Indian wars.

"Look at me," he said smiling. "I am a half-breed in more ways than one, and I have never really felt good about myself until the American Indian Movement came along. Now I am feeling good inside for the first time in my life. I suppose you could call me a scout and an interpreter; anyway, I feel good and a part of the advance party."

His figurative applause for the militants now means months of legal preparation and court appearances to defend the tribal revolutionaries. He is representing more non-paying clients in one month than he has ever defended.

Roubideaux filed a complaint with supporting affidavits against many of his old white friends in high places. The complaint is a class action alleging that government officials and law-enforcement officers deprived tribal people of rights to free speech and assembly, and the right to travel without intimidation and harassment. More than a dozen defendants, from the governor of the state to police officers, are named in the complaint.

"The justice system in South Dakota has mentally and physically brutalized Indian people. In the past, I have rationalized the situation, but I can't pass it off any more," Roubideaux said. "I've always been militant, but not to the point of violence. I have been saying what Dennis Banks has been saying for twenty years, but I was saying it in committee rooms."

Roubideaux has learned that white people respond to violence. He watched white people who had never expressed concern before react with fear and racial hatred to the presence of A.I.M. in South Dakota.

A change in consciousness is only the beginning, but tribal people in South Dakota are fortunate to have a voice in Roubideaux. He knows the law, and he knows where to argue the institutional changes that must be made to free tribal people from legal and economic injustices.

He is one of many professional tribal people who have lost faith in social assimilation and justice in the hands of the dominant white society.

1973

✛ Racism on Frontier Circle

Telephone Larry Lytle, president of the Rapid City Common Council, and ask him how to get to his house. He will tell you to take Arrowhead, turn right on Tomahawk, turn right again on Stockade to Frontier Circle.

When you get there, his wife will welcome you in and tell you that she has been teaching her children the differences between "good Indians and militant Indians."

"If you really want a story," she said in a hushed voice, "then you should investigate the shoplifting those militants have been doing . . . and if you like the seedy side you should talk to the white women they have been sleeping with."

Lytle, a dentist and former schoolteacher, was appointed to the Council and has been re-elected twice without opposition. He represents a ward with a golf course and expensive homes in the hills. He also represents the most conservative law-and-order views of the community.

He has no affection for the presence of the American Indian Movement in Rapid City. "They have damaged our city . . . When people see Indians on the street now, they ask if they are here for peace or violence.

"This is unfortunate," Lytle said, "because we have made great progress in the plight of the Indian . . . housing and jobs for example, but even though we have tried to hire Indians, they are not able to hold jobs for very long

178

. . . We even have an Indian on the Council and one on the school board."

Lytle seems proud of the intensity of his position against militants, claiming that others are afraid to speak out against violence and lawlessness. He installed heavy metal mesh over the windows of his dental office.

"No matter what people say, I am not a racist," he emphasized. "I have always treated people the same. My friend Art LaCroix is on the council, but I don't consider him an Indian."

Arthur LaCroix, soft-spoken tribal person who was raised among white people, has served one term on the Council. He was elected from a ward where several thousand tribal people live. He speaks of Lytle as a close friend.

"I am probably criticized from several sides, white and Indian, for holding my tongue," LaCroix said during an interview at his carpet-and-linoleum store.

"I don't think the American Indian Movement will help local Indians . . . but it is too early to tell if the ends will justify militant means.

"It is better now to support the good, to be optimistic about something like this, but it has made the city government more aware of the problems," said LaCroix.

LaCroix is sensitive to the issues, but says he is not able to speak for tribal people because he was not raised on a reservation. He was not aware that many of the leaders of the A.I.M. are from urban centers.

Lytle, on the other hand, feels it is his personal calling to speak for tribal people because, he said, "many Indian people need me to speak for them . . . They have a hard time speaking for themselves."

Lytle is either not a very good listener, or he has ignored what he has heard from tribal people and militants. Lawyer Ramon Roubideaux demanded that Lytle be removed from the council for racism and for supporting a measure before the Council calling for the removal of nonresident

179

tribal people from Rapid City before anything was done about the problems.

"The tactics of the American Indian Movement have done more to intimidate white people than we have ever done to intimidate Indians," said Lytle during an interview at his home on Frontier Circle.

Rumors have been circulating that Lytle was using the racial issue to oppose Mayor Donald Barnett in the city election. He denied the rumor.

"The mayor could not confront the half-truths and false rhetoric from the militant leaders, but I could," Lytle said. "He had to continue his calm negotiations. We have different views now. You could say we are at a fork in the road, but we are going the same way and we will be back together again."

Barnett agreed, saying, "He took some of the heat off of me for negotiating with the militants."

Lytle repeated several times that the "mayor is very young and dynamic . . . I will not run for his office. I do not wish, nor could I afford, to be mayor."

The moral behavior and lawlessness of the militants was not all that troubled the president of the City Council. Lytle seemed to want to negotiate himself, but he was very disturbed that A.I.M. leaders would not put their demands down in writing.

"I had hoped this would have been kind of like solving the Vietnam War," Lytle explained without humor. "We will do certain things and you do certain things and we will settle this. But we never knew what they wanted . . . They never put anything down in writing when they terrorized our white community. They contradict themselves with false rhetoric . . . but when I speak, I speak the facts."

Lytle grew up in a sod house near the Pine Ridge Reservation, he said, and takes pride in the fact that he attended school with many tribal children. Many were his friends.

180

LaCroix said he grew up during the Depression and lived with many white people. Many of his friends are white.

"Compared to cities in the East," LaCroix explained, "people out here are only about fifty years from the frontier. They are more inclined to take matters of law enforcement into their own hands . . . It makes sense to hold your tongue.

"There are serious concerns beyond the problems raised by the militants, because they have stirred up the old animosities toward Indian people. Many Indian people need the trust of white people to live out here."

The personal tragedies are many and the ironies are fathomless. Lytle emphasized that hundreds of tribal people have called him in opposition to the militants, while LaCroix pointed out that hundreds of white people have called him, willing to offer assistance to stop the militants—

181

including a group of white vigilante cowboys who were ready for a shoot-out at sundown on Main Street. LaCroix held his tongue; Lytle did not.

The Black Hills are white, and it will take a long time to discover the depths of racism and even longer to change it. Rapid City has many good people working on the problems. Lytle should join an encounter group and take a course in human relations to learn how to listen. Tribal people have been asking for equal justice for centuries. Lytle has even closed off the screaming.

1973

✛ Urban Radicals on Reservations

The American Indian Movement is a radical urban organization whose followers have dreamed of returning to the
ideal reservation as the new tribal warriors.

Reservations are not ideal, and the behavior and political
rhetoric of the urban militants does not reflect direct personal reservation life experiences. Many of the militant
leaders were radicalized in prison and found white people
the first to listen.

The political ideologies of the militants is a reaction to
racism—that much all tribal people have in common—and
to prison life and the experiences of alienation in urban
centers. The language of the leaders was not learned from
tribal people on reservations.

The simulation of a new tribal warrior captured the
imaginations of many romantic white people. Supporting
tribal symbols and traditional dreams were no sacrifice on
the part of the dominant white society.

Dressed in turn-of-the-century tribal vestments and telling of past atrocities in the first person, militant leaders
have led a revolutionary caravan of young adventurers
from a series of symbolic confrontations with white people
and institutions to confrontations with elected tribal leaders on reservations.

From Plymouth Rock to Wounded Knee the rhetoric, the
constituents, the enemy, the audience and the problems
and solutions have changed from place to place.

183

WHO ARE THE CONSTITUENTS?

The militants speak a language of confrontation and urban politics. They were not elected to speak for reservation tribal people, nor were they appointed to represent the feelings and political views of elected tribal officials.

When the militants provided services to urban people, they were supported and defended by those they served. Since the direct services have ended and the issues have become symbolic, the constituents have become the followers, and they change with each confrontation. The followers are young and alienated. Many have dropped out of high school, and some have dropped out of college, to be part of what they believe is a revolution.

There is no formal constituency, but many urban and reservation tribal people share the excitement and the dreams that white people and tribal leaders will change. Those tribal people who have suffered the greatest misfortune in a racist society are the strongest supporters of the militants.

WHO IS THE ENEMY?

When the Movement was first organized eight years ago, the enemy was white and the problems were poverty and oppression.

Since then the leaders have tired of railing against white people and have redefined the enemy. Elected reservation tribal leaders have become the new enemy.

The appeal to higher authority has also changed in the past few years. Militant leaders once called upon white people for money and reservation leaders for support, but now the militants are calling upon the federal government to remove tribal leaders from elected reservation offices.

Militants have charged Richard Wilson, elected president of the Oglala Sioux on the Pine Ridge Reservation, with alleged corruption and nepotism.

George Mitchell, one of the founders of the American Indian Movement

Wilson was elected after defeating five candidates in a primary election. Wilson has said that the militants "believe in paternalism" because they have called upon the federal government to challenge the elections on a reservation.

White people seem to find it easier to support militant demands for the removal of tribal leaders from office than to accept themselves as the enemy.

When tribal people are successful in the dominant society and accepted by white people, they are not always understood by reservation people. Tribal people who have stayed on the reservation very often speak traditional tribal languages. Few militants speak traditional languages, and to reservation leaders *they* have become the enemy. But in time the militants may unite with elected tribal leaders and redefine the old enemy—white people.

Militant leaders are coming back to reservations with the consciousness and idealism of urban politics. Tribal leaders are charged with corruption and nepotism, and now the militants are demanding that white people solve the problems on reservations.

But not all militant leaders have deserted programs and services in the urban centers for an audience of white people. In a few cities militants have supported symbolic confrontations while maintaining the support of urban tribal people through continued services.

Eddie Benton, director of the St. Paul chapter of the American Indian Movement, has led and participated in many confrontations while carrying on an impressive cultural education program for tribal young people. He has also directed a legal-advocates program for juveniles and advises public-school officials on cultural activities.

The dedicated experience of urban militant leaders is needed in the urban centers to continue the work that was started ten years ago.

The only way to learn the language of reservation politics is to move back. Symbolic confrontations bring national attention to problems, but institutional changes require more than an audience with government authorities.

Many reservation leaders who have been criticized by militants have been reelected to tribal offices. Reservation people get what they vote for—urban tribal ideologies will not change that. Reservations are functional for the people who live there, and favoritism toward friends and relatives is often a way of life.

Rather than calling on the federal government to solve the problems on reservations, the militants should be negotiating with Wilson and the Pine Ridge Reservation Tribal Council for changes. The federal government has been the problem on most reservations for more than a century. The source of the disease is not the cure.

"The present occupation of Wounded Knee is more a symptom than a problem in itself," said Senator Edward Kennedy in a prepared statement. It is the surfacing of a "hundred years of submerged oppression, dissatisfaction and resistance to assimilation."

Resisting assimilation, the urban militant leaders have declared sovereignty at Wounded Knee. The symbols will never be buried again, but reservation life and politics will probably go on as usual when the militants return to the city.

1973

✛ Candidate Russell Means

What began as a symbolic occupation of Wounded Knee to protest the oppression by federal and tribal governments may soon become a radical political movement with a reservation government of its own.

An analysis of the primary election returns from the Pine Ridge Reservation indicates that Russell Means, a leader of the American Indian Movement, which declared a sovereign nation at Wounded Knee last year, probably will be elected president of the Oglala Sioux Tribal Council.

Means, who is on trial in federal court for alleged violations of federal laws in connection with the occupation of Wounded Knee, is challenging incumbent president Richard Wilson in one of the most sensational tribal elections in reservation history. Means is a defendant in federal court and a candidate for the same political reasons—to change the leadership and form of government on the Pine Ridge Reservation.

The candidate Means announced at least three dramatic things he will do if he is elected president of the Oglala Sioux Tribal Council:

Abolish his job and establish a traditional form of consensual government with a rotating presidency;

Establish "customs checkpoints" around the reservation, prohibiting the transportation and sale of alcoholic beverages or drugs;

Investigate the use of tribal lands and "jerk those leases" held by white people living off the reservation.

In short phrases, mixed with radical-urban and conservative-reservation political metaphors, Means argues that the existing tribal government is oppressive and corrupt because it was established by the federal government. In his view, the Oglala Sioux people have never accepted the existing constitutional government on the Pine Ridge Reservation because it has violated the sovereignty of traditional hereditary leaders. The constitution of the Oglala Sioux Tribe was approved in 1935 by a vote of 1,348 to 1,041.

Means will prohibit alcohol and drugs because, he said, most crimes are "alcohol related . . ." He emphasized that with prohibition "crime will disappear" on the reservation. Treating the symptoms is not always the cure, but it may garner the sympathy of whites and draw votes from prohibitionists.

His third campaign announcement reflects a century of agony over the sale and leasing of tribal lands, which has left tribal people in this nation landless on their own reservations.

But, the hopeful and aggressive candidate said in a much softer voice, "Nothing is going to happen overnight."

Presidents of the Oglala Sioux are elected for two-year terms. In more than three decades of the constitutional government that was established by authority of the Indian Reorganization Act of 1934 under the colonial administration of the Bureau of Indian Affairs, no elected president has ever succeeded himself in office on the Pine Ridge Reservation.

"Two years as an elected tribal leader is just long enough to be oppressive," said Sam Deloria, director of the American Indian Law Center at the University of New Mexico, "but not long enough to get anything done."

189

Means opposes the Indian Reorganization Act. It is not so much the act, but the way it has been administered by federal agents for the Bureau of Indian Affairs, that is the problem. The act provides that a reservation tribe "shall have the right to organize for its common welfare, and may adopt an appropriate constitution and bylaws . . ." In the past the federal government influenced what has been "appropriate." If a majority of tribal people support a consensual or parliamentary form of government, then that should be appropriate for that reservation.

Students at the American Indian Law Center point out that the act created the authority to establish constitutional governments on reservations and in fact recognizes inherent tribal sovereignty.

Exuberant over his victory in the primary election, which he said was a mandate to dismiss all charges against him in federal court, candidate Means, like many politicians, may be promising more than time and experience will allow. In two years, but not overnight for sure, he said he will change the tribal government, cause crime to disappear and recover leased land. Promises may be difficult to keep.

If defendant Means is found guilty of violating federal laws, there will be arguments over the interpretation of the Oglala Sioux Tribal constitution, which states that "any member of the tribal council who is convicted of a felony or any other offense involving dishonesty shall forfeit his office."

If elected, and once in office, Means must abide by the constitution that sanctioned his election. The existing constitution, designed by anthropologists for the Bureau of Indian Affairs and adopted by many tribal groups, does not provide a clear separation of powers: Judicial, legislative and executive authority rests with the elected tribal council. The president of the council may vote only in case of a tie. The president could call for a referendum to amend the constitution or to hold a constitutional convention to plan a

190

new government, but such an action would first require a petition signed by eligible voters on the reservation.

All of those potential actions will require interpreters to translate and explain in Lakota—the tribal language spoken by more than half of the people on the Pine Ridge Reservation—the legal problems in forming a new government.

Richard Wilson, the incumbent, is the first mixedblood president who does not speak Lakota. If Means defeats Wilson, he will be the second mixedblood president who does not speak the language of the people.

But even in English, without an interpreter, according to the results of the primary vote, Means may have communicated more than enough hope, through his vociferous allegations of corruption among tribal officials, not only to win the election, but also to change the form of government that has been identified with the colonial exploitation of tribal lands by federal agents.

In the election a vote for Means may be a vote against Wilson and alleged corruption, but the votes may not necessarily indicate support for a new consensual government of hereditary tribal leaders.

It is conceivable that Means could use the existing constitutional election only to defeat Wilson, and then, if the entire council and a majority of the voters agree, he could reject the existing constitution and operate as an unofficial consensual government. What troubles some observers about radical governmental reform is the possible interruption of income and federal services to citizens on the reservation.

Few tribal governments have a stable administrative bureaucracy, because the federal government has controlled the delivery of services to the reservation. Idealists argue that there should be a clear division of executive, legislative and judicial functions in tribal governments and a reservation civil service system with political immunity. As it is, the spoils system operates on many reservations.

191

Means has distinguished himself as a resolute radical organizer and leader, but when it comes to political diplomacy outside the militant camp and the management of government programs in health, education, welfare, economic development, law enforcement and transportation, his skills are less obvious.

If Means becomes president of the Oglala Sioux Tribe, changing the form of government will be only the beginning. It will not be enough to show his sorrow and anger to white audiences for the suffering of his people. Offering hope to tribal people on the reservation may obligate him and every radical to produce more than anyone has ever produced in the past.

1974

✚ Speaking for Mother Earth

*If the indigenous way of life has been subjected to
misery, persecution and other adversities, the people
seek relief—from their frustrations and sufferings in
religious ways . . .*

VITTORIO LANTERNARI

The American Indian Movement has a new image. Since
the occupation of Wounded Knee, radical leaders of the
movement have been speaking a mellow language of spiritual revivalism.

After several years of angry and violent confrontations
and condemnations of dominant social values and institutions, Russell Means and Dennis Banks, in their opening
statements to jurors in federal court and in public
speeches, are now emphasizing in prophetic monotones
their traditional religious connections with Mother Earth
and the regeneration of tribal values and life styles.

Banks and Means, radical leaders of the movement,
were on trial in federal court for alleged violations of federal laws in connection with the occupation of Wounded
Knee.

Means, in his opening statement to the jurors, said, "We
believe that all living things come from our sacred Mother
Earth . . . the green things, the winged things of the air,

193

the four-leggeds, the things that crawl and swim and, of course, the two-leggeds . . .

"It is our philosophy that because all living things come from one mother, our Mother Earth . . . we have to treat one another with the same respect and reverence that we would our own blood relatives.

"But the important thing in our philosophy is that we believe we're the weakest things on earth, that the two-legged is the weakest thing on earth because we have no direction."

In poetic metaphors Means expressed a collective tribal consciousness that there is spiritual significance in every form of life.

"We have looked around us and . . . we saw that every living thing has direction and a role in life to play. The green things, the sacred cottonwood trees, the eagle . . . the spider, the snake all have a direction and role in life, every one of them" except the two-legged people.

"And so we built our civilization on what they could teach us, and this is our philosophy . . . because we are the weakest things on the earth, we do not have a license to exploit or manipulate our brothers and sisters . . .

"And so the spirituality of the red man is why we welcomed with open arms the man from across the sea . . . in every instance we welcomed him."

Means went on to tell the jurors in the undulating tones of an evangelist that the treaty rights that protect traditional tribal life have been violated throughout history by the federal government.

Banks, a Minnesota Chippewa, told the jurors that he now is a member of the traditional Oglala Sioux Sun Dance religion, which he said is a "very sacred religious event where men warriors offer themselves to the great spirit to seek a vision . . .

"We must prove to Mother Earth and all the female objects of this planet, to all the female things . . . the men

194

warriors would like to share some of the pain . . . that our mothers had when we were born."

The Sun Dance is a ceremony in which vows are made in the belief that spiritual visions will follow. Some participants in the ritual, puncture the skin on the chest with a wooden skewer—which is then tied to a sacred tree—and dance in the circle of the sun until the skewers are torn from the flesh.

"The piercing of the skin," Banks told the jurors, "is a reminder to me that I truly owe myself to Mother Earth . . . and when the flesh was torn from me I suddenly realized what a great sin, what a great injustice, it would be to lose the Oglala Sioux religion."

While Banks may reflect a sexist male-dominant view by referring to women as "objects" and "things," he appears to be a man of peace and spiritual visions. He no longer rails at white people in an angry voice, and he no longer practices disruptive tactics at public meetings. He speaks in mellow tones now, and his gestures are gentle.

Tribal people have suffered and survived the oppressive subterfuge and malignant deception of the federal government—they have survived the shifting policies of cultural genocide and segregation on reservations and forced assimilation.

A century ago tribal people were slaughtered by federal troops and given poisoned food and blankets infected with smallpox disease. Tribal children on reservations were forced to attend federal schools, where they were given arbitrary English-language names and forbidden to speak the languages of their visions and dreams.

Tribal people everywhere share a growing collective consciousness of oppression, and some have responded to cultural genocide and racism with violence and spiritual movements.

The American Indian Movement, presented by Means and Banks as a new tribal spiritual revival, may become one of many religious groups in tribal history that have re-

195

sponded to oppression with a collective spiritual belief that the traditions of the past will be regenerated.

At the turn of the century, followers of the Ghost Dance religion on the plains believed that the white man would be exterminated and that tribal lands and sacred traditions would return. They fought the white man and lost.

In contrast to the Ghost Dance, the tribal followers of Peyotism—a subsequent spiritual movement based on visions and hallucinations that is now identified as the Native American Church—did not oppose the white man with violence, but believed in an adjustment to existing conditions of life with religious independence.

Leaders of the American Indian Movement may have learned from history and experience that the white man cannot be defeated by force or political rhetoric. The mellow vision of a religious revival is not only a good defense posture in federal court, but a strong connection with the growing expressions of spritiualism rather than materialism.

1974

PART 4
NATIVE AMERICAN EDUCATION

✛ Senator Mondale at Rough Rock

You damage a child still more when you destroy
his first stone of identity, when you tell him his
language is no good, when you tell him that his
color is not right or imply it by surrounding him
with people of a different color, habits, and status.
You tell him that what his parents have taught him
is no good, that he should not do so and so, or be
what is.

KARL MENNINGER
Menninger Foundation

"These children aren't as unhappy as people say they are
. . . they're only lonely for about a month." The principal
of the Tuba City, Arizona, Bureau of Indian Affairs boarding school was speaking, first brushing the ubiquitous Arizona dust off his desk.

"Senator, look out here," he said, next brushing the dust
from his hands, "do you see any lonesome, poorly kept
children?"

Outside, a neat column of Navajo children moved past
the window. The March wind tossed their hair. Nothing
else seemed spontaneous.

One thousand Navajo children attend the Tuba City
boarding school. Less than half speak English when they

arrive, but their native language soon becomes secondary
. . . something less than English. The Indian parents have
no voice in the way their children are efficiently central-
ized, processed and alienated in a white school environment. Happiness and education are systematically measured by career bureaucrats, many of whom have no
sensitivity or training in education. Cultural brutalization
begins.

Minnesota's Senator Walter F. Mondale, a member of
the special Subcommittee on Indian Education of the Committee on Labor and Public Welfare, had been told that the
Tuba City school was one of the worst in the federal system. He went to Arizona specifically to compare federal
schools to the Rough Rock Navajo Demonstration School
which is entirely run by the people—that is, the Indians
themselves.

The Tuba City principal, leading Mondale on a tour of
the classrooms, pointed with pride to a plywood hogan
built in the corner of one room. The *token* hogan, you
might say. "You know," the principal ventured pleasantly,
"it sure is interesting how the children first use the modern
kitchen play things and then inevitably return to the
hogan."

Later in the day Mondale flew over Black Mountain to
meet with the all Navajo elected school board at Rough
Rock. He was accompanied by a member of his staff, a reporter, and Dr. Robert L. Bergman, Public Health psychiatrist on the Navajo reservation.

Four of the five Navajo school board members at Rough
Rock do not speak English and have never been to a formal
school. Through an interpreter, Mondale learned about the
people's school.

"When I travel here I see the mountains," said school
board member John Dick, "and I cannot see what goes on
in Washington . . . They have been operating schools for
over one hundred years. We have never been part. The

school here is open to everyone . . . you'll see the difference.

"We have four kinds of schools—long coats schools,
Washington schools, white schools, and the people's
schools . . . In our school here we talk about the identity,
the Indian identity. Children knowing who they are, that's
what's important. They will be better off in the world . . .
This is good for the people."

Through the interpreter Mondale told John Dick that his
description was the best he had heard. "Until parents feel
it is *their* school we will not reach anyone. You have done
us a favor showing America the truth about education.
Your school is a symbol of quality in Indian education."

Mondale asked the school board members if they would
trust the Bureau of Indian Affairs if the Bureau admitted it
had been wrong about education and said it would
change. The laughter needed no interpretation.

During the five hours the board and Mondale met, more
than fifty parents and teachers gathered to listen. John
Dick invited Mondale to continue the late hour discussion
in a traditional sweat house. "We could both use it,"
Mondale said, slapping his stomach. But there wasn't
room for an interpreter in the sweat house. Next day
Mondale attended a sand painting ceremony at the hogan
of John Dick held in honor of a child who had laughed for
the first time. Rough Rock was originally built by the Bureau of Indian Affairs but, before it opened, it was turned
over to the Navajo in 1966. It has been operated by the
people on an experimental basis for two years. Funds are
provided by the Bureau, the Office of Economic Opportunity, and private foundations.

The curriculum is based on the people's language and
heritage. The comforts of education are identity. Students
are encouraged rather than punished for speaking their
native language. The more than four hundred students at
Rough Rock receive instruction in both Navajo and English, since in Arizona it is unlawful to teach in a foreign

Navajo children at Rough Rock

language unless it is a second language. The principal at the Bureau school at Rock Point, the third institution Mondale visited, said the Bureau attitude is that it does "not intend to be an ambulance for a dying language." Contrary to Bureau tradition, the principal *has* made an effort to teach Navajo in his school.

Medicine man and board member Ashie Tsosie said: "We like the older folks to teach our children philosophy." Medicine men can train students at the Rough Rock school. In every classroom there is a Navajo mother at a loom. While the women weave and tell the legends of the people, the children listen and learn in the Navajo tradition by watching.

At the Tuba City boarding school there are only two

202

Navajo teachers. The Agency Superintendent, who is not an educator, said they have a problem getting qualified Navajo teachers "because they get the bright lights in their eyes and stay in the cities." At Rough Rock more than half of the teachers are qualified Navajos.

Board member Yazzie Begay told Mondale that the Navajo teachers came to Rough Rock because "they don't have traditional things in other schools."

About half of the employees in the Bureau of Indian Affairs are of Indian descent. Only sixteen percent of the teachers are Indian. Less than five percent of those teachers are assigned to teach in their own tribal groups. Federal civil service requires efficient random placement of teachers.

At Rough Rock the parents take an active part in the school and work in the dormitories. The principal at Tuba City said some parents visit. "We have an open door policy, but they don't often stay over night because they want to get back to the sheep."

When Mondale left, the Tuba City boarding school classes were over for the day. The recreation room was closed and the playground was empty. The only children in sight on a warm spring day were those doing exercises in front of a dormitory.

Two weeks later, during a session of the Subcommittee on Indian Education, Mondale told the Commissioner of Indian Affairs what he saw and felt at Tuba City and Rough Rock.

"It was the difference between a semi-military setting and a setting which was the kind that one would want to educate his own children in," Mondale told Commissioner Robert L. Bennett.

"In the Bureau of Indian Affairs system I found only two Navajo teachers . . . In the smaller Rough Rock school, I found ten Navajo teachers . . . in the dormitories in Tuba City, I found cold, really humaneless structures for these children . . . at Rough Rock . . . they used the mothers and parents of the community to live with the children so that they had a friend, a supporter, counselor and adult, just like every child needs at that age.

"They have a permissive environment . . . the parents were encouraged to sleep over night with the kids. Wherever you went, Navajos were moving freely in and out of the classrooms. I didn't see any of that at the Tuba City school.

"I saw an exciting bi-lingual program at Rough Rock . . . Navajo textbooks developed by Navajo illustrators and under the supervision of Navajo leadership. I saw the creative use of local Navajo talents, so that side by side with the white teacher or with the Navajo teacher there was a mother teaching arts and crafts and telling the traditional stories of Navajo lore.

"I saw exciting adult education systems at Rough Rock, not at Tuba City.

"I saw a system at Rough Rock where *they* hired and fired the teacher, where the school board determined the policy, what I hear at the Tuba City school was all to the contrary.

"More than all of that and in an indefinable way, I saw a spirit and pride and excitement of people who realized for the first time they had something to say about their own lives.

"I think the difference was the difference between night and day. I am not an expert in the field, but I think I know how to assess human feeling. I came away from Rough Rock committed to doing the best I could to tell the American people what I saw."

Commissioner Bennett quickly agreed with Mondale, but in the same sentence he defended the Bureau and testified that the subcommittee should also look at public schools where Indian children are educated and supply the Bureau with more money to do the job right.

"I don't have any argument at all . . . because this is the

same goal to which we are working as far as the Bureau of Indian Affairs schools are concerned," Bennett testified.

The Bureau of Indian Affairs, which operates through Division of Land Management under the Department of the Interior, has been laying the quoins of an inflexible bureacracy for more than a century. Indians expect to see the day when there will be more Bureau employees than Indians. Indians frequently contend that if all the Indians left the United States it would take the Bureau a century to phase itself out of existence.

Bennett said he graduated from a federal boarding school and has worked for the Bureau for thirty-six years. He is of Indian descent. In a speech in Minneapolis shortly after he became Commissioner, he was not critical of the Indian policies of the past because, he said then, he thought the "policies of the past were well intentioned."

"The motivation was good and so were *all* the people. There is no question that the decisions which were made many years ago were the best that could be made at that point in history."

The Commissioner probably did not intentionally mean to include the autonomous authority of Indian agents on the reservation, inhuman tribal relocations, exploitation of Indian land, suppression of Indian language and religion, and cultural genocide.

Now that the dominant society seems bored with suppressing Indians and making them white, the Bureau stands between the people and their ambition to run their own lives. The burdens of the people are many, but Rough Rock is a symbol that Indians are alive and breathing on at least one reservation.

Testifying before the Subcommittee, Bennett said he believed "there had been" an attitude of paternalism by the Bureau, but he stated that "this was one of the attitudes which had to be eliminated . . . and for three years I have worked on it."

205

"We are performing to the maximum of our ability with the resources that are available," he testified, adding that he believes the Bureau can manage the problems of Indian people.

Before the Subcommittee Bennett took credit for creating a full division of education within the Bureau; he was agreeable to criticism of the Bureau from members of the Subcommittee, but blamed everything on the "various winds" and unthinking critics.

"Indian needs are so many and varied one scarcely knows where to begin . . . we get swept around by the various winds and currents of the national policy," he told the Subcommittee.

Bennett himself is symbolically the best measure of the Bureau and its relationship to Indians. He sidesteps criticism, speaks like a bureaucrat carrying out policy directives on the one hand, and pretends that Indians are planning and making the decisions for the Bureau on the other. He is not unkind, but defensive, confused, inconsistent and difficult to follow. Indians educated by and working for the Bureau strongly support him, others want to believe him because he is an Indian, but Bennett is unclear. His language shows his own identity problem.

He refers to the "profoundness" of the Indian in his testimony, but it would take more than a profound Indian to unravel the policies and guidelines of the Bureau.

Bennett does not question the intentions of his administrators and seems to believe that the Bureau has never made mistakes. He testified that the "current critics in Indian affairs tend to blame the education programs of the Bureau of Indian Affairs for all the social, economic and political ills of Indian people that, in actuality, are the cumulative results of a century of neglect, misunderstanding, prejudice and paternalism."

"*I am not very profound in Indian affairs,*" the Commissioner of Indian Affairs told the Subcommittee, "because I have been associated with *them* too long and that during this period of association I have developed a great respect for their profoundness."

But Bennett has not demonstrated his respect for that "profoundness" by allowing the people to run their own schools. He testified that it is the policy of the Bureau to move toward local control only if the tribe requests it.

Mondale, pointing out that the year before President Johnson directed the Secretary of the Interior to establish Indian school boards for federal Indian schools, asked Bennett how many school boards have been established.

Bennett: "So far, there have been two established because of the guidelines necessary to implement the President's message."

Mondale: "One of them is at Rough Rock. Where is the other one?"

Bennett: "Blackwater on the Pima Reservation."

Mondale: "At the present rate of establishing the school boards, how long will it be before the President's directive is fully carried out?"

Bennett: ". . . *we leave this up to the Indian people.* We don't believe that we should go out and force them into school boards."

Mondale: "Are the Indians resisting local control?"

Bennett: "There are a variety of reactions . . . *our policy* is not to force this upon them. *They have the guidelines* and the appropriate requirements for applying for the administration of their schools."

Mondale: "Is it the intention of the Bureau of Indian Affairs that the so-called advisory boards come within the meaning of the President's directive?"

Bennett: "No sir; it is not. These are strictly people *selected* at large from the Indian community that advise us in the development of *our* educational policies and also *our* school operations . . ."

Mondale: "I was very impressed by the pride and the involvement of the board of education at Rough Rock and the parents in the community. If there is anything I heard from everyone I talked to, it was their pride and delight for the first time in their history of having something to say about the quality and direction and sensitivity in the education of their own children, *something which every other American has had for generations.*

"What is it about Indians that makes them any less desirous of local control and having something to say about the education of their children than anyone else in this country?"

Bennett: "I don't think there is any difference. I think *they* have wanted to do this for a long time. This is why *we* have the present policy."

Mondale: "Why has a century gone by and yet there are only two systems in the country where that is true?"

Bennett: "It might be because of the fact for many years *American Indians did not accept an education program of any kind."*

Mondale: "Is it your testimony that the Indians didn't want their children educated?"

Bennett: "My testimony is they evidently weren't satisfied with the education they were getting because *they* weren't sending *them* to school."

Mondale: "I think that is right. I agree with that . . ."

Bennett testified that when the Bureau tried to bring Indian heritage and bilingual education into the educational system "there was an uproar in education circles about the fact that *we* were trying to teach Indians to be Indians . . . we get swept around by the various winds . . . "

Mondale: "Right. As long as it is federally controlled, it will continue to be, won't it? In other words, if the Indian children of this country are going to be educated pursuant to the *notions of the current white power structure that controls Washington,* you are going to have winds of change for the next century . . .

"No other parents have that problem. If you told the school district where I was educated that we had to have a handy-dandy new national policy which was going to be

Navajo federal boarding school

controlled from Washington, complete in every detail—
hiring, firing, curriculum and the rest—and that the bud-
get bureau in Washington was going to determine through
some unknown bureaucrat the nature of our education,
you would have a *revolution, you would have a war, and I
think it would be a justified one.* Yet, this has been going on
for a century in Indian education."

1969

✛ Red Lake Truant Officer

The truant officer for the Red Lake public school looked over his list of absentees for Tuesday.

Sixty-nine absent—about 10 percent of the student body. An average day. Absenteeism is highest on Mondays and during the wild rice harvest, he said.

Raymond Oliver knows where just about every family lives on the reservation. As he drove from house to house he talked about his job as a truant officer.

"Most of these kids are bright but they don't have the initiative to stay in school," he said.

His first stop was at a new three-bedroom home. He picked up a fifteen-year-old boy who said he had overslept. Oliver drove him back to school. The boy had missed eleven days of school in three months.

"I don't care what culture or society you come from, the problem all goes back to the family," Oliver said as he stopped in front of a home near the sawmill.

He knocked on the door and stepped in. No one was there.

Next stop was a two-room tarpaper house buried in the snow. An old man met the truant officer on the road. He seemed to recite. He said his granddaughter was sick. He said she would return to school the next day.

"This is not a job where you make friends. I only took it because no one else wanted it," Oliver said.

210

He retired from the Air Force a few years ago and moved back to the reservation to build a home. His wife is a reservation policewoman and a member of the school board. They have five children.

Oliver works five hours a day as a truant officer and in his spare time supervises the only Boy Scout troop on the reservation.

Next stop was at the home of the Adams family three miles west of the school. A sixteen-year-old girl had been absent for two days and her fifteen-year-old brother had been absent for more than a week.

No smoke was coming from the chimney. The two-room house looked abandoned. Oliver's footsteps squeaked in the snow. The only other sound came from the torn plastic window covering flapping in the cold wind.

It was noon. He knocked and then slowly pushed the door open. The door bumped against the bed where Debbie Adams, an attractive, above-average eleventh grade student was sleeping.

Across the room Patrick Adams, an above-average ninth grader, was buried beneath several blankets, clothing, and a foam rubber pad for warmth.

The house was cold. In the middle of the room was a converted oil barrel wood stove. The fire was out. There was no running water. The outside well was frozen. They had to melt snow for drinking water.

They did not have an axe to split the green logs piled on the front porch. On a box near the stove was an empty pail and a large jar of surplus commodity peanut butter.

Florence Adams and her youngest child were huddled in a third bed. Two other children were sleeping in the second room.

"Are you sick, Pat?" Oliver asked.

"Yes," Patrick answered from beneath the covers.

"Are you going to school tomorrow?"

"Yes . . . I think so," he answered after a long pause.

211

Oliver left the house, checked off the names of Debbie and Patrick on his absentee list and drove to the home of the next student on his list.

"I don't know what's wrong with the mother," Oliver said, "she probably needs some mental therapy. I told the social worker when I was out here last. They were in the same shape then."

Debbie and Patrick's teachers speak of them as good students, mentioning that Patrick shows ability in public speaking. Debbie likes to read. School officials suspected problems in the home but the only person from the school to visit the family was the truant officer.

It is rare that a teacher visits a family on the reservation. Most of the faculty live in nearby towns and leave the reservation at the end of the school day.

Neither absent student complained about school. In evaluating her education, Debbie said the system was too lenient. She said she was rarely assigned homework. She complained that many of the assigned books were the same ones she read in earlier grades when she attended school in Brainerd, Minnesota.

Florence Adams explained that the family had been living in Brainerd until last summer when her husband left her for a younger woman. She said she recently had surgery for an aneurysm.

"I tried to maintain our house . . . the children liked school there," she said resting in bed, "but we were three months behind in the rent.

"Welfare finally helped us, but they couldn't pay the back rent so we had to move."

Debbie and Patrick were bitter about their father leaving the family. They said their home in Brainerd had running water and was always warm. There was so little to worry about there. The family wished they could move into one of the new homes on the reservation.

Patrick has assumed the duties of the man of the house. He feels responsible for his two younger brothers now. He said he would probably end up working in the sawmill on the reservation.

Debbie said she wanted to be an artist when she graduates from high school.

"I would like to go to the Minneapolis School of Art, but I don't like the idea of living in the city," she said.

Leather Indian costumes decorated with beads were hanging in the closet. Since the family moved back to the reservation they had not been able to dance together at a pow wow.

"I did a lot of bead work in Brainerd and we danced all the time," Florence said, "We felt better as Indians there."

1969

✛ Protecting Tribal Identities

Two generations ago tribal children on reservations were forced to attend federal boarding schools away from their traditional homes. At the schools their hair was cut short, and they were given arbitrary names and forbidden to speak tribal languages.

The efforts of the federal government and institutions of the dominant society to force assimilation by invalidating tribal traditions and values have not succeeded. Today, at the beginning of a renaissance of identity, tribal people are more often using the courts and new civil-rights legislation to protect traditional expressions and styles of life.

For example, Chip Pokrywka, and his brother Pat, were expelled from the public elementary school they attended in Keenesburg, Colorado, because the length of their hair did not conform to school policy. The Sioux boys, with the support of their parents and a tribal holy man, have been wearing their hair in traditional tribal braids.

At a hearing on the issue, representatives of the school board defended the policy, emphasizing that short hair on males promotes discipline and orderliness in the school.

Tom Fredericks, a Mandan Indian with long hair and an attorney for the Native American Rights Fund, defended the right of the boys to wear their hair in braids on the grounds of freedom of expression and religion and on grounds of sex discrimination. The length of hair on female students in the same school is not regulated.

Navajo children

Leonard Crow Dog, tribal holy man for the American Indian Movement and religious leader of the two boys, testified before the school board that he taught the boys "the sacred peace pipe and the life of the generations . . . I told them, you must respect your brother's vision and you must observe the sacred things that have been given to the American Indian people."

Crow Dog explained that "the belief the Sioux people have is whenever you cut your hair you mourn any close relation you have . . . That means you are mourning . . . My Indian people never cut their hair . . . We never go to the barber shop and cut our hair and put it down the drainer."

The boys lost their case for masculine pride, religious expression and tribal identity in a white institution. The school board sits in judgment of the merits of its own rule on short hair—a throwback to the arbitrary authority of federal agents on the reservations. If the local juvenile court upholds the decision of the school board, the case will be appealed to the Colorado Court of Appeals.

In a racist society the legal process protecting the rights of tribal identity is expensive and time-consuming, but in the past there were few choices, few privileges of appealing arbitrary and absurd rules—and very little hair.

1973

PART 5
NATURAL TRIBAL RIGHTS

✝ Leech Lake Agreement

Elected representatives of the Leech Lake Reservation have reached a tentative agreement with the Minnesota Department of Natural Resources regarding original treaty rights to hunt, fish and gather wild rice within the boundaries of the reservation.

The agreement, which must be approved by the state legislature, relinquishes the right to commercial fishing within the reservation and includes a special restrictive licensing system.

Simon Howard, President of the Minnesota Chippewa Tribal Executive Committee, and Governor Wendell Anderson announced the agreement at a press conference held on the reservation. David Munnell, Chairman of the Leech Lake Reservation was hospitalized and could not attend the meeting.

Sharing the announcement at the press conference were Robert Herbst, Natural Resources Commissioner, Kent Tupper, attorney for the Leech Lake Reservation, and other officials and visitors from the community, the Leech Lake Reservation Business Committee and the state and federal government.

Governor Anderson listed the following provisions of the agreement:

1. Relinquishment by Leech Lake Indians of any right to commercial fishing within the boundaries of the Leech Lake Reservation.

2. A licensing system which allows the Leech Lake Indians to charge a $1.00 fee for non-Indian hunting and fishing within the reservation.

3. Wild ricing, previously regulated by the state, is to be controlled by the Tribal Conservation Committee.

4. Leech Lake Indians are to have the exclusive rights in the taking of rough fish.

The taking of game and fish by tribal people living on the reservation for their own consumption is to be regulated by the Leech Lake Reservation Tribal Conservation Committee under a new game and fish code for the reservation.

"I believe the settlement serves the best interests of the Leech Lake band and the people of Minnesota," the governor said. "This agreement is fair, it is honorable and in my judgement it is one the legislature and all citizens of Minnesota should support."

Three years ago the Minnesota Chippewa Tribe and the Leech Lake Reservation brought suit against the State of Minnesota, seeking original treaty rights to hunt and fish on the reservation without state restrictions. The tribe was joined by the United States Government in asserting that they were free of all restrictions on the reservation according to treaty rights.

In January 1972 Federal Judge Edward Devitt ruled that the Leech Lake Band of the Minnesota Chippewa Tribe had the right to hunt, fish and gather wild rice on the reservation without restrictions from the state.

Since then the Department of Natural Resources and elected leaders of the Leech Lake Reservation have met to resolve the issue. The agreement reached yesterday must be approved by the state legislature when it convenes next year.

Robert Herbst pointed out that the agreement "envisions full cross-deputization of enforcement officers so that Minnesota enforcement officers will have the power to arrest under the Indian code and trained Indian enforcement officers will have like powers under the Minnesota game and fish laws.

The agreement further provides, Herbst continued, "a licensing system permitting the Indian Band to charge an extra fee for non-Indian hunting and fishing within the reservation.

"The state will sell this license and will turn the proceeds over to the Band. Although the parties have agreed that the Band may charge as much as fifty percent of the existing state resident license fee, the Band has stated that it intends to charge $1.00 on all licenses.

Reviewing the history of the issue, Simon Howard pointed out that "in effect we offered the same plan to the state about two years ago with no money payment attached, but they (the state) were good enough to refuse it then and now we have the money."

Referring to the elected reservation leaders, Governor Anderson said "they were the toughest possible negotiators, but they always demonstrated understanding . . . they represented their people well."

The governor said that "while the tentative accord applies only to the Leech Lake area, we are hopeful that the pattern established here will be adopted for all open reservations in Minnesota."

Herbst emphasized that under the agreement as approved, "no resident of Minnesota will forego any right which he now possesses.

"Nothing has been taken from the non-Indian citizens of the state and the rights of the Indian community are fully recognized.

"The new licensing system will allow the state to insure the protection of our resources by banning commercial taking of game and game fish."

Simon Howard explained that the tribe has never been interested in commercial fishing. "Everybody is worried about the amount of fishing done by Indians," he said. "We have taken a survey which shows that only about two

221

percent of the reservation population engages in hunting and fishing, which is minimal and will not deplete the fish and game population."

The agreement reached yesterday includes the original treaty boundaries of the reservation. Generally these boundaries run west from Boy River south of Leech Lake through Walker Bay, and then northwest through Kabekona Bay; the line that generally runs north through Steamboat Lake including Cass Lake, Little Wolf, Big Lake and west including Winnibigoshish. The boundaries also include Round and Bow String Lakes and south including Ball Club Lake.

1972

✛ Treaties and Tribal Rights

In the past century the federal government negotiated several treaties with tribal people for land. Reservations were created in exchange for large woodland areas in the state.

Since then tribal ownership of reservation land has been diminished, but recent federal court decisions have protected the rights of tribal people to use the natural resources within the original boundaries established by treaties.

Recognition of these rights has compelled the state government to negotiate for the public use of tribal lands rather than assuming jurisdiction over natural resources on reservations.

Tribal leaders are now more cautious in negotiating with the state than their grandparents were when they signed treaties with the federal government.

For example, the Minnesota Chippewa Tribe has opposed the offer to negotiate a special state hunting and fishing license for use on all six reservations within the jurisdiction of the unified tribal governments.

The White Earth Reservation filed a suit in federal court claiming that the Minnesota Department of Natural Resources does not have jurisdiction to regulate or enforce state game and fish laws within the original boundaries of the reservation.

Robert Herbst, Commissioner of Natural Resources, who argued against a similar suit involving the Leech Lake

David Munnell and Simon Howard, 1972

Reservation, disagrees with the claim that tribal people have sovereign jurisdiction over natural resources on the White Earth Reservation.

In the Leech Lake suit the court ruled that the rights of tribal people to hunt and fish and to gather wild rice have survived federal legislation and other jurisdictional claims to reservation land within the original boundaries of the treaties. The rights to hunt and fish were not subject to state jurisdiction. Herbst and tribal leaders negotiated a settlement that permits the public to hunt and fish on the Leech Lake Reservation with the purchase of a special license.

224

State officials are now concerned that if White Earth wins its case in federal court, tribal leaders may then demand an agreement similar to the one negotiated with Leech Lake. Herbst has argued that the prospect of issuing several special licenses for hunting and fishing on different reservations would be a difficult and complex system to administer.

In a recent letter to Harry Boness, president of the Minnesota Chippewa Tribe, Herbst encouraged tribal leaders to consider an agreement that would "permit the state to offer a basic unrestricted hunting and fishing license valid on all reservations involved."

But tribal leaders emphasize that not all reservation governments in the state are interested in opening their lands and resources to public tourism and recreation. White Earth, for example, does not attract as many tourists or people who hunt and fish as does Leech Lake, and may choose to close the reservation to the public.

The Grand Portage Reservation has for several years controlled its own natural resources by issuing special tribal hunting and fishing permits to nonmembers of the tribe and may consider that the state plan of one basic license for use on all reservations is not in their best interests.

The Minnesota Chippewa Tribe is a unified constitutional federation of six elected reservation governments in the state—Leech Lake, White Earth, Mille Lacs, Nett Lake, Fond du Lac and Grand Portage.

Kent Tupper, legal counsel for the tribe, told Herbst in a letter that the state must resolve hunting and fishing rights with each reservation government, "which does not necessarily mean a complex state licensing system."

Tribal leaders have indicated that none of the reservation governments has expressed a desire to enter into special licensing agreements with the state.

A century ago, Tupper said in his letter, the United States first entered into treaties with the whole tribe and then later entered into treaties with smaller individual tribal groups, or bands, for areas of land sought by the government.

"The Minnesota Chippewa Tribe," the letter said, "in recognition of the fact that hunting and fishing treaty rights should be regulated by the appropriate reservation tribal governments, has delegated all tribal authority over hunting, fishing, trapping and gathering of wild rice" to the six individual reservation governments.

Because of the unique status of each reservation and because of differences in land-ownership patterns affecting the development of natural resources, it appears that tribal leaders may have obligated the state to negotiate with each reservation for the possible public use of tribal lands.

1974

PART 6
TRIBAL PARAECONOMICS

✛ Custer Died for Pantribal Pop

Harold Goodsky was born in a small village on the Nett Lake Reservation in Minnesota. The first language he spoke was *anishinaabe*, the woodland language of the tribal people now named the Chippewa. Goodsky first saw the world through the humor and spiritual power of tribal families, but these traditional identities were not enough to survive.

Goodsky needed money. When he was ten years old he embarked on a capitalistic adventure of capturing frogs— his first foray in the commercial language of economic exploitation of natural resources.

Goodsky was a paraeconomic survivor. (The meaning of paraeconomic is derived from the combined definition of being irregular and dependent on the dominant economic systems of production, consumption of goods and services, and the distribution of wealth.) There were two ways for young Goodsky to earn honest money on the reservation: he could have worked for corrupt tribal capitalists or for corrupt white capitalists. Tourists had more money so he decided to sell frogs to white people fishing on the reservation. His paraeconomic aspirations in the reservation frog market were inflated. His first commercial venture was a failure.

"We were in the frog relocation business," Goodsky explained. "But on our way to the white market we bumped into a giant bear and dropped our frogs . . . we lost every-

Harold Goodsky in Minneapolis, 1967

thing." The frogs jumped home to a cool tribal ending in a placid pond.

Goodsky was influenced by the dominant capitalistic system. Discouraged by his experience in the frog market he earned money cleaning boats for white people, collecting beverage bottles and selling his own authentic tribal made sling shots to tourists. His simple objective was to earn money to survive in a new mechanical culture. Trees are cut and sacred mesas are stripmined for the same reasons.

Leaving the reservation for military service, Goodsky has since worked in corrections and social service programs in urban centers. He is now a college student. His capitalistic interests have shifted from frogs to the production and sale of tribal pop sweat shirts and bumper stickers inscribed with racial and cultural bromides. His market is much wider than the reservation. Goodsky travels to national tribal peepshows and conferences and earns several hundred dollars from the sale of his printed novelties.

"Indian and Proud," Goodsky said, has been his best selling bumper sticker. Two other pantribal pop bromides have also been selling well, they are: "Custer Wore Arrow Shirts," and "Custer is Alive and Well in Washington."

From the reservation frog market to commercial pantribal pop, Goodsky remains a traditional person in his religious beliefs. He speaks the woodland language of his people and participates in tribal social and ceremonial events on the reservation. *Anishinaabe wanaki*, a place of peace among woodland family people.

In the past twenty years Goodsky has lived under the jurisdiction of four governments. He has also experienced the effects of segregation, assimilation, termination, cultural pluralism and several other federal policies.

Tribal people must respond to federal policies and jurisdictional caveats as an act of paraeconomic survival, while re-echoing the claims of exploitive state and local governments, and, unlike white people, be responsive to reservation governments and corrupt tribal officials.

Tribal reservations may be the least tolerable environments for anarchists. There is too much government, too many jurisdictional arguments, and too few individual rights. Notwithstanding the grim realities of reservation life, thousands of tribal people have survived with high spirits and good humor. Three generations after his death,

231

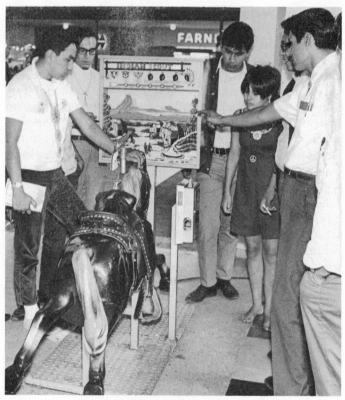

Harold Goodsky and Clyde Bellecourt inspecting 'Indian Scout' at Apache Plaza shopping center in Minneapolis, 1969

General Custer is helping Goodsky supplement his income.

The federal government adopted termination policies while Goodsky was capturing frogs and selling sling shots. His paraeconomic survival was little changed by federal resolutions. While he was serving in military service the government shifted from termination to policies of assimilation and self-determination.

Goodsky and thousands of tribal people have prospered in the dominant culture from assimilation programs—from termination. He is now a paraeconomic survivor with a college scholarship and a thriving pantribal pop business. At the same time he expresses good humor he shows deep bitterness because of the racist policies which keep so many tribal people poor and dependent on federal exclaves.

"The world has changed more on paper than it has on the reservation," said Goodsky who is a romantic participant in tribal nostalgia. "Imagine how many reservation trees it has taken for the whiteman to solve our problems on paper."

While many tribal people have suffered from poor mental and physical health, others, living in the selfsame situations, have reaped personal profits from economic and political adversities. One successful tribal person however, is neither a measure nor a model for the remaining reservation population.

Some tribal people may think catching frogs and selling pantribal bromides is a sure way to derail the commodity gravy train.

1975

233

✚ Wampum and the Presidents

The traditional style of ceremonial consumption and the ways in which tribal people made use of natural resources was in great contrast to the ambitions of white people who accumulated wealth and competed for political power.

Harold Hickerson in his book *The Chippewa and Their Neighbors*, writes that the industrial and ideological systems of tribal people were "geared to the simple needs of small communities whose members exploited a rather difficult environment without using artificial means to produce animal or plant food." The exploitations of several thousand tribal people, who used little more than they need from day to day, is less obvious an exploitation of natural resources than the waste left by large corporations.

The fur trade interposed the first anomalous economic burr on the traditional survival rhythms of woodland life and the equipoise of tribal spirits. Tribal people from the mountains, plains and waterways of the woodland, transcended or ignored their religious beliefs and family totems by killing millions of animals for peltry. Muskrat, beaver, marten, fisher, the sacred otter, mink, wolverine, fox, bear, moose, raccoon, and other animal pelts were exchanged for intoxicants, material goods, services, and sundries. Tribal people volunteered, they were not forced, to participate in this exploitation of natural resources.

But the personal reminiscence of tribal people is often in sharp contrast to the voices of exploitation around them in the woodland. Nodinens, for example, an old tribal woman, gave this information about her life to Frances Densmore almost fifty years ago: "When I was young everything was very systematic. We worked day and night and made the best use of the materials we had. My father kept count of the days on a stick . . . He cut a big notch for the first day of a new moon and a small notch for each of the other days."

The American Fur Company was one of the first large private corporations operating in tribal country more than a century ago, before reservations were established. When the frivolous market for beaver felt hats, and other pelts, waned in favor of silks and other materials, the big fur companies with all their overlords of the trade, partners, interpreters, clerks, guides, canoemen, and tribal hunters at various woodland trading posts, diversified their business operations and capital investments into mining, timber, transportation, banking, manufacturing, and land. Little of the enormous wealth accumulated from the fur trade was ever returned to the area for economic development. The wealth was used to build huge corporations, powerful banking institutions in urban centers, and national political organizations to favor the future accumulation of wealth.

Following their first commercial transactions as laborers and low cost factors in the fur trade, tribal people, except those who had intermarried and were canting to assimilation, were left to the spiritual spasms of cultural reunions on segregated exclaves.

The low cost of labor and available natural resources are still the fundamental reasons why private corporations locate on reservations. But since the fur trade, with the exception of timber and mineral and natural gas resources, commercial interests in reservations has been minimal. It has been what tribal people have in terms of natural resources, rather than who they are as human beings that attracts businesses from the economies of the white world.

235

William Lawrence and Francis Brun, Bemidji, Minnesota, 1970

In his report, *Industrial Development on Indian Reservations in the Upper Midwest,* James Murray points out that notwithstanding attractive business incentives, private firms are not moving to reservations in large numbers, and those which do, fail at a higher rate than the national average of business failures.

"One of the disappointing aspects of the effort to industrialize the reservations has been the rather large numbers of newly established firms which have failed or shut down after relatively short periods of operating on reservations," writes Murray, an economics professor, in his report published five years ago.

Poor management is the most frequent cause of business

236

failures—reservation locations are no exception. In a ten year summary of business failure on reservations across the country, inexperienced management was the reason most often given for failure. In the ninth federal reserve district, lack of developed markets and under-capitalization were other reasons given for business failure on reservations.

"In a private enterprise economy, management, rather than creditors, material suppliers, laborers," Murray writes, "receives with its right to make decisions, the primary responsibility for the outcome of those decisions. To attribute business failures to bad management, therefore, is not very helpful to those who are attempting to reduce the rate of these failures.

"Also, in the process of locating on the reservations, firms have had the advantage of feasibility studies, employment assistance, and other services provided by federal agencies . . . This causes many people to wonder why the record of failure is as bad as or worse than the national average."

The first corporations which were attracted to locate on reservations, Murray continues, "are often firms which would probably not start at all, or would not locate on reservations, except for the added promotional effort on the part of development specialists and political bodies at all levels of government.

"Many of the firms which have failed appear to have been firms which would not have been initiated if they had to rely on normal channels for credit, and would have had to bear the full cost of training their work force, constructing a building, and determining the marketability of their product.

"In the struggle to create employment opportunities on the reservation, both tribal officials and government agencies may overlook certain facts which would suggest problems for the firm. This may be encouraged by the fact that they are evaluated in terms of the success they achieve in producing jobs in a short period of time rather than in terms of the permanence of those jobs."

One of the most perplexing realities of paraeconomic survival on reservations is the constant paternalistic, and in some cases socialistic, efforts of federal and tribal governments to create and to control jobs on reservations rather than inspiring capitalistic profit making enterprises, which would benefit tribal organizations and individuals. The challenge is how to increase jobs and profits and reduce paternalism at the same time.

Leon Cook, who has several years experience in tribal economic development, argues that tribal people have "internalized colonial attitudes of creating jobs rather than being motivated by profits which is the rule in the real world . . . people should go into business to make money." He is critical of the fact that so many tribal development organizations are nonprofit corporations.

Exceptions to the development of paraeconomic tribal enterprises include commercial fishing and logging operations, oil and mineral leases, and several construction companies. The Minnesota Chippewa Tribal Construction Company is an outstanding example of a tribal government diminishing the need to depend on contractors in the white world. The profit corporation was established two years ago by the Minnesota Chippewa Tribe—a federation of six reservation tribal governments. Where contracts for work on six state reservations were offered to competing white contractors in the past, the work is now done by tribal people working for a profit making tribal owned and managed corporation.

Most reservations do not have an independent functioning economic system through which social and political experiences are shared by those living in the communities. Most of the money earned in wages on reservations is spent in the consumption of goods and services in white communities off the reservations. With private and tribal enterprises controlling most reservation employment there

238

are too few employers and not enough tribal people in small businesses offering their goods and services to people living on the reservation.

Elected tribal politicians who measure economic development by the number of jobs available must spend much of their time relating to white people and government officials who represent interests in the dominant economic system. Depending on federal programs as solutions to social and economic problems on reservations only perpetuates paraeconomics. Paternalistic programs spawn dependencies and limit personal expectations and aspirations for economic growth.

A decrease in reservation unemployment—underemployment and unemployment are serious problems on reservations—puts more money in the hands of individuals, but when most of that earned money will be spent off reservations it does little to reduce dependencies on the dominant economic system. Few communities are able to function without benefits from the dominant economic system, but interdependence on goods and services will diminish paraeconomics and strengthen social tolerances and sensitivities. Poor white people living in rural areas near reservations have shared the interdependent realities of unemployment and social problems in the past, but tribal people as a group have been excluded from the profits of white economic systems of the present.

Tribal people will continue to survive in a paraeconomic system without the independent and interdependent development of enterprises owned and operated for profit by tribal people living on reservations.

William Lawrence, law school graduate and former industrial development specialist for the Red Lake Reservation, proposed an impressive and ambitious development plan for the reservation, ranging from private enterprises offering goods and services, tribal owned businesses, such as a liquor store, golf course, airport, motel, and water and power associations. His economic development philoso-

239

phy was to increase the number of reservation employers and encourage individuals and independent corporations of tribal people to establish enterprises on the reservation. His ideal was to have tribal people earning and spending— exchanging goods and services and sharing economic risks—on the reservation as a way of reducing dependencies on off-reservation businesses and government institutions. His was a long range plan that may never be realized because of cultural attitudes and tribal politics.

The political power of elected reservation leaders has increased in proportion to the number of jobs tribal governments create and control through private corporations or tribal enterprises operating on reservations. On several reservations, political discussions and government decisions are made in tribal languages, while the language of proposals for economic development originate from the values of the dominant society. These are political realities which limit economic change from the perspective of modern theorists.

Few reservations have a tribal civil service system to protect workers from political influences and abuses. Such a system would be too expensive for a small tribal government to maintain, but on a regional or state wide basis the idea is worth consideration.

"As a consequence of their experiences," Murray points out, tribal people "are often inclined to view political activity as more important than business acumen in achieving social and economic objectives . . ."

Perhaps one reason so few private firms are inspired to locate on reservations is because of the unskilled labor available. Tribal politics may be another reason. In the dominant economic labor market, workers are paid well above minimum wage rates because they are productive and because of collective labor union organization. Murray emphasizes that there is a common misconception that "high wage industries have a difficult time competing in international markets.

240

"The opposite is in fact the case. Our high wage industries are also those where labor is the most productive but wages do not reflect the full potential of that productivity because of the ready availability of labor from industries with low productivity. Thus the industries with highest productivity are likely to have the greatest advantage of labor unit costs. It is the low-wage, low productivity industries which are threatened by foreign competition . . ."

If the firms are labor intensive with no methods of mechanization it would be difficult to increase the productivity of the laborers to compensate for a higher minimum wage. "In such firms, productivity differences depend largely upon differences in human qualities," Murray continues.

"While individuals can differ greatly in their ability to perform certain physical tasks, large groups of individuals seldom display the same degree of disparity. That is, in any community one can find certain people" who can work more quickly and efficiently than others.

"But, except for cultural or environmental differences relating to these activities, you can probably find a similar percentage of talents in almost any area in the world. It is, therefore, extremely difficult for any community to become substantially more productive than others in labor intensive activities, and even more difficult to maintain this advantage over time.

"In exploiting the pool of unskilled labor, it would seem wiser to pursue opportunities to perform custom work which is labor intensive rather than standardized work."

The Brunswick Corporation operating on the Fort Totten Reservation and the MDS-Atron Corporation located at Belcourt on the Turtle Mountain Reservation, both in North Dakota, are successful examples of firms employing tribal people to perform customized work. Brunswick has a contract with a tribal development corporation and federal agencies for the customized manufacture of camouflage netting for military use. The operation has not only pro-

241

vided more than two-hundred new jobs on the reservation but profits have also been realized by the tribal development corporation.

The MDS-Atron electronics operation at Belcourt has grown in the past three years to about fifty employees, most of whom are tribal people classified as electrical assemblers trained on the job in core memory stringing, hand soldering, and miniature wiring. The plant is located in a building owned by the tribal government.

John Miller, who is director of manufacturing and responsible for the operation has pointed out that the apparent unwillingness of corporations to offer contracts to reservation businesses is not by design, but rather a problem in the systematic methods of purchasing from subcontractors. Habits and associations are difficult to change. Miller repeats the success of customized operations, but points out that operations on reservations also need diversification in production. Other experienced observers agree, and stress diversified production as a means of providing real economic choices which can be supported with education and training.

There are many other successful customized production facilities located on other reservations. For example, the electrical components operations on the Fort Berthold Reservation, the jewel bearing manufacturing plant on the Turtle Mountain Reservation, electronics operations on the Rosebud Reservation and the Mille Lacs Reservation. There are also numerous customized wood products manufacturing operations on several reservations.

In his report, James Murray questions the extent to which reservation industrial development provides a satisfactory solution to the economic problems of tribal people. ''In spite of the very encouraging activities of many reservations, the present rate of industrialization will not provide the employment opportunities required to significantly reduce the rate of unemployment among the rapidly growing Indian population. After ten years of activity by the staff of the Bureau of Indian Affairs and other agencies, coupled with the various incentives, about one-thousand jobs have been created in the five state area of the upper midwest . . ."

In the next decade the tribal population in this area may increase by more than 20 percent. "During that time approximately three-thousand additional jobs will be needed," Murray predicts, "assuming that the same percentage of the Indian people remain on the reservation as have in the past.

"With new resources, greater interest and experience on the part of tribal leaders, and, hopefully, the passage of legislation to assist in financing the effort, the industrialization program should be much more successful in the next ten years than in the past ten. However, even if it is twice as successful, it will provide only about ten or fifteen percent of the positions needed to really solve the problem, and there will be several thousand more unemployed Indian people living in poverty than there are now."

Since his report five years ago there have been dramatic changes in the potential for economic development, but no dramatic decrease in unemployment on reservations. Various federal service programs have increased the number of jobs on reservations and a few new plants have opened, but when federal programs are concluded, so will most of the jobs. Reservation tribal life is still a paraeconomic survival experience.

In the past five years the number of tribal owned businesses has increased and several tribal governments are now contracting for the administration of federal programs in education and public services, which are all promising half steps toward reservation economic independence or at least interdependence. There has also been important litigation in federal courts favoring tribal jurisdiction over natural resources—such as tribal jurisdiction over hunting and fishing within treaty boundaries on the Leech Lake Reservation.

243

The most significant potential changes have been the organization of the American Indian National Bank and passage of the Indian Financing Act, which will make more money available to tribal governments and individual reservation enterprises.

Bernard Granum, who identifies himself as a resource economist for the Bureau of Indian Affairs, is optimistic that new sources of credit financing will relieve capitalization and industrial expansion problems on reservations. He believes in one national economic system.

"This nation can tolerate diversities in religion and in many other areas of life," said Granum, who remarked that he knows of no differences between the economic aspirations of tribal people and white people. "But we can tolerate only one economic system, and that is the world of work . . . in that system you either fit in or you are counted out.

"We all have the same economic system . . . it functions the same way, even though the objects have changed from wampum to pictures of the presidents."

1975

✛ The Politics of Paraeconomics

In the Ninth Federal Reserve District there are more than a dozen different tribal groups living in hundreds of distinct reservation communities. The individual tribal people in these diverse cultural groups speak of themselves as Anishinaabe or Chippewa, or Dakota or Sioux, two of the largest tribal groups in the area, or Crow, Cheyenne, Assiniboin, Hidatsa, Mandan, Menominee, and other plains and woodland tribal groups. Each group, each reservation, and individual tribal people, project unique and complex identities.

"We have to get back to the ceremonies that put us close to Mother Earth," said Pine Ridge Reservation born Edward McGaa, a law school graduate and former combat fighter pilot.

"I have a tribe," he told a group of rural white people, "we are still holding together, we still got our religion, we still got our ways and we are going back . . ."

The direction he was referring to is a linguistic retreat to the romantic comforts of the traditional tribal past. He speaks of the future in terms of pantribal religious values of the historical past, but he lives and breathes in the technological present tense.

The traditional cultural elements which emerge in the language of pantribal movements are derived from complex sources. Evon Vogt points out that a "high proportion of these elements are drawn from plains cultures.

"These elements have become symbols of Indianness to the Indians themselves to a degree that bears little relationship to the aboriginal facts. And it is probable that their importance as symbols derives in part from the fact that these elements are central features of the prevailing white-American stereotype of the American Indian.

"They are the features of Indian culture which white tourists expect to find when they attend intertribal ceremonials, and Indians are rewarded by the whites for behaving in conformity to the stereotype."

Some tribal people appear at times to be living in two different worlds and moving in opposing directions from the present. Emotional statements about the past seem authoritative, but the language of the future is spoken without the conditional future tense. Most of those listening to tribal revivalists are white people. Reservation tribal people are too preoccupied with survival to afford the luxuries of linguistic retreats from the present.

Thousands of urban educated tribal people, some adorned with pantribal vestments made of plastic and leather, are withdrawing from civilization and driving back to the reservation to live the way they have projected tribal life to be several hundred years ago. And they are met by thousands of tribal people leaving reservations to attend colleges and find work in metropolitan areas. Neither group is in conflict with the other.

The romantic movement back to the reservation is new in the experiences of tribal people; following military service and assimilation and relocation programs, tribal people returned to reservations to live and work sans the intensive revival of the traditional past.

The movement corresponds to a general ecological temper and radical consciousness, but those abandoning the realities of urban life may soon be outnumbered on the roads back to the reservation by tribal people with technical skills and college educations returning to manage new tribal programs and industrial enterprises.

246

Alfred Nickaboine returned to the Mille Lacs Reservation after twenty years in an urban center. He now operates his own bumper repair business.

Donald Bibeau, who was an instructor at Bemidji State University, and thousands of other young tribal people have returned to teach, manage, and administrate tribal and federal programs and enterprises.

Bibeau earned his college degree in philosophy, served four years as a military policeman in the service, worked for an insurance company in the claims department, wore conservative suits and white shirts, and then returned to the reservation to rest and write. But he has not been able to do much of either because of demands to teach and to assist in the development of social and educational programs on the reservation.

"I came home to rest, to cleanse and cure and understand myself after a long period of urban angst," Bibeau said. "But it was the beginning of new movements on the reservation . . . I was involved and had little time left for a romantic rest."

More tribal people talk about returning to reservations than those who make the actual move. There are some who would never return because of social and economic securities found in metropolitan areas. But between those who leave, those who stay, and those who are returning to work or dream, are thousands of families returning to reservations for visits several times a year.

Going back to the reservation to live and work is not a simple transition. True, there are more housing, employment opportunities, and social services for urban escapees, but tribal politicians have discouraged more than a few tribal people from returning.

The political ambiance of most reservations is conservative and often based on loyalties to individual tribal leaders. Young tribal people who have left reservations for training and education tend to be more liberal and aggressive. When they choose to return to reservations, their at-

247

titudes may conflict with reservation conservatism. The most obvious conflicts are with those urban tribal people who espouse radical ideologies demanding immediate changes in tribal governments. Most older political leaders speak tribal languages which younger aspirants seldom understand, but the unique experiences of the older leaders is often limited to political acumen, while the college educated are speaking technical languages of law and economics.

From different levels of appreciation, tribal people are discussing potential changes and new reservation developments in tribal jurisdiction, contracts for federal services, government reorganization, management of natural resources, pantribal assimilation, national business associations, comparative cultural differences in economic aspirations, the potential for incorporated families in private businesses on reservations, and numerous other issues.

In 1950, before the assumption of state jurisdiction on reservations in several states, Luther Youngdahl, Governor of Minnesota, organized a fifteen state conference on tribal problems. Tribal leaders and government officials from Montana, North Dakota, Wisconsin, Minnesota, South Dakota, and other states, discussed treaties and claims settlements, the restrictions of tribal people on reservations as wards of the federal government, housing conditions and unemployment on reservations, and the need for occupational training programs.

There was little discussion of tribal economic development; the participants were more concerned with improving the living conditions of individuals and families.

Youngdahl stimulated national attention to tribal problems. He advocated the support of several states in proposing federal legislation to assist tribal people. Proposals and programs backed by the united support of a dozen states would have much better chances of success than action requested by a single state.

248

Three years later the federal government responded, but not to Youngdahl, with policies of termination and legislation authorizing certain states civil and criminal jurisdiction on reservations.

In 1972 the Leech Lake Reservation challenged the jurisdiction of state conservation laws. A federal court judge ruled that the rights of tribal people to hunt and fish and gather wild rice have survived federal legislation and other jurisdictional claims to resources within the original boundaries of the reservation. The right to hunt and fish on the Leech Lake Reservation was not within state jurisdiction.

At the same time there is growing interest in returning civil and criminal jurisdiction to tribal governments, there are intense arguments over the need to reorganize tribal governments. Most existing reservation governments were patent democratic republics designed by social scientists working for the federal government. Tribal people had the choice of accepting the new constitutional governments, but they were not instructed that they also had the right to choose the *form* of government they wanted to live with on the reservations.

Radical leaders of the American Indian Movement have opposed the Indian Reorganization Act which created existing constitutional tribal governments. The problem is not so much in the legislation but in the administration of the measure. The act provides that a reservation tribe "shall have the right to organize for its common welfare, and may adopt an appropriate constitution and bylaws."

Tribal people may still decide what is *appropriate*, which means that by referendum or constitutional convention, the existing tribal governments could be changed to consensual, parliamentary or other forms of government organization.

Sam Deloria, director of the American Indian Law Center at the University of New Mexico, pointed out that the

249

act created the authority to establish constitutional governments on reservations and in fact recognizes inherent tribal
sovereignty.

The Leech Lake Reservation has an annual income from
the sale of licenses to hunt and fish on the reservation,
which is a dramatic shift from paraeconomics to an interdependent economic system. The tribal government is using that income to invest in the development of tribal enterprises.

Tribal leaders on the Northern Cheyenne Reservation in
Montana are discussing alternatives to strip mining in an
effort to better manage their natural resources on the reservation. The tribal government there has petitioned to
void the coal leases for strip mining. Tribal jurisdiction has
been recognized but the disposition of the leases will depend on future court decisions.

James Youngblood Henderson, a lawyer who teaches at
the University of California—Berkeley, argues that the major legal and economic problems on reservations are not internal. "The causes of tribal problems are external to the
reservation."

Federal institutions have discouraged tribal government
reorganization, Henderson points out, while at the same
time stimulating the need among tribes to "form tribal and
intertribal corporations which could bring exclusive tribal
business within the jurisdiction and control of state and
federal governments."

Tribal governments are increasing their demands for exclusive jurisdiction over natural and human resources on
reservations. Many tribal groups are taking over contracts
to control federal services on the reservation. Control of
mineral exploration and mining, timber and water resources, will benefit tribal people in the future sale of these
resources.

If federal courts continue to recognize the jurisdictional
rights of tribal people according to past treaties, and if

tribal governments manage reservation resources with success, then paraeconomics may not survive.

Concurrent with the increase in the control of tribal resources and the development of tribal enterprises, there should also be an increase in the development of independent tribal businesses on reservations. The traditional independence of tribal people should not be ignored.

There are no obvious differences when the economic aspirations of white people are compared to those of tribal people, but the most obvious cultural difference is in the manner of consuming goods and services. Tribal people tend to invest less personal resources in chattel or real estate as a presentation of social and economic class position.

There may be a possible cultural link with the past in the proposal to incorporate tribal families on reservations. Before the effects of the fur trade altered tribal social and religious values, families were the primary political and economic unit. That basic cultural survival unit has been forgotten and ignored in the efforts of the federal government to assimilate and individualize tribal people. Families are still strong and functioning on reservations. Not as powerful as in the past, but the frequent allegations that nepotism is practiced in tribal enterprises is evidence that families are still political and economic units of survival. The federal government, as it has never done, should encourage tribal families to incorporate and establish businesses on the reservation.

There is some opposition to the idea from tribal people. Roger Buffalohead argues that the differences in individual experiences, political affiliations and styles of economic survival would work against common identities in families.

Leon Cook questions the proposal of families in business because it would "institutionalize nepotism on the reservation, which is enough of a problem now." People should go into business to make money, Cook repeated. Making money is competitive, and that kind of competition may

251

not be the best experience for families. Cook referred to successful farm families on the reservation, but explained that while families live together on a communal basis they are not able to work together in a competitive system.

"Economic survival is an individual problem now," Cook said, "not a gathering of past cultural experiences for a mutual communal survival . . . the individual still sees himself surviving as himself, because he has lived in his own poverty."

It appears that reservation paraeconomic systems, weakened by tribal jurisdictional control of natural resources, new reservation enterprises and sources of credit and aggressive industrial development corporations, can only survive in the future with poor management. With educated and experienced management of tribal enterprises and enlightened political leadership, paraeconomics on the reservation will not survive.

1975

✛ Indians Are Great Sharers

"Too many white people are waiting for someone on the reservation to stub his economic toe," said James Bianco, canting backward in his black leather chair and huffing on a stout imported cigar.

His leather chair, the expensive furnishings of his office, and the way he offers cigars to his friends and important depositors, is where the stereotype of a conservative banker ends. Bianco is known among tribal people on the Leech Lake Reservation as an honest person. His systematic banking experiences have not hardened his humor and respect for the poor.

James Bianco is president of the First National Bank of Cass Lake, one of the few banks located within the boundaries of a reservation. He is serious about his status on the reservation and feels a real obligation to loan customers from the reservation because of the substantial deposits made by the tribal government and individual tribal people. Tribal people living on trust land have less to offer as collateral in securing a loan than a white person who owns property. In some cases collateral can be based on inventories and equipment if tribal people are involved in business enterprises.

But Bianco is not tied up all the time with banking regulations. Near his desk is a handsome cigar box where he keeps small amounts of cash for personal noninterest loans to tribal people facing daylong emergencies for food, and,

253

in some cases, hairtonic, as friends of the bank call intoxicants. The borrowed money is all returned in time without interest. Bianco said he once accepted a finger print from a tribal person who spoke only her native language and was not able to sign her name to a loan document.

Daylong needs are important, but borrowing larger amounts of money is more difficult because of collateral requirements.

Reservation land which is held in trust by the federal government for individual tribal people can be mortgaged with the consent of the owner and the approval of the Secretary of Interior. Obtaining approval is difficult enough, without further complications of heirship. When a tribal person dies, if there is trust land as part of the estate, the heirs are identified but the land is not divided or sold. Obligating land with several heirs requires the approval of the federal government and all of the heirs to the trust land.

Solutions to these problems must seem impossible to most tribal people. The legal complications surrounding the use of tribal land, trust land, heirship, and jurisdiction on reservations, has made it almost infeasible to negotiate with banking and financial institutions. Many bankers are reluctant to loan money to tribal people living on reservations because of the jurisdictional problems and the presumed legal obstacles in collecting or recovering debts.

A summary report on the establishment of the American Indian National Bank prepared by Montana State University, stated that tribal people have limited access to financial services and less credit available to them than do white people.

The report concluded that there is a need for a "financial institution that can use more effectively resources that are available but highly fragmented. As a matter of fact they are so fragmented that many ordinary Indians have difficulty in discovering how and where to apply for financing . . . And after they obtain financial resources, they need

254

management assistance to implement the plans they have made . . .

"The proposed American Indian Bank would seem to be the kind of institution to build a bridge between existing financial institutions and Indian financial needs. It also would provide a means for the Indian to move toward his goals of participation and self determination."

The American Indian National Bank was chartered in 1972 by the Comptroller of the Currency. The bank is a member of the Federal Reserve System and is subject to the same regulations and requirements as other banks in the system.

The main office is located in Washington, D.C., with future operations planned on reservations in tribal communities across the nation. The chairman of the board of the bank is Ben Reifel, former congressman and enrolled member of the Rosebud Reservation in South Dakota. Barney Old Coyote, former professor at Montana State University, is president of the bank.

A profile of proposed services includes all those services offered by a full service commercial bank. The primary stockholders will be tribal people or tribal governments or organizations. The bank "intends to become an innovative and profitable banking institution that will provide a favorable return on investments to its Indian shareholders."

The American Indian National Bank will operate a trust department and will make loans to tribal groups and organizations for "worthwhile purposes" and will "accept both time and demand deposits from persons, groups and organizations desiring to assist the American Indian, as well as from those that wish to establish normal banking relationships."

But the American Indian National Bank will not be the only new source of money to tribal people and organizations in the next few years. Last year the Indian Financing Act was enacted with an amendment proposing appropriations of fifty million for direct revolving fund loans to

255

Leech Lake Reservation Housing

tribal people and tribal organizations, twenty million proposed for a loan guarantee and interest subsidy program, and ten million for tribal business development grants.

The policy of the Indian Financing Act is to "provide capital on a reimbursable basis to help develop and utilize Indian resources, both physical and human to a point where the Indians will fully exercise responsibility for the utilization and management of their own resources and where they will enjoy a standard of living from their own productive efforts comparable to that enjoyed by non-Indians in neighboring communities."

The public law provides through the revolving loan fund that loans may be made for any purpose which will promote the economic development of individuals and tribal groups.

The new financing law emphasizes loans to tribal people

256

and organizations on reservations and excludes tribal people who are living in metropolitan areas. Individuals living in urban centers, if they can be determined eligible for any loan, may be obligated to make application through their tribal governments on the reservation. Some tribal people can be expected to oppose this legislation, or seek an amendment to include tribal people living off reservations.

The intent of the Indian Financing Act is to assist people living on reservations in a paraeconomic system to develop their resources in an independent economic system. Tribal people living in metropolitan areas have had more access to services of financial institutions than have reservation residents.

"Indians are great sharers," said James Bianco, "but they are not savers . . . they have so little to save."

1975

257

PART 7

NEW TRIBAL SCENES

✛ Inside Toilets

*If obeying one law means violating another, I have
a right to decide which I would rather have on my
conscience.*

LORETTA BEAULIEU

When the area director of the Bureau of Indian Affairs in
Minneapolis walked into his carpeted office one morning
he found a young Anishinaabe twirling in his expensive,
high-backed swivel chair.

Unaware of history, the boy twirled and twirled until he
got bored and left for a tour of other offices in the building.

The office of the director had been seized by members of
the American Indian Movement. They arrived early and
announced that they were staying on the federal carpets,
among the drapes and pictures of the Presidents, until
changes were made in archaic policies controlling the lives
of the people on the reservations and in the city.

The people have had thoughts about taking over the Bureau of Indian Affairs for more than a century, but the actual plan to seize the area office in Minneapolis was organized in less than a week. Militant leaders, young and old
Oshki Anishinaabe, residents of the city and the reservation, and whole families were sitting in the director's office
waiting for history to be changed.

261

The people believed their courage would change the world. In time they would learn that nothing had changed.

Wearing a beaded headband and moccasins, an Oshki Anishinaabe, a new tribal person, asked the director of the area office how long he had been working for the Bureau of Indian Affairs.

"Thirty-one years," he answered without hesitation. "And I have a very, very good reputation."

"Would you say that you have enjoyed your work and the bureau has done a good job?"

"Yes, a very good job," the director said with pride. "I have many Indian friends."

The people groaned and then laughed, drowning out the last words of the director. They did not see themselves as Indians, nor as his friends.

It was a bad day for the white director. He was being held responsible in one day for all the known and unknown sins that have been committed against the people by the federal government.

Time passed slowly for everyone. The excitement was wearing thin on the faces of the militants. The area director sat at his desk attempting to discuss the demands made by the leaders of the occupation. The room was filled with smoke. The Oshki Anishinaabe children were rubbing their eyes. Questions were never answered. Discussions were never completed. The telephone rang and tempers flared when the director referred to the progress the bureau had made in working with the people on the reservations.

An Oshki Anishinaabe in long hair and knee-high moccasins asked how many reservation people served on the school boards of federal boarding schools.

A woman asked the director if he was a racist.

An Oshki Anishinaabe child asked if he could have something to eat.

The questions were repeated.

The area director seldom answered.

Dennis Banks and Kahn-Tineta, 1968

Responding to a question about his salary, the director said he earned over twenty thousand dollars a year.

"Do you know how many people can eat in one year for that salary?" an Oshki Anishinaabe woman yelled, wagging her finger at the director. Her husband had left her and the children on the reservation. She moved to the city and receives welfare assistance.

The telephone rang.

The militant leaders demanded that the Bureau of Indian Affairs be restructured to serve both the urban and reservation people equally.

The leaders demanded that an immediate investigation of the bureau be conducted by an all-Indian team . . . *exemption of Indians from federal and state taxes . . . an appropriation of half a million dollars for urban Indian programs . . . turn all jobs in the bureau over to the people . . . construct hospitals on every reservation in the state . . . return to the people exclusive hunting and fishing rights on the reservation.*

The director explained several times that most of the complaints were out of his hands because the bureau was responsible only to the people living on reservations. He said the demands should be made to a legislative body, not to an administrative office of the government.

"When has the bureau ever helped the people fight for what they want?" George Mitchell snapped. "Why don't you people help us just once fight for what we want?

"Everything is the reservation," Mitchell snarled. "But this is the largest reservation right here in the city . . . when will you help the people living here?"

The area director tired of the confrontation and called the city police to clear the building. One police officer arrived, and the people told him to leave because the building belonged to the people and it was *their* bureau. They were the people the offices were staffed to assist and they were staying.

The area director took a long lunch on the first day of the occupation, and on the second day he signed a complaint which gave the police the authority to clear the building.

Nine Oshki Anishinaabe were carried from the building by police officers and taken to the city jail in a police van. Dennis Banks, director of the American Indian Movement, stood in the door of the van with his arm raised and his fist clenched—the symbol of the oppressed expecting to be oppressed. The doors of the van were closed to the steady beat of a tribal drum and the voices of Oshki Anishinaabe singers.

While the militants were on the way to jail the director hired a private detective agency to protect the building from the people it was established more than a century ago to assist.

For several months the private detectives sat inside the front door of the area office and questioned everyone who

264

Dennis Banks and Clyde Bellecourt

passed . . . *what is your name, what is your business, do you have an appointment, whom do you want to see.*

Only people with dark skin were detained and questioned at the door. The director was safe. People with white skin were not questioned. Some things never change.

"The people have a love-hate relationship with the bureau," said Ronald Libertus, who was born on the Leech Lake Reservation. "Neither can function when they depend on each other for love and hate at the same time. The whole world is going to hell and the bureau guards the door to federal services."

The militant leaders have charged the bureau with racist hiring practices, but very few Oshki Anishinaabe show in-

265

terest in working for the bureau. The demands were being made by urban Oshki Anishinaabe and not by residents of the reservations, where the people are more dependent on the bureau. Some believe that urban people are expressing a need to be as dependent on the bureau as reservation people.

Ray Lightfoot has worked for the bureau for more than thirty years. He said the "militants always demand more jobs, but at the same time they discourage people from working for the bureau." There are about two dozen tribal people working in the area office. Most of them are women in clerical jobs.

Within a year of the occupation of the area office by militants, Lightfoot was promoted to area director. For the first time, an Oshki Anishinaabe was in charge of programs on reservations in four states. But his appointment did not change bureau policies, and the militants objected again. This time they were critical of a man they had originally supported.

The American Indian Movement was organized by Mitchell, Banks, and Harold Goodsky. There are more than a thousand active members, with branches in several cities across the country. The purpose of the organization and the philosophy of militancy was best expressed in a statement by Banks on the second anniversary of the movement: "we must commit ourselves to changing the social pattern in which we have been forced to live . . . the government and churches have demoralized, dehumanized, massacred, robbed, raped, promised, made treaty after treaty, and lied to us . . . we must now destroy this political machine that man has built to prevent us from self-determination.

"We must never allow another one to be built. We must never again take a back seat to anyone . . . we must, ourselves, build machines that will prevent this—not a political-type machine—but a machine built on beliefs, self-determination, freedom from oppression, and on the difference between what is *morally right and wrong* as opposed to what is *legal and illegal.*"

One of the most enduring objectives of the movement is to work with Oshki Anishinaabe young people in the community.

"If we are going to have any community action at all, it will be with the young people who are working out their identity at the same time they are working with adult leaders," said Ronald Libertus, who has helped raise funds for youth programs in the city.

Militant leaders argue that there should be a special school for the Oshki Anishinaabe who have moved from the reservation to the city.

"In a struggle with his own identity," George Mitchell said, "the young Indian must find himself before he can relate to an alien society and its institutions. Too often a relationship has been forced."

Clyde Bellecourt is seen as the most controversial militant leader ever to emerge among the Oshki Anishinaabe. He is both intense and soft-spoken, a fist-clencher and affectionate, a table-banger and mitigator—he is angry and gentle, headstrong and yielding. He is complex when he is angry and very warm and affectionate to the personal needs of others when he is not angry. Bellecourt is Oshki Anishinaabe, and the people find in him everything they are themselves and dislike in others.

He was born on the White Earth Reservation and attended a parochial elementary school until he was eleven years old, when he was committed to the state training school for boys as a delinquent. He was committed for being absent from school.

The next fifteen years of his life he spent in and out of correctional institutions. While in prison on a burglary sentence, Bellecourt and another Oshki Anishinaabe inmate organized a group of reservation people to discuss the meaning of culture and religion. It was then, he said, that he began to understand himself.

267

Bellecourt voices the bitterness of inhuman experiences not only as a person of dark skin but as a man who has been committed to a correctional institution.

"They told me I already had two strikes against me," he said about the past, while leaning against the door frame in his office. "First I was an Indian, and second I was a convicted felon."

Some Oshki Anishinaabe think the leaders of the movement are interested in little more than seeing their names in the newspaper, their faces on television, and their cars rigged with short-wave radio telephones. Some believe the militant leaders are receiving a good salary for organizing their own personal complaints. And a few Oshki Anishinaabe see the militants as nothing more than opportunists who should be ignored.

But most Oshki Anishinaabe support the purpose of the movement while differing at times with the tactics of the leaders. But those who have experienced the frustrations of trying for change are respectful of the energy the militants give to changing the conditions of life for the people.

A militant leader seldom has a moment of personal peace. The people need him at all times of the day, because a leader who is trusted is depended upon by those who trust him. That trust and dependency call for a total life commitment. There are no vacations and quiet evenings at home for the militant leader. And there are no retirement programs.

College-educated Oshki Anishinaabe generally support the causes of the militants but are not certain confrontation is always necessary when an issue might be negotiated. But every Oshki Anishinaabe leader who has worked for a few years in the institutions of the dominant society agrees that because of what the militants are doing the changes from within the structure of the dominant society are much easier and more immediate.

There is some truth in all the responses to the Oshki Anishinaabe militant movement, just as there is truth in the various ways of understanding and changing the conditions which have caused the problems.

"This country is sympathetic and willing to serve Indian programs," said Lee Cook, showing his concern that there might be a backlash in the dominant society. "We don't have the numbers as a small minority to risk having the doors closed by a backlash to political militants. What we really need now are more diplomats . . .

"If the militants have used every other means to express the problem and change the quality of life for themselves first and then others," Cook continued, "then they have no other way to speak out than as militants.

"But the question is whether militancy is an experience of futility," he said, looking off and pondering the question himself.

"People would be better off on their own without the federal government . . . do your own thing instead of crying about having someone else do it for you.

"The militants think they are doing a new thing, but we did the same thing ten years ago," Cook said, pitching his hands to express a reference to time. "The cry has changed from food and clothing and shelter to politics now.

"If the militants have not lost their perspective they will see that all the crying has been done before . . . the people want a program of their own now, not a new cry every year."

Cook is a persuasive diplomat but at times he is the most militant of leaders. For two years he served the needs of the people in the city, and he has never forgotten the cockroaches zipping across sinks and hiding behind a hot water pipe that runs cold. He was no diplomat when he saw children sitting on bare mattresses close to space heaters in cold, dimly lit rooms, watching television to escape the reality of poverty. Lee Cook is a good diplomat because he was a good militant who did more acting than crying.

Most of the Oshki Anishinaabe families living in the city live in substandard housing. They pay more for broken

269

windows, doors without locks, broken hinges, cock-roaches, leaking gas stoves, cold water, and the fear that the landlord will evict them in the middle of the winter. Every Oshki Anishinaabe has either lived in or knows about the conditions of life that make the best diplomats and the best militants.

Many people in the city have been down so long they see what they have as a good life compared to the past on the reservation. For decades the dominant society has ignored the problems of poverty because the people have not complained. When militant leaders educate the poor about their poverty, the militants are often criticized by white people for creating the problem.

For more than a century the Anishinaabe have been listening to missionaries and government officials and expert anthropologists and teachers tell about the good life and the many opportunities for success in the world. But the meaning of life in the city for many Oshki Anishinaabe families is little more than an inside toilet.

"The one thing you can always get from a white man is a drink," said George Mitchell with bitterness. "Someone will always buy you a drink or give you a few pennies to buy a cheap bottle of wine, but try to get some money for a program. It seems to me that the white man would like to keep the people begging for a drink."

1972

✚ Stealing Tribal Children

Ten little Injuns standing in a line, one toddled home and then there were nine.

Nine little Injuns swinging on a gate, one tumbled off and then there were eight.

Eight little Injuns . . .

That decreasing musical verse by Septimus Winner is a forbidding poetic measure of the number of tribal children who are stolen each year from their ancestral homes. Stolen, declared Lee Cook, for adoption and foster care by social workers in the dominant white society.

Testifying before the Senate Indian Affairs Subcommittee on the welfare of tribal children, Cook said that "one out of every six Indian children in Minnesota were adopted in the last couple of years . . . at the rate of eight times the number" of white children adopted.

Tribal children are "stolen from their parents under one guise or another," said Cook, who is a professional social worker and an elected tribal representative from the Red Lake Reservation.

He asserts that children are removed from tribal homes without due process of law and are adopted or placed with white foster parents because of prejudicial standards established by white social workers who have jurisdiction on many reservations.

Seventy percent of all reservation homes are judged to be substandard because of space limitations and the lack of

271

many modern middle-class conveniences. Few reservation homes meet the rigid requirements of foster-care certification.

But the problem is not just the want of more space and household devices. For centuries the dominant society has assumed through the systematic administration of assimilation programs that reservation families and tribal cultures were not only substandard, but primitive and dangerous to the health of developing children.

"Separating Indian children from their parents and tribes has been one of the major aims of governmental services for generations," said Robert Bergman, director of mental-health programs for the Indian Health Service and a psychiatrist on the Navajo Reservation.

"The assumption," said Bergman, testifying before the same subcommittee, "is that children, and particularly those in any kind of difficulty, would be better off being raised by someone other than their own parents. The purpose of the first boarding school on the Navajo Reservation as stated in its charter was 'to remove the Navajo child from the influence of his savage parents.'

"Thousands of Indian children are sent each year to boarding schools for a variety of reasons, all of which basically have to do with the opinion that children cannot be brought up right at home.

"Foster-care practices for Indian children has been damaging," Bergman testified. "Given the least excuse, substantial or rumored, children are removed from their homes and placed in the home of a white person."

Bergman told the members of the Subcommittee that it is his professional opinion that many children who were removed from their homes "would be better if left with the parent or a close relative . . . For some unexplained reason, current laws in many states provide a relative with less foster-care subsistence than a stranger."

At the same time, according to a report by the Association on American Indian Affairs, almost all tribal children placed under foster care are removed not because of parental abuse, but rather as a result of cultural misunderstanding and the imposition of dominant white values.

"Many social workers," the report said, "untutored in the ways of Indian family life and assuming them to be socially irresponsible, consider leaving a child with persons outside the nuclear family as neglect and thus as grounds for terminating parental rights . . . Tribes that were forced onto reservations at gunpoint are now being told that they live in a place unfit for raising their own children."

Bergman emphasized that white people should stop legislating morals and respect tribal people who "know best what is right for their own children."

In the past, such humanistic advice has seldom been heeded in the dominant society. For that reason, and many others, tribal people in the past few years have demanded control of all services and programs that affect their lives on the reservation.

1974

✝ Departing from the Present

*Do not measure time by saying, there was
yesterday and there shall be tomorrow.*

KAHLIL GIBRAN

Once upon a time, a teacher of future studies and a tribal
revivalist came down from the city to talk to people in
Waseca, Minnesota about the values of man and the land.

Eighty farmers and local residents listened to two speakers evacuate by words the present tense of this pleasant
town for the romantic tribal past and the fantastic galactic
frontiers of the future.

"I think it time to begin designing our futures," said
Arthur Harkins, who evacuated the present for the future
in a half-hour speech. "History is in the present and the
future is in the present . . . For powerful people time col-
lapses but for powerless people there is a tendency to live
in the past and push the future back indefinitely."

Edward McGaa, former combat fighter pilot and law
school graduate, evacuated the present for the tribal past.
"We have to get back to the ceremonies that put us close to
Mother Earth . . ."

Harkins, an expert on tribal education and reservation
life styles, is now specializing in future studies and teaching at the University of Minnesota. Time seemed to stand

275

Edward McGaa at a tribal ceremonial in South Dakota

still as he told the people here that they should prepare themselves by demythologizing their present beliefs and develop alternative technologies and value systems for the future.

"Until we develop the technology on the basis of solar power, or fusion power to take us away from this vale of tears," said Harkins with the subtle humor of an after-dinner speaker, "we are pretty much bound by a conservation ethic . . ."

McGaa, an Oglala Sioux and co-chairman of the Bicentennial Commission, said that all the problems in the world are caused by excessive materialism and because people have lost respect for their mother.

"Our ways come from a woman, your ways come from a man," he told the people in Waseca, referring to his Mother Earth concept.

"Anytime you get away from the natural way you're going to get into trouble," he said in conversational tones, "you have to get back to tribal thinking . . .

"I have a tribe," said McGaa, who was born on the Pine Ridge Reservation in South Dakota. "We are still holding together, we still got our religion, we still got our ways and we are going back . . ."

Harkins considers it practical to think of the future, but impractical to think of the present and the past, because, he said, people depend on myths to explain the meaning of life and the cultural and racial differences between them: "How do we design ways of looking at things in which we can step beyond the traps of rhetoric, the traps of history?

"To really know ourselves is to become at least temporarily alien to ourselves . . . In order to advance as humans we may have to become temporarily other than human . . . In order to see what we are, it may be necessary to be other than what we are," he said in a roundabout way, "but then when we find that we can see what we are, we find that we are seeing only what we were, because that alienation that enabled us to see has created a new reality, and in order to really understand that we have to get outside it . . . and so it goes."

And so it went.

Closing with a fatalistic understatement, McGaa, who flew over a hundred combat missions as a jet pilot over Vietnam, said: "If atomic war comes . . . we'll learn that

277

mister Indian really was right—these weapons that have been developed through materialism are extremely dangerous . . . we will go back to a bow and arrow and to a spear."

Harkins, the intellectual of the future, who thinks about self-alienation as a new basis for identity, had the last word before time and the audience marched on home to income-tax forms, the energy crisis and seed catalogs, "I think that we are all faced with the problem of controlling technologies whether it is a chemical compound or a tomahawk."

McGaa seemed to be the more popular of the two speakers. He signed up over a dozen people to take part in a sacred sweat lodge ceremony this summer. The public forum was funded through a grant from the Minnesota Humanities Commission.

1974

✛ Claims to the Grand Canyon

While this nation is restoring historic battlefields and preparing to celebrate two centuries of independence, a small group of tribal people gathered at the bottom of a canyon is struggling to restore aboriginal title to a small portion of its traditional lands on the plateaus above.

The Havasupai, a people of enormous endurance and peaceful instincts of survival, have been minding their culture and gardens—and in recent times grazing cattle—for over a thousand continuous years. Since the arrival of the white man, their land has diminished from the spacious plateaus to a small plot at the bottom of the Grand Canyon. Three hundred people live there now on a few hundred acres of arable land. They are poor and unable to cultivate enough food to survive in good health, but in spirit they have endured with the belief that the federal government will restore some of their land.

A century ago, the government assumed control of millions of acres of plateau land to protect the Havasupai from the encroachment of independent prospectors and miners. Since then the tribe has been permitted to use portions of its original land for grazing cattle. But year by year, since the creation of the Grand Canyon National Park, the Havasupai have been excluded from living on the plateau and were driven down the winding eight-mile trail to the bottom of the canyon.

Congress is now considering a measure to double the size of the park—an action which would be a denial of use and title to traditional tribal land. The Senate passed the bill several months ago. The Havasupai are appealing to the House Committee on Interior and Insular Affairs for title to only a fraction of the land they once used. "They are not going to build a dam or put up a factory, or launch a tourist extravaganza," said Edward Kennedy, senator from Massachusetts. "Rather, they are intent upon preserving and protecting the natural, undeveloped and unspoiled beauty of their homeland." Barry Goldwater, senator from Arizona, implored his friends in the House to "correct the bill and insert language which will be proposed for the immediate expansion of the Havasupai reservation."

Alfonso Ortiz, president of the Association on American Indian Affairs, said that the "Havasupais have through the centuries evolved a complex and responsible pattern of everyday usage of the area in question, from gathering medicinal plants and herbs to grazing stock . . . In the name of simple justice they should be granted trust title . . ." The Havasupai have a moral, if not legal, right to land on the canyon plateau. This nation has an obligation not only to protect tribal land rights, but to respect the dignity of a people who have lived near the canyon for more than thirty generations.

1975

✝ Water Rights on Reservations

Many school children have learned from romantic class-room lectures that tribal people on this continent not only shared their lands and resources with white settlers but taught the first settlers how to grow corn and other foods.

The one-sided myth of sharing is in sharp contrast to the grim facts that tribal people were forced to live on desolate reservations as colonial subjects under arbitrary govern-mental authority.

The assumption of educators seems to have been that children are better prepared for the future if they are de-nied the realities of malignant violence and the knowledge of the systematic oppression of tribal people. But igno-rance and benign beliefs fostered in classrooms may have made it possible for the government and private industry to continue the exploitation of tribal lands and resources, which according to hundreds of treaties should be pro-tected as sovereign rights.

Precious water, along with the myth of sharing, is flow-ing from several reservations to the toilets and fountains of Albuquerque and Los Angeles and Salt Lake City and other great western cities. The water from reservations flows because treaty rights have been ignored.

Several courts have ruled that reservation water rights are inherent and protected by treaties but few federal agen-cies have advocated the protection of those rights. Steve Nickeson, writing for the Race Relations Reporter, said that tribal people have lacked a "sophisticated knowledge of their rights and how to get them." As a result, water from many reservations has been diverted to urban centers or sold to private industry. As the water flows away, some reservations are becoming even more desolate.

The protection of reservation water rights may soon become a problem in Minnesota if pollution continues. If more lakes in the state become unsafe as a source of drinking water, some communities may drill wells near reservations which could lower the water tables on tribal land. This, along with water-diversion projects and irrigation systems, could be interpreted as a violation of water rights protected by treaties.

The realities of pollution around reservations do not justify the continual exploitation of tribal resources. The issue of reservation water rights should not be distorted now or in the future by the one-sided myth of sharing with the dominant society. Tribal people may choose to sell their water in the future. Selling may not be an old tribal custom, but it could be a modern act of survival.

1974

✛ Changing Personal Names

Thomas Edward Kill petitioned a court for legal permission to change his name because he hopes to become a medical doctor.

Kill did not think his last name would inspire confidence or offer a comforting bedside meaning to his future patients.

Thousands of people each year, in what seems to be a growing practice, are changing their names for various reasons.

Occupational or professional idealism is one reason. Other reasons range from identification with spiritual and cultural movements to escapism and belief in divergent sexual and political ideologies.

Several years ago Milton Williams, a Minneapolis black educator and writer, changed his name to Mahmoud El-Kati for spiritual reasons. The first El-Kati was an African historian.

Donald DeFreeze became known to the world as Field Marshal General Cinque of the Symbionese Liberation Army. The first Cinque was an African tribal chief who led a slave ship to freedom.

James Morris, a distinguished journalist and travel writer, following transsexual surgery, changed his name to Jan Morris with the understanding and approval of his wife.

Patricia Hearst said she was given the name Tania when she decided to join her revolutionary kidnappers. Other members of the Symbionese Liberation Army also changed their names: Nancy Ling Perry became Fahizah and Patricia Soltysik changed her name to Mizmoon.

Esther Nahgahnub, a tribal activist on a Minnesota reservation, said she assumed the name of an Anishinaabe hereditary tribal leader to emphasize her identity.

There is nothing new about people changing their names, but in recent years the reasons for choosing new names seems to have shifted away from the historical period of assimilation—or the melting-pot of social acceptance—to the expression of unique individual identities through personal names.

"Taboos are applied not only to acts and objects, but also to words, and to none more than names," wrote Sir James George Frazer in *The New Golden Bough*.

A few people who change their names believe that they are escaping their past with the hope that they will become new persons with new names. But such fantasies of identity are not always true. Shakespeare wrote in *Romeo and Juliet* that "a rose by any other name would smell as sweet."

El-Kati, who assumed his new name on a spiritual trip to Africa, said that changing his name was an act of "personal freedom." Many black people, whose heritage was oppressed during slavery, are now rejecting the names associated with white slave masters.

The Honorable Elijah Muhammad writes in Muhammad Speaks that the "black man should be free in name as well as in fact . . . freed from the names imposed upon him by his former slave masters. . . ." The editor of the black religious newspaper is identified as Charles 67X.

A century ago the names of many immigrants were changed by immigration officials because they were too difficult to pronounce or spell. Other immigrants have voluntarily changed or shortened their names to avoid exclusion or the embarrassment of being identified as foreign-born.

But changes in names did not always mean a change of heart or cultural identity. The President of the United States was first known by his birth name Leslie Lynch King until his stepfather changed his name to Gerald Ford.

Twenty years ago the poet and novelist Feike Feikema changed his Frisian-language name to Frederick Manfred because he said he was "sick of having to spell that name . . . Why not have a name in the language of the culture I live in now?"

At the same time that there is an increase in the number of people who change their names, there seems to be a growing interest in the history of names.

Harold Hazelton, director of the New York Genealogical and Biographical Society, told a reporter for the New York Times that "there has been a resurgence of interest" in genealogical research.

Kenn Stryker-Rodda, president of the National Genealogical Society, pointed out that "grandparents no longer take the youngsters on their knee and tell them about their grandparents. The sense of human continuity is lost, sad to say, and there is a growing realization that it is something precious."

While there is a growing interest in the history of names and an increase in the number of people changing their names, many women, more than any time in history, are declaring their independence and retaining their birth-certificate names after marriage.

Those who change their names—or women who keep their names after marriage—seem to be depending more upon the historical or personal meaning of their names as a source of unique identity rather than upon occupational roles or social status.

Kurt Vonnegut, the novelist, wrote that "we are what we pretend to be, so we must be careful about what we pretend to be."

1974

✝ White Earth Remembered

"The novelty of a newspaper published upon this reservation may cause many to be wary in their support, and this from a fear that it may be revolutionary in character . . .

"We shall aim to advocate constantly and without reserve what in our view, and in the view of the leading minds upon this reservation, is the best for the interests of its residents . . ."

Those salutatory remarks were written by Theodore Beaulieu, the editor of *The Progress* — a newspaper published on the White Earth Reservation three generations ago.

Following the publication of the first issue of the newspaper, federal agents confiscated the press and ordered the removal of the publisher and editor — both of whom were tribal members — from the reservation.

Several months later a federal district court ruled that they could publish their newspaper without interference.

"Now that we are once more at sea," the editor wrote in the second issue of *The Progress*, "fumigated and out of quarantine . . . we will spare no pains in guiding you to a higher civilization."

Civilization was in grim transition then. While one generation of tribal people was removed to live on segregated reservations — giving way to white settlements — thousands in the next generation were forced to leave reservations.

286

Way Quah Gishig, like many tribal children, was forced to attend a federal boarding school hundreds of miles from his woodland home where he was given the name John Rogers and taught that his traditional culture was inferior.

Rogers is unusual, not because he learned to read and write under cultural duress, as many tribal children did, but because he used his new language to write a sensitive book about his experiences on the White Earth Reservation at the turn of the last century—about the same time as the publication of *The Progress*.

After six years at a boarding school, Rogers writes in his book *Red World and White* (published by the University of Oklahoma Press), he returned to the reservation to find his parents separated and his mother living alone in a wigwam.

"I was anxious to see my mother and be home again," the author remembers. "Mother was seated on the ground working on some fish nets . . . As she stood up with outstretched arms her eyes sparkled as does the sun on laughing waters . . ."

In spite of his adverse experiences in a racist world, Rogers writes with a sense of peace about his changing woodland culture. He is suspicious at times, but his memorial prose is not bitter or consumed with hatred for white people.

"She started talking joyously, but we couldn't understand very well what she said," Rogers wrote about his mother, "for we had forgotten much of the Indian language during our six years away from home.

"During the days that followed we had a happy time getting acquainted after those long years of separation . . . I was pleased to feel that I would grow into a strong young brave, and so I tried very hard to please her and to learn once more the Chippewa language.

"Mother promised to teach me the ways of the forest, rivers and lakes—how to set rabbit snares and deadfalls,

287

how to trap for wolves and other wild animals that roamed this land . . .

"Soon came the time for the leaves to turn brown and yellow and gold. The forest was beautiful and the wind rustled the dry leaves. We just couldn't resist the temptation to gather those beautiful colored leaves and the empty bird nests.

"At school, if we brought in a nest or a pretty leaf, we were given much credit, and we thought we would also please Mother by bringing some to her. But she did not like our doing this. She would scold and correct us and tell us we were destroying something—that the nests were the homes of the birds, and the leaves were the beauty of the forest."

His gentle thought rhythms and simple metaphors show a deep love for life. A love for nature without philosophical hesitation.

"I had learned to love the primitive life which had for so many, many generations influenced and shaped the existence of my ancestors . . . Nothing the white man could teach me would take the place of what I was learning from the forest, the lakes and the river.

"I could read more in the swaying of the trees and the way they spread their branches and leaned to the wind than I could read in any books that they had at school.

"I could learn much more from the smiling, rippling waters and from the moss and the flowers than from anything the teachers could tell me about such matters.

"I could gain knowledge from my daily walks under the trees where the shadows mixed with the shifting sunlight and the wind fanned my cheek with its gentle caress or made me bend, as it did the trees, to its mighty blasts."

His praise of nature as a spiritual teacher and his resistance to formula knowledge is not unlike the conflicts voiced by tribal people today. The difference is in experience. Three generations ago the author was living two lives in two real worlds. Today, many urban tribal people

288

who have not lived in the wilderness express romantic instincts rather than real experiences. The conflicts have changed and so has the language of cultural survival.

Rogers reveals with poetic affection the contrasts and contradictions in his experiences on the reservation. For example, while attending the boarding school at White Earth he was appointed to climb to the top of the water tower and oil the gears of the windmill.

"As I stood there breathing hard from my climb upwards I noticed how some trees were taller than others. And then I knew for the first time how the forest and fields and lakes looked to the bird that sailed so freely and happily about . . . Looking down again on the school grounds, the children appeared like dolls as they walked along the paths or ran about at play.

"As I observed all these things, I did not, for a moment, regret my leaving the forest home." Rogers then questions himself: "Perhaps there were advantages that would make up for what I had left behind!"

The author never lectures. His telling of life experiences on the reservation is gentle, more like whispering a great and lasting secret to the reader.

1974

✛ Tribal Newspapers

In the past decade thousands of periodic newsletters and newspapers have been published by tribal people.

The circulation of the newsletters is often small, but the number of publications on so many reservations indicates a strongly felt need among tribal people for more news and information by and about themselves.

For example, the *Leech Lake Reservation Newsletter* contains information about tribal governments, employment opportunities, health care programs, training programs and general news and editorials about changes on the reservation. Newsletters in many communities have provided a source of accurate information in place of gossip as a means of social communication.

Several tribal newspapers have a national circulation. For example, *Wassaja*, a national newspaper of Indian America, published by the American Indian Historical Society in California, is one of the most ambitious and successful newspapers published by and for tribal people.

Other major tribal newspapers include the *Navajo Times*, the *Tundra Times* and *Aswesasne Notes*.

Several hundred tribal newspapers are listed in the *American Indian Media Directory*, which was published this year by the American Indian Press Association.

The association is a Washington-based news service that publishes regular reports on federal legislation and policies

☞ READ THE PROGRESS.
THE ONLY PAPER
That Fearlessly and Truthfully
Advocates the Cause of the Red
Man, Justice and Fair-play.

THE PROGRESS.

☞ STUDY THIS ISSUE!
Observe the Defects of the Human Race, but Don't Lay all
the Short-Comings at the Door
of the Red Race.

"A Higher Civilization : The Maintenance of Law and Order."

VOL. 1.   WHITE EARTH AGENCY, MINNESOTA, SATURDAY, JUNE 23, 1888.   NO. 37.

The Indian : Right and Wrong.

RACE PREJUDICE.

A serious obstacle to the satisfactory adjustment of the Indian problem, is the

Absurd Race Prejudice,

which exists in the minds of so many. The Indian as judged from what seems to be his normal condition, is looked upon as the typical representative of all that is slothful, ignorant and inestimable.

He is looked upon as a being incapable of advancement to that plane, which, in this century, and in this country, is deemed a necessary requirement, by those who desire to occupy a recognized position in social life. We do not mean here, social life, as gauged by conventionalism, but social life in its broadest and best sense; that is, as the term which expresses conditions of living under principles voiced in the words,

Liberty, Equality and Fraternity.

Not, indeed, in the sense of the French revolutionists, but in that sense which our national parties would recognize.

It is to be regretted that public estimate is based upon observations biased, by preconceived notions, or by local sentiment, engendered by agrarian utilitarianism, or even by a sentiment kindly enough intentioned, but impatient for immediate results.

In what we have to say as an answer to these various modes of estimating our national character, we would call attention to history, and then leave inference to candid and impartial minds; believing that those who are really anxious to see the Indian problem solved will learn to judge charitably and hope, and strive for better things.

We do not doer that any one seeking the tenor of Indian reservation, will witness squalor and ignorance beyond measure, enough to make true the derogatory statement of comparison is to be instituted from conditions as they are now seen.

What surprises us, is that often literary tons have lose control of the historic instinct, and institute comparisons not falling under the guidance of sound judgment. As an illustration we may imagine some one advancing as true, a statement that "the Indian is distinctly inferior to the white man in intellectual and moral capacity." Such a man we should charge with

Lack of Literary Acumen,

or with absolute deficiency. For any one desirous of being honest in the discussion of etnology, must come armed and equipped with the observations of centuries. He must base his argument, not on a limited personal observation, nor upon the superficial reading of modern opinions.

Under this principle, we hold that he who draws comparison between the Cancasian of to-day and the Indian of to-day, commits a serious blunder, and we would remind him, that the impartial student of sociology compares epochs; stages in progression, rather than appearances as they are presented in parallel times.

If any of our readers occupy the platform of our fictitious individual, we would say to him: "turn to the pages of history and review the early condition of your own ancestry." Says a recent lecturer on "Anglo-Saxon history vs. Latin Imperialism." "Our Saxon-English ancestors were indeed savage,

ruthless, heathen worshippers of WOOD AND THUNDER !"

Mr. Taine in his remarkable, successful book on English literature seems to take a French relish in describing these "fine old English gentlemen of the real old kind." He says of them :

"Huge white bodies, cold blooded, with fierce blue eyes, reddish flaxen hair, ravenous stomachs filled with meat and cheese,

Heated by strong Drink !

of a cold temperament, slow to love, home-stayers, prone to brutal drunkenness, pirates at first; fond of all kinds of hunting, the manliest most profitable and most noble. They dashed to sea in their two sailed barks, landed anywhere, killed everything, and having sacrificed in honor of their gods the tithe of their prisoners, and leaving behind them the red light of their burnings went further on to begin again." A fine picture.

Suppose that some of the contemporary nations, whose civilization dated far backward, had said of them : "They are a people distinctly inferior, intellectually and morally," how the men of this century would turn with disgust at the hypercriticism of ancient civilization. And yet on the grounds of much of modern criticism, these ancient critics would not have been much out of the way.

In all this we argue that our social conditions in the country is but identical with that of the Anglo-Saxon of past ages.

How many centuries he lived as a savage and heathen we do not know, but we do know that his civilization and enlightenment are of comparative recent date, and more than that, were not indigenous, but importations, having dawn and zenith in what is now termed the "effete East." To the proud Caucasian we may say "at la brute."

Modern enlightenment according to the tend of individual exponents speaks sympathetically or neuradfully of the "far Orient." Manx laxey says that history has a tendency to repeat itself; in his mind's eye he saw the New Zealender gazing from the bridge upon the ruins of London ! Pursue the analogy, and might not the future red man gaze upon the ruins of New York and Brooklyn from their great suspension bridge ?

We believe, on the whole, that there is no justification in assuming any real distinction in the intellectual vitality and capability of the two races in question. The term 'white man' is too universal in definition to stand opposed to the red man in any true comparison, and from which results, such as are commonly held, shall really follow.

We are inclined to think that in most instances, comparison has been made rather from the conditions of the average red man and the educated white.

Let it be remembered that there are thousands upon thousands in the slums of American and European cities whose conditions, intellectually and morally, are

Far below Those of the Average Indian.

They are the dregs of humanity; the scum of civilization, whose conditions are what they are through lack of opportunity to rise in the scale of social life, and are less to blame for their inferior condition than the lawmakers and the less efforts of many christians.

Moreover we hold that intellect, being a common heritage, cannot be one thing in one race and another thing in another. It differs not in kind, however it may in degree, and we hold that opportunities being equal the white, red and black man will not, on the average, exhibit even the difference in degree. The position of the negro in the days of slavery (deferred him from the exercise of his intellectual powers, hence there arose instances in his history until recently of refined intellectual exhibition.

The isolation of the red man placed him in somewhat similar position, but still we may see that his freedom afforded him some opportunities for the exercise of his mind and to give exhibition in certain directions of talent and genius of no small order. Inter-tribal war, and conflicts between the native and the white intruder afforded means for exhibition and growth in statesmanship, diplomacy and military genius.

Holding to our definition of intellect, we ask, whether General Braddock exhibited greater powers than the leaders of his lawny foe? We ask whether the victories of Miles Standish were due so much to superior intellect as to the avowed superiority of powder and ball over bow and arrow? Have there been no Kino Philips, no Tecumsehs, no Logans, no Red Jackets, no Hole-in-the-days, no Sitting Bulls, and Black Hawks to contest the claim of Caucasian ? Have there been no Grand Guards to invent alphabets, no Parkers skilled in engineering and state craft ? What valiant christian soldier has done more in the service of the Master, than has the venerable Rev. J. Johnson-Enwegawung ?

It almost seems that some minds merely through force of inherited and, in some instances, cultivated prejudice, take as a text the oft asserted position of "Caucasian mental superiority;" and seek to ring it on the public at every occasion.

Some may assert that there is no "royal road to the equality we demand. They will most assuredly not "must prove" our inability to be what we claim. And we reply *that of the Indian is given the opportunity he CAN PROVE IT!*

We recognize that times have changed, and that the tide of the tide of times being on in the heaten paths of industrial arts. But we would not always be "hewers of wood and drawers of water."

This coupling of the ideas of "intellectual inferiority," and the "eternal necessity of physical toil" we decry. And if our wisest friends have no better advise to offer us than to be content to remain "physical toilers," they must excuse us if we do not accept.

We feel that our prosperity rests in the "persistent appeal to the conscience of the nation," and to this we do appeal and not to the unchristian prejudice of a narrow bigotry which would exclude one race from participation in the blessings of this country. Furthermore, we appeal to the conscience of the nation to repair the wrongs inflicted by the

Power of Physical Might

by placing the Indian upon an equality with the white man, distinctionally and politically.

We appeal to the conscience of the nation to furnish the opportunity for development intellectually. Give us the chance and we will exhibit the capability in due season to rank in with even the vaunted assertions of 'mental superiority." We do not expect to become existing examples at once, for we owe to deficiencies, that we must needs outlive national traits and characteristics, the results of heredity.

We say to this country "take us to your arms as you do the peasantry of foreign shores, cast us into the molds of your national methods, assimilate us, and we shall in time be a credit to you. Men of the country! We know that we lay before you a multifarious task, but you who are wise and noble, just and true, create a sentiment which shall *frown down* **our RACE PREJUDICE;** begin at once and lay the foundation for the change, by ample provision for our improvement in mentality and in industrial culture ; put your hands to the plow of reform and never look backward.

—WAR-MOORE.

THE PROGRESS.

JOB

WORK

—AND—

Printing

Establishment.

All kinds of Job Printing, such as Bill Heads, Letter Heads, Blanks, Cards, Tags etc., soit tile Work Warranted and Satisfaction Guaranteed.

affecting tribal people. The reports are mailed to media subscribers.

But this is not the first time in tribal history that so many newspapers have been published on so many reservations. A century ago more than a dozen weekly newspapers were published by reservation tribal people from Minnesota to Oklahoma.

For example, in 1843 the first issue of the *Cherokee Advocate* was published in Thalquah, Oklahoma, then known as Indian Territory. It was printed in both English and the Cherokee language.

Other weekly tribal newspapers of the time (all published in the Indian Territory) include the *Indian Arrow,* published at Fort Gibson; the *Chickasaw Enterprise,* published at Paul's Valley; *Our Brother in Red,* published in Muskogee; and the *Indian Citizen,* published at Atoka. Most of those newspapers continued as weekly publications for several years.

James Melvin Lee wrote in his *History of American Journalism* that another tribal journal, *The Vindicator,* published for the Choctaws and Chickasaws, merged with the *Oklahoma Star.*

In his history of newspapers and journalism, Frank Luther Mott wrote that "since whites could not own land in Oklahoma until after the opening in 1889, the papers published in the territory were designed chiefly for Indians. . . ."

There were many more newspapers published by and for tribal people a century ago, but one of the most interesting was *The Progress,* published on the White Earth Reservation in Minnesota.

The *American Newspaper Directory* for 1888 had the following entry for *The Progress:* "The only paper outside of the Indian Territory published and edited by Indians. A true friend of the Indian and his cause. The champion of the coming citizen and a fearless exponent of truth and justice."

Justice and Fair Dealing for every Indian who desires to become a good Citizen.

THE TOMAHAWK.

"Truth before Favor."

Published in behalf of, and to secure the welfare of the Indians of the United States.

MINNESOTA HISTORICAL SOCIETY

Vol. XIV.　　　White Earth, Becker County, Minnesota, Thursday, June 15, 1916.　　　No. 8.

THE TOMAHAWK.

GUS H. BEAULIEU,　-　-　Publisher

White Earth Agency, Minnesota.

Entered at the Postoffice at White Earth, Minn., as mail matter of the second class.

SUBSCRIPTION: $1.50 PER YEAR IN ADVANCE

FOR UNITED STATES SENATOR MOSES E. CLAPP.

It is probably the desire of every member of the Chippewa bands of Minnesota to have tribal affairs settled upon a basis that will give to the credit, in the United States Treasury, the share of each person who is entitled to participate in the tribal funds of the Chippewas of Minnesota.

Chippewa matters have been and are in towards a settlement by Senator Clapp and it is to the

UNITED STATES SENATOR MOSES E. CLAPP.

interest of the Chippewas that they should not neglect to take the day off on the 19th of this month and go to the polls and vote for him.

Senator Clapp has been a true friend to all the Chippewas of Minnesota, and has been in fact, as ex-Commissioner Dat S. Hall expressed it last year, the best United States senator Minnesota has ever had.

So far as the Chippewas are concerned it is up to them to now show their gratitude for the good work Senator Clapp has done for them in the past since he has been in Congress, by supporting him solidly at the primary election.

The Nomination Of Justice Hughes.

For nomination of Justice Hughes of the Supreme Court of the United States, by the Republican party, as its candidate for President of the United States, is being pressed by the Republicans generally with a grimace.

To sum it up briefly Justice Hughes was not the candidate a very large majority of the voters wished to see nominated. Col. Roosevelt was the choice of the people, but the fictonite alliance defeated the nomination of Hughes by agreeing to give him about three million German votes of the country.

For low-and Americanism of the American party is briefly this; it was cold for the votes of the German alliance by a few politicians who had the matter in charge at Chicago. The German citizens of the United States do not like Roosevelt for his outspoken sentiments in favor of America as against Germany, and they injected the master into American politics.

Neither do the American Germans like President Wilson's policy towards Germany, and for this reason they intend to punish him at the election next November in the same manner they have punished Col. Roosevelt. True Americanism will not stand for this.

FORTY-EIGHT YEARS AGO YESTERDAY

Chippewas Settled Upon This Reservation.

EVENT NOW BEING CELEBRATED AS USUAL.

Yesterday was the 48th anniversary of the arrival of the Chippewas upon this reservation from the Chippewa reservations then in Crow Wing county.

Of more than forty persons that were of the party that first arrived here, less than a dozen of them are alive today, and these are now taking part in the celebration that is now in progress to commemorate the event.

The establishment of this reservation resulted from the numerous Indian wars that existed in the northwest at that time as it became necessary for the government to consolidate each tribe up-

Candidates For Re-Election.

Among the candidates for re-election to a state office this year is Ira H. Mills, who is now one of the railroad and warehouse commissioners.

Mr. Mills is well and favorably known among many of the residents of this reservation. For years he was a United States Commissioner at Moorhead, which position he held until his election as a railroad and warehouse commissioner.

It is hoped that Mr. Mills will receive a good and substantial vote among his friends on the reservations, for one good turn deserves another and Mr. Mills did many good turns for some of the boys while he was a United States commissioner and not always in an official capacity.

Indian Office Extends Greetings.

The Indian office at Washington has extended greetings, through Assistant Commissioner of Indian Affairs Merritt, by telegram to Julius H Brown, president of the 14th of June Celebration, in the following words:

"The Indian Office extends to the Minnesota Chippewas on the occasion of their annual celebration, our cordial greetings and wishes ab to the harmonious time, fraught with good will towards one another and friendship towards your Sioux brethren, who come as your guests. May this meeting work an epoch in closely uniting all Chippewas and the Sioux in a lasting brotherhood and broadening your influence as American citizens and a deeper appreciation, love and respect for the glorious flag."

Minnesota Woman of Old Indian Days Dies.

Mrs. Mary Elizabeth Woodbury, a daughter of Major Lawrence Taliaferro, the first Indian agent in Minnesota, died at the age of 89 years at the home of her son, Lawrence, in Santee, Neb. Through her father, who was stationed at Fort Snelling from 1819 to 1840, she was closely associated with the early history of Minnesota.

Mrs. Woodbury was born in this state. When her father returned to Pennsylvania after resigning his post she remained behind and afterwards married Warren Woodbury of St. Paul. She is survived by two children, Mrs. Hannah Oliver Gammell of St. Paul, and Lawrence Woodbury, the postmaster at Santee, and a granddaughter, Mrs. N. M. Anders of St. Paul.—Minneapolis Tribune.

on a limited number of reservations so as to be better able to control them.

In those days the Indians were practically uncivilized, and, we are loth to add, a more inhuman set ran as a whole than they now are; they undertook, at the risk of being exterminated, to convince the government, in their wild way, that its field employee were not what the Indians and Congress expected them to be, and failing to bring the administrations to a realization of this fact, they invariably took to the war path.

Rev. J. Johnson (Enemegahow) who organized the 14th of June Celebration.

were of the party that first arrived here, less than a dozen of them are alive today, and these are now taking part in the celebration that is now in progress to commemorate the event.

Eventually, principally through the efforts of Capt. Pratt, who established the Carlisle Indian

Clement H. Beaulieu who aided Rev. Johnson Enemegahow to organize the first 14th of June Celebration in June 1875.

Peter Roy one of the interpreters of the treaty establishing this reservation.

school, the policy of educating Indians was adopted by the government, and as young Indians became educated, Indian wars ceased to exist. Today the celebration is being conducted exclusively by educated Indians, and they are doing this in a manner that is a credit to themselves and the Chippewas they represent.

Apropos to the cession of the six Chippewa reservations near the Mississippi in Crow Wing county, it is very doubtful whether the Chippewas made even a fair bargain, for it is upon their old reservations that a number of iron mines are now in operation, and many million dollars worth of iron has already been found there and is being shipped. But at that time no thought was given to iron, or any other kind mines, in Minnesota, except the little restriction

that took place at Vermillion Lake regarding the alleged discovery of gold in 1866, which soon died out, and on account of the futility of the soil here the government reported to make every Indian a farmer.

It will not be many years before the annual celebration here will cease entirely, for those who take a deep interest in the matter will cease to do so, and the younger element will no doubt fail to be impressed by the sentiment that now causes the genuine members of the tribe to observe the day.

ANDERSON VISITS WHITE EARTH.

A. G. Anderson, candidate for Congress against Halvor Steenerson, visited this place yesterday and got acquainted with many of his friends here, or those who wish to see him elected to Congress.

Mr. Anderson sustains his reputation of being a good mixer and there was nothing strained about him for the purpose of creating a good impression.

If any conclusion can be reached from indications Mr. Anderson will in the next congressman from the Ninth Congressional District.

EGGS FOR SALE.

Single Comb Rhode Island Reds for hatching, 75 cents per 15, $4.00 per hundred. Also day old chicks.

Max Blacknik, Waubun, Minn.

293

Augustus Beaulieu, publisher, and Theodore Beaulieu, editor, issued the first number of *The Progress* on March 25, 1886. They were critical of the Bureau of Indian Affairs, which had arbitrary authority on reservations then, and of federal legislation that allotted collective tribal reservation lands to individuals.

Following the publication of the first issue, federal agents confiscated the press and ordered the publisher and editor removed from the reservation.

Several months later, following a favorable federal court decision, publication of *The Progress* was resumed and continued weekly until 1889, when the name was changed to *The Tomahawk.*

The Progress published reports about tribal people and national news, but the editorial comments were the most controversial. For example, the following headlines were printed over a two-column, front-page report: "Is it an Indian Bureau? About some of the freaks in the employ of the Indian Service whose actions are a disgrace to the nation and a curse to the cause of justice. Putrescent through the spoils system."

Almost a century later, leaders of the American Indian Movement use similar language in criticism of the Bureau of Indian Affairs.

Similarities in history are difficult to resist. Today, as a century ago, tribal people are publishing their own newspapers and voicing the same intense criticism of the Bureau of Indian Affairs and other state and federal agencies.

Following the last gust of tribal publications a century ago, the federal government enacted policies of assimilation. But forced assimilation has not been successful. Reservations still exist; tribal people are still voicing the same criticisms, and there are many more tribal publications declaring tribal sovereignty.

1974

✝ Deerskin Simulations

The name of American Indian Movement leader Dennis Banks is familiar to tribal people in thousands of reservation homes. Familiar not because the radical spiritual and political leader has visited every reservation, but because he has been named in more newspaper reports than any other tribal person in recent history.

Banks uses the media without shame to advance his image and the cause of his organization, but he has also been a constant critic of newspaper reporters for their coverage of tribal issues. His motives in using the media may be challenged, but his general criticism of newspapers is well-founded from a tribal point of view.

Notwithstanding his disapproval of the media, the image of tribal people in local newspapers has expanded and improved in the past two decades. Twenty years ago it was not uncommon to read about tribal people as if they were somnolent cultural artifacts or uncivilized pagans living on wilderness reservations.

White people then were most often those consulted and quoted as authoritative sources of information about tribal people and their problems assimilating with the dominant society. But in the past few years the emphasis in newspaper reports has shifted from the patronizing views of white "experts" to tribal people as authentic sources of information about themselves. As a result, the diversity of tribal people has been recognized.

The shift from dominant white views to authentic experiences of tribal people corresponds to changes in public attitudes toward minority people.

The romantic tales of tribal traditions or the denigrating judgments of reservation life styles have given way to factual reports on such issues as industrial development on reservations or new programs in health and education.

These observations are based on an examination of several hundred newspaper reports and editorial columns which were published in the *Minneapolis Star* and the *Minneapolis Tribune* in the past two decades.

Twenty years ago, for example, the *Minneapolis Tribune* published a series of stories about tribal life on a reservation by a person named Deerskin. The stories told of traditional experiences.

The editors wrote that they had checked into the background of Deerskin and found him to be "eminently qualified to write about Indian tribal life." Several people responded to the series by writing letters to the editor.

Don Foster, then the local director of the Bureau of Indian Affairs, commented in a letter to the editor that he thought the stories were accurate. "They will meet with great public interest, and we think they should be widely read."

Helen Clapesattle, then editor of the University of Minnesota Press, said that the "narrator's level of literacy, vocabulary, is obviously much higher than his description of himself and his way of life would lead one to expect."

Another example was the late Jay Edgerton's series of editorial columns for *The Minneapolis Star* about the Nett Lake Reservation. The columns implied a sense of cultural superiority. "Out of the hard rock of Spirit Island in Nett Lake a series of crude pictographs holds a special significance for these remote Chippewa Indians living in the deep north woods . . .

"For some Chippewa," Edgerton wrote, "especially the older ones, the pictographs are said to have a connection

with their ancient tribal religion . . . with practices curiously like voodoo . . . which is having a revival among the
Chippewa. More progressive Indians deny this."

In another report about the wild-rice harvest Edgerton
wrote that "money will flow into the reservation again,
and provident Indians will prepare for the year between
harvests. Storerooms and freezers will be filled and old accounts settled.

"But for many more the harvest will mean a series of
sprees, poverty and even destitution . . ."

These are examples of newspaper reports which have
perpetuated the image of tribal people as hapless artifacts
of traditional reservation life. The articles are denigrating
and inaccurate and fail to show the rich diversity and personal aspirations of tribal people.

The most significant shift in the emphasis of newspaper
reports about tribal people occurred a decade ago, about
the time of the founding of the American Indian Movement and the first confrontations of radical urban tribal
people with the Bureau of Indian Affairs and other agencies.

The *Minneapolis Tribune* in 1966 reported on the emergence of "Indian Red Power." In the following three years
there were hundreds of reports on urban tribal issues and
numerous articles about Dane White and Thomas White
Hawk. White committed suicide after being held six weeks
in jail awaiting a juvenile court hearing. White Hawk was
sentenced to death by electrocution in South Dakota for
the murder of a white man. His sentence was commuted.

Ten years ago national attention was focused on the
problems of all minority people through the creation of
federal poverty programs. Journalists were writing more
about the issues of minority people because they had more
knowledge of urban problems and were able to understand the language and experiences of urban tribal people
better than those living on reservations.

Although the issues surrounding the American Indian
Movement have dominated the news, newspaper reports

Gaming facility to open in Walker

Questions about HUD funding persist

By Mark Boswell
Editor

A new casino-style gaming and lounge facility is expected to be opened this summer in Walker by the Leech Lake Reservation Business Committee.

Renovation of a 6,000-square-foot building located in Walker at the junction of Highways 371 and 200 is expected to cost $400,000. Martin Jennings, tribal planning director for Leech Lake said that the RBC will put up $200,000 of the project. An additional $200,000 is expected to come from the Department of Housing and Urban Development Community Development Block Grants.

Questions about the legitimacy of funding such a project with tax dollars were met with statements stressing the economic development aspects of such a project.

Jennings said that the positive results will outweigh the negative criticism. "Whenever you're doing something with public dollars, you can always find some type of criticism," said Jennings. "The way that we look at it is that if we can create new jobs, we're going to be taking those people off government assistance." Preliminary projections expect between 12 and 15 new jobs to be created by the project.

The Walker location was chosen for several reasons, said Jennings, but mainly to tap into a new market and make gaiming more accesible to other areas of the reservation.

Bill Atkins, Block Grant Representative for the Walker area stated that the facility was "a unique situation for which there is a set aside fund specifically for Indian reservations. Decisions for funding such a project under would have to be made by HUD directly."

The Minneapolis Office for Small Cities Programs representative Steve Johnson said that Community Development Block Grants were consolidated in the early 1980's. "The Chicago office now handles all of the Indian Housing and Community Developments..."

According to Leon Jacobs, Director of the Office of Indian Programs East of the Mississippi including the Leech Lake area, HUD does not fund such programs. Jacob's office, located in Chicago, oversees the funding of such projects through a similar fund. "There are funds available under the Community Development Block Grant Program which is a special set aside to assist tribes with a variety of community improvements such as community facilities and economic development. Bingo is an eligible activity under that program."

Asked whether or not HUD Block Grants should still be considered for projects such as the fpcility Jacobs explained: "they need to talk to their congressional representatives. The Congressional representatives have taken the position that it is economic development. We're not talking about gaming facilities, we're talking about Bingo halls, which in most states is categorized under a different statute."

Despite Jacob's stressing the point that the facility was for Bingo and not "a gaming facility", a press release presented by the project developers "envisions a Las Vegas-style casino where guests can take chances on some of the latest high-tech gaming machines in an informal and relaxing atmosphere."

Accordingly, public notice published in the Bemidji Pioneer requesting comment on the project stated: "The requested funds will be used for the economic development purpose of establishing a legal gaming facility..."

Bob Larson, tribal gaming officer looks at it differently. "I don't see us being in th gaming business. It is an activity that takes place here, but we are more into the entertainment business. We're trying to provide a forum for people to enjoy themselves."

"It is a game that people play and nobody plays it more than the Catholic Church," said Jacobs jokingly.

Jennings said the RBC has also discussed opening another facility on the eastern side of the reservation. The Walker location was chosen for several reasons, siad Jennings, but mainly to tap into a new market and make gaming more accessible to other areas of the reservation.

"The reality is," explained Jacobs,

Bingo/ see page 11

Features Page:

The Lac Court Oreilles are one of six Chippewa bands in Wisconsin that retain the right to hunt, spearfish, gather food and cut timber off reservation under court-affirmed 19th Century treaties. The *News* examines the issues surrounding the battles being fought to retain this right and the repercussions both in Wisconsin and elsewhere. *See page six.*

Voice of the Anishinabe

Fifty Cents

The Ojibwe News

Founded in 1988 | Volume 2 Issue 14 | February 7, 1990

A Bi-Monthly Publication

Bemidji, Minnesota 56601

Council of Indian Students powwow held last weekend in Bemidji

The Bemidji State Univerisity Council of Indian Students hosted the 1990 Winter Powwow at BSU last weekend. The powwow opened Friday evening to a crowd of about 1,000 participants and spectators who made the event a major success by the final dance on Sunday evening. Many drum groups were also in attendance, pictured are the Kingbird Singers. Photo by Jim Johnson.

Allery files brief

The *News* recently obtained copies of brief's filed by attorneys for Alan J. Allery and the United States Attorney's Office for the District of Minnesota.

The brief's were filed as a result of the appeal by Allery from his convictions by a United States District court jury on two counts of defrauding the Indian Health Service of over $15,000 in travel funds.

As a result of his conviction, Allery was sentenced to serve one year and one day in federal prison, to make restitution to the United States Government in the amount of $22,320, and to be placed on probation for a period of three years to commence upon his release from prison .

Allery's attorney Steven J. Meshbesher of Minneapolis, Minnesota, appealed Allery's conviction on the following two grounds:

(1) that the evidence presented in this case is insufficient to find the appellant (Allery) guilty beyond a reasonable doubt, and

(2) the trial court erred by refusing to give the jury, upon their request, an enlarged copy of the government rule and regulation regarding what constitutes temporary quarters.

Assistant U.S.Attorney James E. Lackner prepared the brief on behalf of the U.S. Government.

In a telephone interview with the Clerk's Office of the 8th Circuit Court of Appeals in St. Louis, Missouri.

The *News* learned that the court will determine in a few days whether oral arguments by the parties are necessary.

Attorney Steven Meshbesher, who is representing Allery, requested oral arguments whereas Assistant U.S. Attorney James Lackner stated they were not necessary.

In the event that oral arguments are allowed, they would most likely be heard in St. Paul, Minnesota, this spring.

Allery, who was former Director of the Bemidji Area Office of Indian Health Service, is currently employed as a consultant to Red Lake Tribal Chairman Roger A. Jourdain at an annual salary of $62,500.

In July,1989, based upon a request by Allery, Federal District Judge Edward Dewitts declared him to be *in forma pauperis* status, which requires that his attorney's fees for his appeal be paid by U.S. taxpayers.

BIA reviewing White Earth fisheries complex

Wilcox leaves in relation to alleged mismanagement

By Mark Boswell
Editor

White Earth Reservation Conservation Department's Head Biologist Dwight Wilcox was fired last Friday because of alleged mismanagement of accounts in relation to the construction of a fisheries project on Ice Cracking Lake.

According to Dan Stevens, District Representative for White Earth, "The budgets weren't turned in on time." He also said that it was just "poor management."

The project is being reviewed so that the problems in management can be worked out. According to guidelines set up by the Bureau of Indian Affairs, from which the project was funded, the money used for the project was meant specifically for renovation. The project, which includes a fisheries building and two expansive rearing ponds was built completely new. Since the funding source specifically stated that the money be used for "renovation", the project has been stalled for review by the BIA.

White Earth fisheries complex on Ice Cracking Lake. Photo by Mark Boswell

Roger Aitken, Superintendent of BIA operations in Cass Lake, is responaible for White Earth's federal funding. He did not return phone calls concerning the status of the fisheries complex situation.

Wilcox had been with the White Earth Conservation Department for 10 years. Despite the backing of the project by the White Earth RBC, Wilcox believes that his return to work there is "seriously doubtful."

"There was some problems with management and we're trying to work it out with the Bureau," said Stevens.

"The Tribal Council is still supporting the project out here," said Dave Renke, biologist working at the fisheries complex. He hopes that the problems in management will be ironed out.

"The Tribal Council is letting it fly and is supporting it. At this point we have two rearing ponds that we hope to raise fish in," he said.

Randy Zortman, fisheries specialist with the White Earth Conservation Department since 1986, believes that the project is a good idea. According to Zortman, the two rearing ponds should produce 500 lbs of fish flesh this up-coming season. At 200 fish fry per pound, the project is expected to produce a substantial amount of the fry that are used to stock area lakes. Walleye fry are raised to stock local fishing lakes to sustain good populations for sport fishing and netting.

"We hope to be on line in April," said Zortman. "We've been needing a project like this since 1983."

"In the past we have raised our own fry in natural rearing ponds," said Zortman. Problems with slow growth and the capturing of the fry have hampered the use of natural ponds as a source of fish fry. Other sources of fish fry have been provided by the Fisheries Department of the Leech Lake Reservation.

Video examining Fetal Alcohol Syndrome to Premiere in Cass Lake

The premiere of The Circle of Life, a video examining teen pregnancy, Fetal Alcohol Syndrome and battering, will be shown at the tribal chambers of the facility center in Cass Lake on Feb. 27, from 2-4:30.

The video, to be distributed nationally, was developed specifically for the American Indian population. Lynn Thunem, video project coordinator sees this program as a positive step toward addressing this issue because "there was a lack of sensitive films available to (Native Americans)."

The documentary is unique because teenagers have been responsible for the direction of the movie, the hiring of the production company, and the filming of the video. According to Thunem, teen involvement is important in such a project. "They are deciding what is relevant to them and we are honoring that."

Thunem and video organizers will be honoring the film participants as well as watching the video at the premiere.

Also present at the premiere will be prepresentatives from the March of Dimes, Blandin Foundation, area school prepresentatives, State Representative Toni Kinkel, and the Reservation Business Committee members.

"This is a movie from the people to the people," said Thunem. "It is a real gift."

Seating is limited at the event; call Lynn Thunem at 335-2911 for more information.

In Depth

Indian Housing:

According to the BIA, Indian country suffers from a 62,000-unit housing shortage. Many Indian families are forced to live in housing that is substandard, and in some cases virtually uninhabitable. The News continues an ongoing examination of the situation in Indian country as published in The Senate Select Committee on Investigations Report.
See page 8.

Ojibwe News, *published by William Lawrence*

in the past decade have also focused on treaty rights, tribal leadership, reservation politics, housing problems, education, cultural diversity and court actions over tribal rights to hunt and fish on reservations.

As the number of newspaper reports about tribal people increased, newspapers also began sampling public opinion. In 1965 the *Minneapolis Tribune* Minnesota Poll found that "six out of every ten persons in the survey contend that Indians on reservations do not have a reasonable standard of living."

Sixty-two percent of those surveyed thought that tribal people have been treated with dishonor by the federal government in the past three centuries.

To some extent the results of surveys on public attitudes and the radical activities of urban tribal people helped journalists expand their views and write with more understanding about tribal people.

Ten years ago both *The Minneapolis Star* and the *Minneapolis Tribune* began to publish several series on tribal people. They included news reports and editorial-page articles.

But the increased attention to tribal issues has not eased the criticism of the media.

Some believe that only tribal people are capable of reporting on tribal issues. The number of tribal people working for newspapers has increased in part because of several special training programs for minority journalists.

At the same time that many newspapers are increasing their coverage of tribal issues, hundreds of small tribal newspapers are being published on reservations and in urban centers across the country.

Wassaja, a national newspaper of Indian America, publishes reports about Banks and the American Indian Movement as often as major daily newspapers. The difference is that tribal journalists are more critical of radical leaders and their objectives.

1974, 1990

✝ Firewater and Phrenology

To be human means to stand in need of solace, of comfort in our grief or loss or in the painful throes of anxiety . . . to experience the pain in concert with our fellows, and to share our perceptions of meaning, however fleeting or partial, amidst confusion and despair is to be solaced, and at a price which, unbearable as it might seem, saves us from resigning our powers of decision to others.

NORMAN JACOBSEN
Pride and Solace

Plain Johnson hunkers over the wads of paper labels he peeled from seven bottles of cheap beer deep in cigarette smoke at the back of the bar. From a short distance he seems to be folded in the narrow booth, at the neck and stomach, a racial monad with swollen fingers. His bare elbows are thick, burnished from the tilt of his trunk, but there is nothing plain about this mixedblood tribal man who resisted social conversion in a foster home and saved his soul from the welfare state. Plain is a high altitude window washer in the afternoon, at night he drinks beer in a bar, and in the morning he writes poems and studies literature at a small private college.

Plain peels another label.

300

Tribal friends, and those who witness the attention that writers and social scientists give to his adverse experiences, find humor in the serious presentation of his past. The eagle feather on his black hat and the beaded floral patterns on his wide belt and watchband remind the white world of his pantribal traditions, while his dark skin determines the distance he feels in the dominant culture.

Plain is not detached from his tribal friends at the bar; he is separated from their expectations of his behavior as he had been from the values of the white foster families where he was placed as a child. He holds his birth name back; a secret, he explains, a sacred dream place where he finds his shadow and spiritual center; but he calls out his birth name in public when he is drunk, when he is aggressive and sentimental.

"Over the course of socialization, people learn about drunkenness what their society 'knows' about drunkenness; and, accepting and acting upon the understandings thus imparted to them, they become the living confirmation of their society's teachings," wrote Craig MacAndrew and Robert Edgerton in their book, *Drunken Comportment*. The authors set aside most commonsense arguments about the effects of alcohol on tribal people and conclude "that drunken comportment is an essentially *learned* affair."

Nancy Oestreich Lurie, in her article "The World's Oldest On-Going Protest Demonstration: North American Drinking Patterns," wrote that in her observation, "Indian people are more likely to get drunk when they feel thwarted in achieving Indian rather than white goals . . . Indian drinking is an established means of asserting and validating Indianness and will be either a managed and culturally patterned recreational activity or else not engaged in at all in direct proportion to the availability of other effective means of validating Indianness."

Mark Lender and James Martin point out in *Drinking in America* that tribal cultures have been the exception to the

301

rules of temperate drinking from the first contact with white colonists. The colonists "remained comfortable about alcohol for themselves," but expressed fear that the use of alcohol by tribal people and blacks "could be dangerous to overall societal stability.

"The colonial view of Indian drinking, that red men could not hold their liquor, was in fact the beginning of a long-standing stereotype of the impact of alcohol on the tribes. Many early settlers believed Indians to be uncivilized—nothing more than 'savages'; therefore, any sign of intemperate behavior served to confirm that image. Some modern anthroplogists have termed the so-called Indian drinking problem the 'firewater myth.' This stereotype not only followed the white frontier line," the authors assert, ". . . but in many respects has survived into the present."

Lender and Martin explain that most tribal cultures were "unfamiliar with beverage alcohol before the invasion of the whites. Most tribes got their first taste from the explorers and adventurers who preceded the influx of settlers." Research has never revealed an unbiased translation of the "firewater myth," nor clinical evidence that tribal people have a genetic weakness or predisposition to alcohol. The authors explain that "some tribes learned to drink from the wrong whites: fur traders, explorers, or fishing crews, all of whom drank hard and, frequently, in a fashion not condoned by the social norms in traditional, settled colonial communities.

"Some whites, for a variety of motives, encouraged binge drinking among the Western Indians," the authors conclude. "Not all tribes succumbed: They either shunned the white man's alcohol or learned to assimilate it without major cultural disruption. But others, like many of the Eastern Indians, fell afoul of fur traders and land speculators who employed established methods of getting Indians drunk before making deals with them. The shrewdest traders refused to negotiate with a sober Indian."

302

Ray Allen Billington, in *Land of Savagery Land of Promise,* asserts that "few observers were willing to admit that drinking was an escape-hatch from the poverty and humiliation that accompanied the shattering of their culture." He participates in the complaisant victimization theme that the "true villains were the storekeepers and traders who plied them with liquor to cheat them of their lands and goods."

In response to these preconceptions and fears of white settlers, the federal government enacted legislation that purported to protect tribal cultures from unscrupulous whites. The new laws, however, regulated frontier resources, economies, and territorial settlements. First the government restricted, and then in 1832 prohibited liquor in tribal communities. It was not until 1953 that the racist law prohibiting the sale of liquor to tribal people was repealed. The federal response to the excessive consumption of alcohol in white families was much less severe: the Eighteenth Amendment to the Constitution of the United States, or the "Prohibition Amendment," which forbade the manufacture and sale of alcoholic beverages, was ratified in 1920 and repealed thirteen years later.

"Perhaps no stereotype has been so long-lasting and so thoroughly ensconced in our social fabric as that of the 'drunken Indian.' Our federal government," Joseph Westermeyer wrote, "gave it official recognition by prohibiting the sale of beverage alcohol to Indian people for over a century. Until recently, many missionary groups required that Indian converts take a pledge of total abstinence." Westermeyer, in his article " 'The Drunken Indian': Myths and Realities," examines the common misconceptions that flow from the "nonlogical stereotype" of tribal cultures and beverage alcohol.

"Indians cannot hold their liquor. This stereotype presumes that Indian people who drink do so to excess and inevitably encounter problems as a result of their alcohol usage. Generally this presumed tendency is felt to be due to some

303

inherent racial trait that results in alcohol's affecting Indians in a specific and unusual manner. . . .

"*Alcoholism rates are very high among Indians.* First, we have the problem of what comprises a case of alcoholism. In the opinion of most people, simply imbibing alcohol or behaving in an intoxicated manner is not a sufficient criterion for alcoholism. . . . Considerable differences exist among tribes, even taking into account the small populations of some tribes that make reliable intertribal comparisons difficult. Also, within tribes there are subgroup differences, and within subgroups there are considerable individual differences. These differences, and the reasons for them, have been neglected in most studies," Westermeyer points out in his article. When "Indian rates are compared with national averages, some groups and tribes do have rates of alcohol-related problems that exceed the mean, and some have rates that are much lower. . . .

"*Alcoholism is the major problem among Indian people.* Even among Indian groups that do have high rates of alcohol-related problems, it is difficult to know whether a given problem is caused by alcohol or by various social, economic, historical, cultural, and/or political factors. Alcohol problems are often associated in a given individual with such stresses as migration from the reservation to a non-Indian community; racial and ethnic prejudice; health impairment; unemployment or marginal economic status; outside interference by non-Indian social agencies in family and community affairs; and lack of control in his own community over the education of his children, law enforcement, religious institutions, and health and welfare resources.

"For any one Indian or group of Indians it is difficult to separate racial prejudice, family disintegration, or economic oppression from alcohol in the genesis of various problems. However," Westermeyer emphasizes, "the danger exists that if alcoholism is focused on as the biggest

problem, urgent political and economic issues may be ignored. This is especially true because much of what is done
regarding alcoholism is done at the individual level, ignor-
ing important social, cultural, and intercultural problems."

Westermeyer points out that tribal alcohol problems
"bear many resemblances to those common to many ethnic
groups in the United States." He concludes that attention
to tribal alcoholism "should not mask or preclude attention
to the many social problems and inequities against which
Indian people now struggle."

The National Institute of Mental Health has reported
that alcoholic related deaths for American Indians are four
to five times higher than among the general public. Two-
thirds of those deaths are caused by cirrhosis of the liver.
Alcohol is also related to higher arrest rates, accidents, homicide, suicide, and spouse and child abuse. In the past

decade there has been a dramatic increase in public funds for research and training and treatment programs in tribal communities for problem drinkers.

The Juel Fairbanks Aftercare Residence, for example, is a treatment center serving alcoholics, most of whom are tribal people, in Ramsey County, Minnesota. Michael Miller and Laura Wittstock, authors of a report on alcoholism, which is based on interviews with tribal people who were treated at the center in St. Paul, estimate that about half of the tribal population in the nation is chemically dependent. Forty percent more are affected as families and relatives. "Virtually the entire American Indian population is affected, directly or indirectly by alcoholism," the authors assert in their report, which was published by the Center for Urban and Regional Affairs at the University of Minnesota.

"Problem drinking and alcoholism are most prevalent among those Indian people who are the least acculturated to urban life," the authors point out. Other studies, however, emphasize the opposite view, that acculturation is *not* the most important factor, that deviant behavior is *not* explained by acculturation.

Plain Johnson seldom drinks alone; he hunkers in a booth at the back of the bar, deep in smoke, with his tribal friends, the friends who understand his gestures and who give meaning to his experiences at the cold intersections in the cities. Plain counts all his tribal friends as his brothers.

Samuel leans back in the booth with a wide smile, a simple pose he likes to strike at least once a night. He drinks gallons of cheap beer and tells trickster stories in the best oral tradition; he is a fine teacher in a small college, and he is a problem drinker.

Cecelia drinks vodka and fruit juices and bears a perpetual cigarette with a short curved ash as she fingers the ends of her tangled black hair. She is a tribal mixedblood, the mother of four children who have been placed in foster care homes because she is an alcoholic. She is at home in the back of the bar with her friends.

Ramon is a medical doctor, the first in his tribe to earn the high honor of becoming a biomedical healer, and he is an alcoholic. He practices medicine on the road, at tribal social and cultural events, and at the back of tribal bars in the cities. This morning he was invited to meet with tribal students at a small college, summoned as a model of tribal achievements, but when he stumbled out of the elevator with his trousers unzipped, and vomit stains on his shirt, the event was canceled.

Harmon has been on the bottle since he lost his right arm in combat. He can trace his descent to a circle of proud warriors. Each morning he begins his series of toasts to his phantom arm, his three wives, and the children he seldom visits.

Charles has never been employed for more than one month at one place because work interfered with his drinking. The old mixedblood trapper was a modern tribal nomad, a severe alcoholic who moved back to the reservation alone last winter and froze to death three feet from the door of his cabin in a snowstorm. Plain Johnson, and all his friends from the tribal bar, remembered the trapper at a traditional wake and tribal burial.

Tribal cultures are burdened with statistical summaries, romantic preoccupations, cultural inventions, social expectations, adverse public attitudes, in both tribal and urban white worlds. The view that tribal people have a predisposition or genetic weakness to alcohol is a racist response to a serious national problem. The notion that tribal people drink to relume their past memories as warriors will neither explain nor mend the broken figures who blunder drunk and backslide through cigarette smoke from one generation to the next. Separations from tribal traditions through marriage or acculturation do not explain the behavior associated with drunkenness. Tribal cultures are diverse and those individuals who are studied at the bar, or on the streets, are unique, alive and troubled, not static entities from museums or the notebooks of culture cultists. There is some humor over the adversities tribal people bear in racist societies, but there is not much to laugh about in the families of alcoholics.

"Outside of residence in a concentration camp," wrote George Vaillant, in his book *The Natural History of Alcoholism*, "there are very few sustained human experiences that make one the recipient of as much sadism as does being a close family member of an alcoholic."

There are two common themes evident in most of the studies of tribal drinking, according to Michael Everett, editor of the book *Drinking Behavior among Southwestern Indians*. The first theme is that tribal drinking is somehow different from other drinking, and the second theme is that tribal drinking, in spite of the problems and abuses of alcohol, "has a number of positive aspects that are often ignored or denied."

Edwin Lemert, for example, studies cultures on the northwest coast and emphasized the positive use of alcohol in the revival of traditional patterns of tribal leadership and ritual when traditional behavior was denied by the white dominant culture. Other studies conclude that tribal drunkenness is a *positive* approach to social integration, a method of survival under cultural duress and the stress of acculturation in the white world.

Stephen Kunitz and Jerrold Levy, in their research on tribal drinking in the Southwest, questioned whether tribal drinking is a "retreatist or escapist response to social disintegration," or whether the behavior is compatible with "tribal institutional values." The authors conclude that deviant behavior associated with alcohol can be explained in terms of social type, and that the "persistence of pattern of suicide and homicide over long periods indicate that neither increased acculturation nor increased alcohol use have been the major factors influencing these types of social deviance."

308

Thomas Hill, who studied tribal drinking in Sioux City, Iowa, wrote in his dissertation, "Feeling Good and Getting High: Alcohol Use of Urban Indians," that "multiple sets of drinking norms or standards exist within the Indian population." He points out that what is acceptable or unacceptable consumption of alcohol depends "upon whose perception we adopt. . . . I have tried to show that at any single point in time many factors may play a role in 'causing' an individual to engage in excessive or problem drinking: social pressure, few social controls limiting drinking, various psychological motives, and biochemical and physiological variables." The tribal people he studied "were not suffering from a massive state of 'deculturation' or sociocultural disorganization."

American Indians resist the traditional methods of treating alcoholism, assert Michael Miller and Laura Wittstock in their report. "For many Indians, drinking is such a central element in social life that to avoid it means to reject friends, relatives," and familiar social places. "The solution to alcoholism has as much to do with improving the conditions of life for Indians as it does with improving treatment programs," the authors explain. "A major difficulty for many Indians in remaining sober is finding an environment of friends and a social life that is free of alcohol. There is a constant pressure to be in social and family situations where alcohol is present." The authors point out that their research "uncovered fewer persons raised by foster parents, particularly white foster parents, than was expected. Studies from other areas have indicated that as many as twenty-five to thirty percent of those surveyed were raised by white foster parents and their alcoholism rates were higher than the general Indian population."

Miller and Wittstock conclude that "alcoholism is but one symptom of the economic and social conditions faced by Indians. Key among these conditions is unequal access to the economic benefits of society."

The problems of alcoholism in tribal communities are as burdensome as some of the theories and proposed solutions. Even to the biased outsider the definitions of tribal alcoholism, and the explanations of drunken behavior, seldom lead to common treatment methods or reliable prevention plans. The diverse experiences of tribal people decamp from simple racial solutions to the problem. Histories tumble with each drink; tribal memories and colonial theories break from the masculine pleasures stored in national advertisements for beverage alcohol.

Kunitz and Levy, for example, contend that "the pattern of alcohol use differs depending on degree of acculturation. . . . To be like a white man means, in part, drinking like one."

Ron Wood, a Navajo who works in a public health program, expresses a similar view, that the "more acculturated a Native American person is, the more his drinking pattern tends to resemble the Anglo pattern of drinking." He points out how drinking habits differ from tribe to tribe. "The Navajo drinking pattern is generally of an open, boisterous manner with friends, while the Hopi pattern is generally of a singular, secretive, or less boisterous nature. To be effective, a Native American alcoholism counselor must be aware of these differences among individual clients."

Research seldom focuses on the "practical issues of treatment," or the prevention of alcohol problems, according to Michael Everett, editor of *Drinking Behavior among Southwestern Indians*, because the studies emphasize the "positive functions of drinking and drunkenness." Everett contends that theories and research methodologies have contributed little to the meanings of tribal drinking practices, "and even less to the development of effective treatment and prevention strategies for Indian alcoholism and problem drinking."

Thomas Hill, an anthropologist, did not consider treatment programs in his studies of tribal drinking in Sioux

310

City, but he concludes, nevertheless, that "a program which attempts to utilize a single treatment approach will be inadequate."

Miller and Wittstock, however, include treatment strategies in their research and report. Based on interviews, the authors are critical of confrontation therapies, those that counter the behavior of alcoholics, because when used by white counselors the tribal clients could perceive the methods "as symbolic of the conflict between white and Indian cultures." The authors conclude that "better treatment programs" should emphasize the need for "Indian staff and counselors, and making use of Indian culture and spiritual values in the course of treatment."

311

Certain traditional tribal spiritual practices, such as herbal or symbolic healing, are culture specific, limited to one cultural experience. Other religious and spiritual events, such as the sacramental use of peyote, have been successful in the treatment of alcohol problems. The Native American Church, which uses peyote in ceremonies, and pantribal fundamentalist movements have been effective rehabilitation experiences for some tribal people.

These are positive methods of treatment and rehabilitation, but there are also punitive approaches to the problem that prohibit the use of alcohol. There seems to be less tolerance of drunkenness at social and tribal spiritual events; signs that prohibit the use of alcohol or drugs appear more often on the doors of tribal centers.

Plain Johnson, and other tribal people at the bar, are marginal consumers of alcohol in the annals of advertisers. Tribal consumption, however, does have some commercial value. Some owners will sponsor social and athletic events for their tribal customers, but most owners of tribal drinking places encourage the consumption of alcohol for personal profits. The federal government collects revenue from the sale of beverage alcohol; the funds that are returned to tribal communities are used to establish new treatment bureaucracies that focus on individuals rather than on larger social problems.

Being Indian, Ron Wood points out, "is not enough qualification to be a successful counselor, nor is the fact that a person is a recovered alcoholic sufficient qualification. . . . A certain amount of technical training is necessary to be a good counselor, but the most important criterion is having a good heart and empathy to help fellow [tribal people]."

National measures that once prohibited the sale of beverage alcohol were never the last words on alcoholism. Legislation has defined and regulated the public use of alcohol: the age, locations, and responsibilities of consumers. Private imbibing of alcohol has been protected as an individual right; the manufacture and sale were prohibited, but not the consumption of alcohol.

Alcohol abuse in the past two decades has been treated as a disease rather than a crime. However, the consumption of beverage alcohol by pregnant tribal women has been cursed as a moral crime; the protection of the fetus has been seen as more critical than the constitutional rights of the mother.

"On some American Indian reservations, the situation has grown so desperate that a jail internment during pregnancy has been the only answer possible in some cases," wrote Louise Erdrich in the foreword to *The Broken Cord* by Michael Dorris. The situation is Fetal Alcohol Syndrome.

Dorris, an anthropologist, dedicated his book to his adopted son who was born on a reservation. The "delivery of my premature son was unlikely to have been a joyous occasion," he wrote. "Most fetal alcohol babies emerge not in a tide, the facsimile of saline, primordial, life-granting sea, but instead enter this world tainted with stale wine. Their amniotic fluid literally reeks of Thunderbird or Ripple, and the whole operating theater stinks like the scene of a three-day party. Delivery room staff who have been witness time and again tell of undernourished babies thrown into delirium tremens when the cord that brought sustenance and poison is severed. Nurses close their eyes at the memory. An infant with the shakes, as cold turkey as a raving derelict deprived of the next fix, is hard to forget."

Doubtless, the disabilities attributed to alcoholic mothers would burden the memories of the most detached constitutional lawyers; however, the incarceration of pregnant tribal women as a preventive measure to protect the fetus from alcohol would be racial paternalism, liberal fascism, and a denial of civil liberties.

"If a woman is pregnant and if she is going to drink alcohol, then, in simple language, she should be jailed," asserted Jeaneen Grey Eagle, director of Project Recovery.

313

Dorris interviewed her on the Pine Ridge Reservation in South Dakota. He wrote that "her words were shocking, antithetical to every self-evident liberal belief I cherished, yet through my automatic silent denial I felt some current of unexpected assent. . . . What civil liberty overrode the torment of a child?"

Dorris holds his compassionate rhetoric for children too close to moral imperatives. He reviews the scientific research on Fetal Alcohol Syndrome, but not the legal and religious discourse over fetal rights and abortion. Neither incarceration nor the termination of civil liberties would end the social burdens of children with deformities.

Indeed, alcohol is poison, but must tribal women on reservations bear the moral and legal responsibilities for those who distribute beverage alcohol and for a government that profits from taxation on the sale of alcohol? Poor tribal women would pay the moral price once more for the sins of the nation and the anxieties over alcoholism. Actual incarceration would be determined by race and economic class; more white than tribal women would have the means to defend their rights. Poor tribal women would be detained as salvation for moral crimes.

To censure tribal women on reservations is simplism, and a star chamber moral warrant based on racial and phrenologic insinuations. Should the federal government and reservations establish alcohol police units to detain tribal women? Would the crimes be based on evidence? Who would decide the moment when a fetus is deformed? Would romantic liberals be sworn as deputies in the crusade?

Dorris is a serious social scientist, but some of his research notions seem to be based on earlier phrenologic diagnoses. For instance, he wrote that a collection of photographs of "children from various ethnic groups" were reviewed by "scientists and physicians." Based on their past clinical experiences the respondents "were highly accurate in selecting the photos of children at risk" for Fetal

314

Alcohol Syndrome. Dorris considers photographic "signs" of the syndrome from an article in the *New England Journal of Medicine:* "Low nasal bridge. Short palpebral fissures, obscure the canthus, or inner corner of the eye, a normal feature in certain species of the Mongolian race. Thin reddish upper lip. Small head circumference. Epicanthic folds. Short nose. Small midface. Indistinct philtrum, an underdeveloped groove in the center of the upper lip between the nose and the lip edge."

Moreover, "bad judgement" is cited as "one of the most subtle, most difficult, but most telling symptoms" of Fetal Alcohol Syndrome. Dorris quotes researcher Ann Streissguth: "This condition had less to do with intelligence than it did with the inability of a person to evaluate the consequences of his or her actions." Such observations would burden the entire population with imperfections in search of a definition.

The phrenologic notions that facial features and countenance indicated mental capacities, moral manners, and national traits were common racial measures endorsed by scholars more than a century ago. Samuel Morton, for instance, wrote in *Crania Americana* that "there is a singular harmony between the mental character of the Indian, and his cranial developments as explained by phrenology."

Dorris wrote that his adopted son lacked a "particular kind of imagination. . . . He existed in the present tense, with occasional references to past precendent. . . . His estimation of consequences was so hazy that it translated into an approach to action so conservative that it appeared to be stubborn."

George Bancroft used similar phrenologic notions in his *History of the United States, from the Discovery of the American Continent.* "The red man has aptitude at imitation rather than invention. . . . But he is deficient in the power of imagination to combine and bring unity into his floating fancies, and in the faculty of abstraction to lift himself out of his dominion of his immediate experience."

315

"Michael and I have a picture of our son," wrote Erdrich in the foreword. "For some reason, in this photograph, taken on my grandfather's land in the Turtle Mountains of North Dakota, no defect is evident in Adam's stance or face. Although perhaps a knowing doctor could make the fetal alcohol diagnosis from his features, Adam's expression is intelligent and serene. He is smiling, his eyes are brilliant, and his brows are dark, sleek. There is no sign in this portrait that anything is lacking."

Scientists are not certain why Fetal Alcohol Syndrome "strikes the children of some alcoholic mothers but not others, and why susceptibility varies among different ethnic groups." Andrea Dorfman reported in *Time* magazine that Native Americans are thirty-three "times as likely as Caucasians to have a child" with the syndrome. Such evidence could suggest a genetic predisposition, "but scientists have not been able to identify the offending gene."

Native American Indian women bear the fantasies of men and the mythic deliverance of civilization. In *The Broken Cord*, tribal women who would poison and wound their children with alcohol are numerical inventions and represent institutional values; the author is the intransitive confessor and the moral archivist. The social science revelations are the technologies of racial politics.

Michel Foucault pursued a discourse on the "technologies of domination" and the "truth games . . . that human beings use to understand themselves." He wrote in *Technologies and the Self* that "we find it difficult to base rigorous morality and austere principles on the precept that we should give ourselves more care than anything else in the world. We are more inclined to see taking care of ourselves as an immorality, as a means of escape from all possible rules. . . . We are the inheritors of a social morality which seeks the rules for acceptable behavior in relations with others."

George Vaillant writes that alcoholism reflects "deviant behavior that can be often better classified by sociologists than by physiologists; alcoholism is often better treated by psychologists skilled in behavior therapy than by physicians with all their medical armamentarium. But unlike giving up gambling or fingernail biting, giving up alcohol abuse often requires skilled medical attention during the period of acute withdrawal. Unlike gamblers and fingernail biters, most alcoholics as a result of their disorder develop secondary symptoms that do require medical care."

Reviewing the treatments and definitions of alcoholism, the author, who is a psychiatrist at the Harvard Medical School, argues that "calling alcoholism a disease, rather than a behavior disorder, is a useful device both to persuade the alcoholic to admit his alcoholism and to provide a ticket for admission into a health care system."

Vaillant has not studied alcoholism in tribal communities, but in general he points out that alcoholism affects one-third of all American families, and the mortality rate for alcoholics is higher, four times the average. The cost of alcoholism, in lost wages and treatment, is fifty billion dollars a year. In the past decade, according to the author, the federal government has invested one-hundred million dollars on alcoholism treatment programs.

Plain peels the last label for the night.

1983, 1989

REFERENCES

Bancroft, George. *History of the United States, from the Discovery of the American Continent* (Boston: Charles Little and James Brown, reprint 1846).

Berkhofer, Robert F., Jr. *The White Man's Indian: Images of the American Indian from Columbus to the Present* (New York: Knopf, 1978).

Billington, Ray Allen. *Land of Savagery Land of Promise: The European Image of the American Frontier in the Nineteenth Century* (New York: Norton, 1981).

Dorris, Michael. *The Broken Cord* (New York: Harper & Row, 1989).

Everett, Michael, and Jack Waddell, eds. *Drinking Behavior among Southwestern Indians* (Tucson: University of Arizona Press, 1980).

Hill, Thomas Warren. *" 'Feeling Good' and 'Getting High': Alcohol Use of Urban Indians."* Unpublished dissertation, University of Pennsylvania, 1976.

Hoffman, Walter James. "The Mide wiwin; or 'Grand Medicine Society' of the Ojibwa," in *United States Bureau of American Ethnology. Seventh Annual Report, 1885–86* (Washington, D.C.: Government Printing Office, 1891).

Kunitz, Stephen J., and Jerrold E. Levy. "Changing Ideas of Alcohol Use among Navajo Indians." *Quarterly Journal of Studies on Alcohol*, 35 (1974): 243–59.

Lender, Mark Edward, and James Kirby Martin. *Drinking in America* (New York: Free Press, Collier Macmillan, 1982).

Lurie, Nancy Oestreich. "The World's Oldest On-Going Protest Demonstration: North American Indian Drinking Patterns." *Pacific Historical Review*, 40 (August 1971).

MacAndrew, Craig, and Robert B. Edgerton, *Drunken Comportment: A Social Explanation* (Chicago: Aldine, 1969).

Martin, Luther, Huck Gutman, and Patrick Hutton, eds. *Technologies of the Self: A Seminar with Michel Foucault* (Amherst: University of Massachusetts Press, 1988).

Miller, Michael, and Laura Waterman Wittstock. "Indian Alcoholism in Saint Paul." *Center for Urban and Regional Affairs Report* (University of Minnesota, November 1981).

Morton, Samuel. *Crania Americana* (Philadelphia, 1839).

Rogers, John. *Red World and White: Memories of a Chippewa Boyhood* (Norman: University of Oklahoma Press, 1973. First published as *A Chippewa Speaks*, 1957).

Tanner, Helen Hornbeck. *The Ojibwas: A Critical Bibliography* (Bloomington: Indiana University Press, 1976). Published for the Newberry Library.

Thornton, Russel, Gary Sandefur, and Harold Grasmick. *The Urbanization of American Indians: A Critical Bibliography* (Bloomington: Indiana University Press, 1982). Published for the Newberry Library.

Unger, Steven, ed. *The Destruction of American Indian Families* (New York: Association of American Indian Affairs, 1977).

Vaillant, George. *The Natural History of Alcoholism* (Cambridge, Mass,: Harvard University Press, 1983).

Vizenor, Gerald. *Tribal Scenes and Ceremonies* (Minneapolis: The Nodin Press, 1976).

_____ . *Wordarrows: Indians and Whites in the Fur Trade* (Minneapolis: University of Minnesota Press, 1978).

_____ . *Earthdivers: Tribal Narratives on Mixed Descent* (Minneapolis: University of Minnesota Press, 1981).

Westermeyer, Joseph. " 'The Drunken Indian': Myths and Realities." *Psychiatric Annals,* 4 (November 1974). Reprinted in Unger (ed.), *The Destruction of American Indian Families.*

✚ PUBLICATION NOTES

"Crossbloods and the Chippewa" was published in a shorter version as "Minnesota Chippewa: Woodland Treaties and Tribal Bingo" in the *American Indian Quarterly*, Winter 1989. "Bone Courts" was published in the same journal, Fall 1986. The *American Indian Quarterly* is published at the University of California at Berkeley.

"Socioacupuncture: Mythic Reversals and the Striptease in Four Scenes" was first published in *The American Indian and the Problem of History*, edited by Calvin Martin (Oxford University Press, 1987).

"Thomas White Hawk" was first published as "Why Must Thomas White Hawk Die?" in the *Twin Citian* magazine, June 1968; "Commutation of Death" was published in the same regional magazine, January 1970.

The six-part editorial series on the American Indian Movement, "Confrontation Heroes," "The Death of Bad Heart Bull," "Bandits in Rapid City," "Good Little Indians," "Racism on Frontier Circle," and "Urban Radicals on Reservations," was published in the *Minneapolis Tribune*, March 1973. The newspaper later became the *Minneapolis Star and Tribune*.

"Candidate Russell Means" was published as an editorial column in the *Minneapolis Tribune*, February 3, 1974; "Speaking for Mother Earth" was published on March 10, 1974.

"Senator Mondale at Rough Rock" was first published as "Indian Education and Senator Mondale at Rough Rock" in the *Twin Citian* magazine, July 1969, and reprinted in the *Congressional Record*, August 7, 1969.

"Red Lake Truant Officer" appeared in the *Minneapolis Tribune Picture Magazine*, a special report on Indian education in Minnesota, March 16, 1969.

"Protecting Tribal Identities" was published as an editorial column in the *Minneapolis Tribune*, November 16, 1973; "Treaties and Tribal Rights" was published as an editorial column in the same newspaper, June 15, 1974.

"Leech Lake Agreement" appeared in the *Walker Pilot*, June 22, 1972.

"Custer Died for Pantribal Pop," "Wampum and the Presidents," "The Politics of Paraeconomics," and "Indians Are Great Sharers" were edited from a special report on reservation economics written for the Ninth District Federal Reserve Bank, Minneapolis, 1975.

"Inside Toilets" was first published in *The Everlasting Sky* by Gerald Vizenor (Macmillan, 1972).

"Stealing Tribal Children" was an editorial column in the *Minneapolis Tribune*, April 15, 1974; "Departing from the Present" appeared on April 15, 1974; "Claims to the Grand Canyon" was published in the same newspaper on May 14, 1974; "Water Rights on Reservations," June 1974; "Changing Personal Names," June 10, 1974; "White Earth Remembered," July 21, 1974; and "Tribal Newspapers," August 25, 1974. "Deerskin Simulations" appeared as an editorial column on August 11, 1974.

"Firewater and Phrenology" includes recent information on Fetal Alcohol Syndrome; the shorter version was first published as "Firewater Labels and Methodologies" in the *American Indian Quarterly*, Fall 1983.

Gerald Vizenor, a mixedblood member of the Minnesota Chippewa tribe, is a professor of literature and American Studies at the University of California, Santa Cruz. He has also taught at the University of California, Berkeley, the University of Minnesota, and Tianjin University in China. Vizenor wrote the original screenplay for *Harold of Orange*, which won the Film-in-the-Cities national screenwriting award and was also named "best film" at the San Francisco American Indian Film Festival. His second novel, *Griever: An American Monkey King in China*, won the Fiction Collective Prize and the American Book award sponsored by the Before Columbus Foundation. In 1989, he received the California Arts Council Literature Award.

Vizenor has published several collections of haiku poems; *Matsushima: Pine Islands* is the most recent. Selections of his poems and short stories have appeared in several anthologies, including *Voices of the Rainbows* and *Words in the Blood*. The University of Minnesota Press has published Vizenor's autobiography, *Interior Landscapes*, as well as *Bearheart: The Heirship Chronicles* and *Griever: An American Monkey King in China*. Minnesota has also published his novel *The Trickster of Liberty* and three of his books on the American Indian experience: *Wordarrows, Earthdivers,* and *The People Named the Chippewa.*